Praise for Failsafe Strategies

"This excellent book provides both tools and processes for expansion of company activities into market areas that may outwardly appear very risky. By developing multiple options, the risks of new moves in the market can be reduced to practical proportions."

—*Jack W. Harley, President, JWH Group Inc.*

"This book offers very sound, worthwhile advice to management concerning a little-reviewed element—substantiating and evaluating risk. It is well worth the effort and should be well received."

—*James A Karman, COO RPM Inc.*

"For anyone who is currently constructing a business case for their organization, stop now. Read this book first. It will assist you in terms of articulating your chosen strategic design, the core objectives that you are trying to establish, and the pure capability that will enable you to successfully execute. This is value to the max."

—*Professor C.H.J. Gilson, author of* Peak Performance: Business Lessons from the World's Top Sports Organizations

"Businesses have long built their strategies on a foundation of profitability first, risk analysis second. Sayan Chatterjee flips the formula and shows how business opportunities are often profitable precisely because of the risk involved. This is a fresh perspective on how to calculate the risks that can derail a strategy—or lead to greater profits. *Failsafe Strategies* provides business managers with a dynamic, accessible framework not simply for avoiding risk, but for converting it into profitability."

—*Ming-Jer Chen, Leslie E. Grayson Professor of Business Administration, The Darden School, University of Virginia, and author of* Inside Chinese Business: A Guide for Managers Worldwide

"Chatterjee helps you take a fresh look at your company's current business model and gives you a roadmap to implement change to align your everyday operations and long-term strategic planning. This book is a must-read for anyone involved in operations and trying to grow a business."

—*Arthur Anton, President/CEO, Swagelok*

"Dr. Chatterjee has been highly effective in assisting our company with business strategy. He has given us new perspectives in strategic management that have dramatically improved our thought processes and performance results."

—*Rick Juve, CEO, Americhem*

"For a practitioner, this book offers a unique and invaluable focus on proactive risk assessment during the design of business strategy...a focus that other authors omit."

—*Ted Zampetis, CEO, Shiloh Industries, Inc.*

"Risk. It's everywhere in today's business world. Chatterjee shows businesses how to cope and prosper in the face of risk. If you don't want to succumb to the downside of risk, this book is a must."

—*Professor Richard D'Aveni, Tuck School of Business at Dartmouth College and author of* Hypercompetition

"Chatterjee takes a unique perspective to strategy. Instead of waiting for a home-run innovation, companies can boost their profits long-term by clearly understanding what causes everyday strategies to fail. What an idea!"

—*Sydney Finkelstein, Professor of Strategy and Leadership, Tuck School at Dartmouth and author of* Why Smart Executives Fail

"The world of risk management is often thought of in the context of models, measurement, quantitative analysis, and geeks. Dr. Chatterjee's book takes the subject to a new level by focusing on the critical role of strategic risk. As a professional risk manager, I was intrigued by how he weaves strategy into the fabric of enterprise risk management. Chock full of real-world anecdotes, the reader will find this book both entertaining and informative.

—*Kevin M. Blakely, Executive Vice President, Risk Management Group, KeyCorp*

Failsafe Strategies

Profit and Grow from Risks That Others Avoid

Ideas. Action. Impact.
Wharton School Publishing

In the face of accelerating turbulence and change, business leaders and policy makers need new ways of thinking to sustain performance and growth.

Wharton School Publishing offers a trusted source for stimulating ideas from thought leaders who provide new mental models to address changes in strategy, management, and finance. We seek out authors from diverse disciplines with a profound understanding of change and its implications. We offer books and tools that help executives respond to the challenge of change.

Every book and management tool we publish meets quality standards set by The Wharton School of the University of Pennsylvania. Each title is reviewed by the Wharton School Publishing Editorial Board before being given Wharton's seal of approval. This ensures that Wharton publications are timely, relevant, important, conceptually sound or empirically based, and implementable.

To fit our readers' learning preferences, Wharton publications are available in multiple formats, including books, audio, and electronic.

To find out more about our books and management tools, visit us at whartonsp.com and Wharton's executive education site, exceed.wharton.upenn.edu.

Failsafe Strategies

Profit and Grow from Risks That Others Avoid

Sayan Chatterjee

Ideas. Action. Impact.
Wharton School Publishing

A CIP record of this book can be obtained from the Library of Congress

Publisher: Tim Moore
Executive editor: Jim Boyd
Editorial assistant: Richard Winkler
Marketing manager: Martin Litkowski
International marketing manager: Tim Galligan
Managing editor: Gina Kanouse
Project editor: Lori Lyons
Cover jacket design: Mary Jo Defranco
Copy editor: Sarah Cisco
Composition: Jake McFarland
Proofreader: Sheri Cain
Manufacturing coordinator: Dan Uhrig

Ideas. Action. Impact.
Wharton School
Publishing

©2005 Sayan Chatterjee
Published by Pearson Education, Inc.
Publishing as Wharton School Publishing
Upper Saddle River, New Jersey 07458

Wharton School Publishing offers excellent discounts on this book when ordered in quantity for bulk purchases or special sales. For more information, please contact: U.S. Corporate and Government Sales, 1-800-382-3419, corpsales@pearsontechgroup.com. For sales outside of the U.S., please contact: International Sales, 1-317-581-3793, international@pearsontechgroup.com.

Printed in the United States of America

First Printing

ISBN 0-13-101111-1

LOC 2004108359

Pearson Education Ltd.
Pearson Education Australia Pty., Limited
Pearson Education South Asia Pte. Ltd.
Pearson Education Asia Ltd.
Pearson Education Canada, Ltd.
Pearson Educacion de Mexico, S.A. de C.V.
Pearson Education—Japan
Pearson Education Malaysia, Pte. Ltd.

Ideas. Action. Impact.
**Wharton School
Publishing**

C. K. Prahalad
THE FORTUNE AT THE BOTTOM OF THE PYRAMID
Eradicating Poverty Through Profits

Yoram (Jerry)Wind, Colin Crook, with Robert Gunther
THE POWER OF IMPOSSIBLE THINKING
Transform the Business of Your Life and the Life of Your Business

Scott A. Shane
FINDING FERTILE GROUND
Identifying Extraordinary Opportunities for New Ventures

This book is dedicated to my parents and my wife, Anita.

CONTENTS

ACKNOWLEDGMENTS

The central thesis of this book emerged from a gradual convergence of ideas from two sources. The first source is my research on risk and value creation. The second source is my consulting and executive development experience. Chance encounters have played a major role in some significant directions that I have taken in my life, and it is fair to say that had Michael Lubatkin not started the conversation in the late 1980s about looking at risk from a strategic perspective, I may never have been drawn into this stream of research on risk. I may have written a book on strategy, but that would not have been half as interesting to me as the risk management lens of strategy.

Although the notion of risk provides the architecture, the bulk of the concepts relating to designing and implementing strategy have come from trying out these ideas on my executive audience and corporate clients. These are the people who have shaped the ideas to the point where I was willing to try and put it into practice. In particular, some people deserve my deepest gratitude. In no particular order they are Tom Sullivan, Arthur Anton, Larry Vandendriessche, Mike Butkovic, Lev Holubek, Kevin Blakely, Jim Karman, and Jack Harley. All of these people have given me some deep insight or helped me verbalize an idea that I was struggling with. For example, the notion of granularity that I develop throughout the book was an observation by Larry Vandendriessche in his effort to capture the basic essence of my methodology.

I would also like to acknowledge conversations with my academic colleagues that have shaped my ideas over the years. In particular, I like to express my appreciation for the conversations that I have had with Vasu Ramanujam, John Aram, Jeane Liedtka, Jay Bourgeoise, Robert Wiseman, and Charles Baaden Fuller. Some of my students who have contributed to this project are Chris Wargo, Gary Wagner, and Baher Abdelmarek. Others have been cited in the book.

The support of Jim Boyd, my executive editor, has been invaluable. I also appreciate the time Russ Hall took in making sense of my manuscript. As always, any errors and omissions are solely my responsibility. One final note: This is a single authored book. However, I have used the "editorial we" in the book.

Finally, I deeply appreciate the support from my wife and best friend, Anita, throughout this process. There were many discouragements, and her support was invaluable to keep me committed.

Introduction

Understanding Risk: The Real Key to Competitive Strategy

This book is aimed at practitioners and scholars of business strategy. Whether you are a CEO of an organization or a functional-level manager, you need to understand not only how to take risks, but also how to navigate around those risks to capture the rewards that prompted the risk-taking in the first place. More importantly, you need to know your role in reducing these risks. You may argue that the responsibility of a strategy lies at the leadership suite, but it is becoming increasingly apparent that the success of a strategy is determined by how much the rank and file understands their role in the strategy. The risks in any strategy are not just in the execution, but also in the design.

The genesis of this book comes from the extensive executive education and consulting we have been involved in over the past 15 years. Many of our session participants have asked us to develop a book based on the concepts developed in these sessions. These concepts have been field tested and refined over the years through our consulting engagements. Teaching strategy to experienced executives in a one- or two-day session is an extremely different challenge from teaching strategy to MBA students over an entire semester. Executives are extremely intolerant about academic theories that they cannot apply immediately to their day-to-day concerns. Our challenge, therefore, was to develop bite-sized examples that help these executives internalize the concepts we were developing in the sessions, while at the same time making the concepts general enough to apply to a wide range of business situations. Our solution was to write numerous short cases that a busy executive could easily read while including enough detail to illustrate key concepts. You will find these short cases throughout this book. We are hoping to re-create the same experience that participants in our executive sessions typically get from studying these cases.

In the remainder of this Introduction, we provide an overview of how this book is organized. This book has two broad sections and an Appendix. The first section develops concepts that allow a firm to clearly understand the nature of the risks in a given business. The second section expands this framework to growth and diversification strategies. The Appendix presents a detailed analysis of the rise and fall of Enron using the risk management lens.

An Overview of the Book

This book develops a set of concepts that allow you to design business models where the risks can be reduced to practical proportions. The risks in any business come from not knowing the demand, threat from competition, and not having the appropriate capabilities.[1] The basic theme repeated over and over again is that to reduce risk, you need to have clarity regarding where the risks are and create choice, or options, in tackling those risks. We use numerous examples of business strategies to illustrate the concepts. But more to the point, the concepts developed in this book enable you to quickly visualize successful strategies as well as avoid the common pitfalls. However, by no means are we claiming that the strategies we use as examples were developed using our frameworks. We are very aware of academic "after the fact" analysis of famous strategies that in no way portrays the reality of how those strategies were developed. Notable examples are Honda, Wal-Mart, and Southwest. This is where our book differs. Rather than looking backward to try to understand these famous strategies, which is often the case with academic analysis, we use these example as "exercises" to help you re-create these strategies using our framework and methodology—a process that should help you internalize our concepts faster.

Section 1
Designing Strategies for Avoiding Risk

Business risks can manifest at two different stages. Risks in the execution of a strategy will always exist. However, quite often the risk is not in the execution but in the design of the strategy that predisposes it to failure. Our operations colleagues tell us that 80% of the life-cycle cost of a car is locked in at the design stage. A well-designed strategy is not immune to execution risks, but very few firms consider capability risks at the design stage and, thus, compound the risks during execution.[2] A major thrust of this section is to demonstrate that firms often miss out on strategies that can avoid or minimize capability risks while designing the strategy. This is precisely the debate surrounding the Iraq liberation. The proponents point to the goal of a democratic Iraq as a high-return venture. Very few people can argue with this objective if it can be attained. However, critics contend that the strategy did not take into account the capability risks, and the objective may have been attainable at much less cost.

Chapter 1
How to See Gold Where Others See Risk: Identify More Choices
to Get the Gold

To embrace ventures that are considered to be too risky by others, you need to be more proficient than your competitors in understanding the nature of the risks before you actually invest in a venture. To do this, you need to have a framework that allows you to understand the sources of risk at a high level and a methodology that allows you to avoid the risks that scare your competitors. The first step in this process is the ability to conceptualize multiple business models that can exploit the same market opportunity. This chapter gives you a framework to identify options that isolate your firm from key risks.

We call this framework "outcome-to-objective." This framework exposes the inherent risk of relying on core competencies and how this perspective leads to an inside-out view of strategy. This chapter also demonstrates why giving lip service to customer needs is not enough, and how the concept of desired outcomes allows you to break the inside-out mindset. Finally, this chapter shows you how to identify *multiple* competitive objectives, the logic behind your business model, that can deliver the same desired outcome while capturing some of the value for your shareholders. When you begin to identify multiple competitive objectives, you take the first step to put distance between you and your competitors in your ability to profit from risky ventures. In summary, this framework increases the odds of profits by enabling you to do two things. First, it allows you to consider opportunities that others would avoid because of the perceived risk and, thus, have the field to yourself. Second, you are able to differentiate your firm from your competitors by reducing the likelihood of loss because you have many more choices at your disposal to help you avoid risk than your competitors.

Chapter 2
Three Steps to Design a Low-Risk Strategy

In Chapter 1, you are exposed to techniques for visualizing multiple possibilities for exploiting the same risky profit opportunity—the choice dimension. Chapter 2 forces you to come to grips with the constraints in exploiting these possibilities—the clarity dimension. Chapter 2 guides you through three steps to crystallize the constraints and the risks of overcoming these constraints as you design the business model. At the end of this process, you will have complete clarity as to what you *need* to deliver. This by no means suggests that you *can* deliver what you need, but at least you will have better clarity about the risk that you may not be able to acquire the required capabilities to deliver what you need to.

The first step to develop this clarity is to understand the broad competitive objective by which a strategy will deliver value to the customer *while capturing some of the value for the firm's shareholders*. Hopefully, with the techniques developed in Chapter 1, you will have many more broad competitive objectives to choose from to profit from the same opportunity as your competitors.

After deciding on the initial broad competitive objectives, you have to take the critical next step of developing core competitive objectives. We define core objectives as a set of specific and measurable deliverables for the business model. Using short sidebar examples, this chapter shows how to precisely define a strategy's core competitive objectives. This precision gives you a much better clarity on the nature of the risks that you will be facing. This precision allows you to track the risks in real-time, so you can pull the plug in case you made a mistake in your assumptions or logic before the strategy completely unravels. The examples also illustrate how companies have overlooked the true risks of a business model when they didn't take time for this precision. Finally, this precision is critical to clearly understand the constraints a firm will be facing to deliver its objectives—its capability requirements. Basically, at this point, you will have clear choices about what you *can* do. Many strategies have gone awry because of the lack of precision in defining the core objectives. With precise definitions, you will be able to avoid the more risky options at the design stage rather than during execution.

Chapter 3
Identifying Multiple Capability Configurations

In this chapter, we develop techniques to identify alternative capability configurations that allow you to learn from a successful strategy and apply it in a different context. We demonstrate this by contrasting the strategies of JetBlue and Southwest, and how JetBlue's strategy has developed with very different inner workings, even though most people think it is basically similar to Southwest. This example should be helpful in understanding how two successful companies in the same business can have different core objectives and supporting capabilities. Further, we also demonstrate that the same core objectives can be used as the business logic in totally different industries. Clearly, the capabilities to deliver these objectives would vary across firms in different industries, but if you can understand the common theme that is observable across such strategies, you may be able to apply the same principle to your own business. We use five short sidebar examples to illustrate this point.

Chapter 4
Designing Strategies with Low Capability Risks

Up to this point, you will have seen how to clearly understand the logic of a business model and how to identify many choices that can *theoretically* allow a firm to deliver value to its customers while capturing some of that value for itself. So far, we have developed frameworks to identify multiple options for what you need to do to be profitable and a subset of these options that you feel most comfortable in your ability to execute. However, the risk becomes a reality when you select one of these options and choose to implement it. Once you make a choice, your firm has to make the necessary resource commitments to build up the capabilities. In this chapter (and in Chapter 5), you learn how you can minimize your risk by using existing capabilities to deliver the core objectives you have identified. So, if you can address the capability risks efficiently, your business model has a much higher probability of success.

This chapter also addresses situations in which a firm cannot leverage its existing capabilities. Those situations are inherently more risky because of the additional investments that have to be made for acquiring new capabilities. This chapter gives you some ideas on how to identify "white space" or "sweet spot" opportunities (we will define these terms later) where the risks of making such new investments are minimal.

Chapter 5
Lowering Capability Risks with Visible and Invisible Outputs

A corollary to the frameworks that you will learn in this book is time-to-insight. Basically, if you can consistently identify business models faster than your competitors, this by itself will allow you to stay a step ahead of competition. However, there are other things you can do besides developing a completely new business model that will make it difficult for competitors to catch up with you. The framework that is developed in Chapter 5 allows you to fine-tune your firm's capabilities by simultaneously making it more efficient, as well as deliver more of the outcomes desired by the customers. The core insight of this chapter is based around the concept that customers value what you can see and touch. If you realign your firm's capabilities so you can offer more of the things that are visible to the customers, you will be able to differentiate your offerings from that of the competition. On the other hand, the components of your capabilities that are invisible to the customer can be reengineered for greater efficiency, which adds to your profit margins. Variations of these concepts are developed in greater detail in Chapter 5 and illustrated with numerous examples. This framework is a very low risk way of modifying capabilities to put distance between a firm and its competition.

This chapter concludes with a discussion on two other sources of risk. These risks can come in two guises—errors in assumptions and errors in logic. In any business opportunity, you have to make certain assumptions about the future. The assumptions that surprise most firms (negatively and positively) is with regards to customer preferences and market demand, because no one can predict the future with 100% accuracy. However, this is a risk you must get used to taking; otherwise, you will be constantly gun shy of taking on any new opportunities. On the other hand, when it comes to assumptions about the capabilities needed to deliver the core objectives of the strategy, a firm has to strive for more accuracy. Often, mistakes in assumptions regarding capabilities reflect a lack of clarity and should be easy to correct with the techniques developed in this book.

The other source of errors comes from poor logic. You have to apply logic to determine which core objectives you will focus on and which set of capabilities you will draw on to deliver the objectives, depending on your risk preference. Unfortunately, even the best companies succumb to logical errors. For example, Dell Computer now admits that its move into retail channels was a logical error because its direct mail capabilities did not match the capabilities needed to deal with retail channels. This chapter goes on to suggest why Dell might be making a similar error at present. Hubris is one reason why even successful companies still make logical mistakes— they have an exaggerated belief of what they can do. In fact, success itself can lead to overconfidence that in turn might lead to a lack of discipline in applying the framework before committing to a venture. The last section of this chapter develops some ideas about how to avoid assumptions and logical errors.

Chapter 6
Organizations That Can Benefit from the Outcome-To-Objectives Framework

One reason why precisely defined core objectives can reduce the risks of failure is because everyone in the organization has clarity regarding what he or she needs to do to make the organization move toward its competitive goals. However, before there is a convergence around a set of core objectives by the rank and file, the wording of the objectives has to be tested to see that those who will implement the strategies can relate to the objectives. In this chapter, we illustrate this step with many examples to demonstrate how successful companies have gone about this process. If an organization defines its core objectives clearly, it will find that its batting average will go up significantly. Even when a firm makes mistakes, it will be able to learn from them.

Section 2
The Risks in Growth and Diversification Strategy

In the first section of this book, you learned how to develop a low-risk strategy for a specific business. This section develops frameworks for understanding the risks in growing the core business or entering markets that are new to a firm. In Chapters 7 and 8, the book develops frameworks to understand the risks of entering an existing market or adapting to a market. In Chapter 9, this book considers the risks in creating a new market or shaping a market. In Chapter 10, we take a dynamic look at how the risks in a strategy evolve over time and how this can be managed by multiple migration paths.

Chapter 7
When and How to Use Differentiation Entry Strategy

The basic risks in adapting to a market are the same as an existing business. You need clarity on how you want to compete (core objectives) in the new business and the capabilities that you need to deliver the objectives with the least risk. However, there is a critical difference when you are entering as an existing business. You have to overcome entry barriers. In Chapter 7, this book develops frameworks to overcome the entry barriers without taking on undue risks. Basically, as a new entrant, a firm needs to attack parts of the value chain where the incumbents are likely to be vulnerable and where it can leverage its existing capabilities. This chapter provides some ideas about how to carry this out with minimal risk. This chapter also presents the argument that early in the lifecycle of a market or in a market characterized by a few players, the low-risk entry objectives for most entrants should be differentiation, and in the mature stage of the lifecycle, the low-risk entry objectives should be low price. This is true irrespective of the generic description of the market you are entering. For example, Lexus entered the luxury segment of the car market in 1989 with a low-price strategy. On the other hand, in 2000, JetBlue airlines entered the low-price segment of the point-to-point passenger air-transport market with a differentiated strategy. There will be entrants that may attempt a different entry strategy. However, apart from a few exceptions, such as Xbox taking on PlayStation with a low-price strategy, we suggest that even for the strongest entrants, such an entry strategy increases risk.

Chapter 7 also develops frameworks to understand the capabilities needed to execute a differentiated or low-price entry strategy, and the risks that the entrant has to consider ex-ante. Chapter 7 explores the differentiation entry strategy in depth, and Chapter 8 does the same with the low-price entry strategy.

Chapter 8
When and How to Use a Low-Price Entry Strategy

The basic risk in a low-price entry strategy is you lack or cannot develop a low-cost capability. In Chapter 8, we use the example of Dell Computer to demonstrate how a firm can leverage parts of its existing capability set by attacking bloated cost structures of well-established incumbents in mature industries. However, Dell has not always succeeded in its low-price diversification strategy, and there are some important takeaways here. The two most important take-aways are the need to have complete clarity in the kinds of markets where a low-price entry strategy is likely to succeed, given a firm's unique capability sets. Deviation from the ideal market profile will increase the risks of failure. Even for Dell, high-margin markets that we argue are not conducive to a low-price entry strategy, such as storage, have proven to be problematic. Also, if a firm absolutely must enter a new segment where it cannot leverage its capabilities, it may be able to reduce the risks under specific situations. We use Dell's entry into the service business as an example to illustrate these situations.

This chapter concludes with an analysis of Dell's and Sony's strategies for dominating the consumer electronics market. Based on the frameworks that you will have learned up to this moment, we encourage you to make a prediction about which of these two strategies is likely to succeed.

Chapter 9
Strategies to Shape Markets: Products, Process, and Platform

Chapters 7 and 8 develop frameworks to understand the kind of entry strategies that the vast majority of companies will be involved in throughout their lifetime——entry into existing businesses. However, a few companies pursue much grander ambitions to shape or create a market from scratch. These types of strategies are inherently very risky because, by default, firms have to acquire new capabilities to succeed in a market that does not exist. Chapter 9 identifies the critical objectives that must be met to give you a chance in succeeding in market-shaping and how to reduce the risks in the significant investments that you must make to develop the capabilities to shape markets. This chapter considers three broad market shaping strategies and how to manage the risks in each. These are using a new product, using a new process, and using a new platform. We not only consider the risks when initiating one of these strategies, but also how to sustain it in the long run if and when competition becomes an issue. An example of a product-based market shaping strategy is the Blackberry. An example of a process-based strategy is a repeatable acquisition process, such as Cisco Systems or Banc One, or a technology infrastructure that enables one firm to take risks that others are unable to handle. An example of a platform is Microsoft DOS or Windows.

Chapter 10
Develop Multiple Migration Paths

In the final chapter of this book, we develop a framework of avoiding risks in a more dynamic context. You need to get comfortable with embarking on a course of action even though you have not managed to clarify all the relevant uncertainties. The good news is that some of these uncertainties become clearer over time. This chapter provides some ideas about how a firm can navigate its way to its competitive objective by avoiding risks that it clearly did not anticipate in the beginning.

The basic concept developed in this chapter is that you do not need to close off all options that you identified while designing a strategy using the techniques from Section 1. The really good companies keep as many options open as long as possible and make the decision regarding closing options based on information that they receive in the future. Even using the frameworks developed in this book, you will never have as much information as you would want to have to avoid all the risks in the options that you do decide to pursue. However, many times, the quality of information improves over time. If you can keep some options open, you can re-evaluate the options at a later date as more precise information becomes available in the future. This will further reduce the risks of undertaking an option that is beyond your capabilities. We call this technique managing the migration paths (to your ultimate goal). This chapter develops frameworks for managing migration paths for adapting to a market, shaping a market, and for developing platform capabilities.

Appendix

In the concluding section of this book, we present a case study on Enron. We realize that most people have a negative impression about Enron and justifiably so. However, there are some things that you can learn even from the likes of Enron, specifically what *not* to do, even if you are successful initially. We argue that Enron first represents a strategy failure because the company did not understand the risks it was taking and then tried to cover up its mistakes by techniques that have been found to be fraudulent. In the context of this book, Enron has succumbed to the risks, and it may be useful to dig below the headlines to understand why and how the concepts developed in this book can be applied to understand Enron's strategic failures.

Some Concluding Thoughts

We thought long and hard before deciding to write one more book on strategy. We genuinely feel that the issue of risk has not been given as much attention as it deserves in the strategy literature. Further, thoughtful strategy practitioners and academics are waking up to this idea of focusing on business risks, and we see an opportunity to stimulate this discussion. The basic message of this book is that to avoid the risks that others may succumb to, you need to have clarity and choice. You need to clearly understand and communicate where the sources of risks are. You need to give yourself more choices than your competitors in navigating your way around the risks. All the frameworks and heuristics that we develop in this book will help you with these twin goals of clarity and choice.

However, we do wonder if by focusing on risk instead of returns we will be perceived as taking a negative perspective on strategy—how we can avoid loss instead of how we can exploit a profit opportunity. If anything, the central thrust of this book is exactly the reverse. We urge you to look for profitable opportunities. The caveat is that most profitable opportunities are profitable because they are too risky for most to exploit. The only way to really exploit a profitable opportunity is to retain most of the profits without succumbing to the risks that keep competition away. Once you understand risks in profitable opportunities, then you can expand your opportunity frontier, which can only lead to increased shareholder value in the long run. You can profit by seeing the profits in risks that others will avoid.

True to this principle, we have taken on a risk that most other management books avoid. Most management books use examples of past successes and failures to justify their frameworks. Of course, this is necessary, and we have also done that to a large extent. However, we have also gone out on a limb and made predictions about the strategies of the best companies in the world. Some of these predictions are not favorable, but if we believe in our frameworks, the true test will have to come in their predictive ability and not by looking in the rearview mirror. Imagine if someone had predicted Enron's problems in 1999!

Endnotes

1 Academics may suggest that there are risks form the five forces identified by Michael Porter. Our argument is the risks are a problem only if a firm does not have the appropriate capability to position it against the forces.

2 Readers familiar with manufacturing techniques will no doubt relate to the concept of FMEA (failure mode effects analysis) that tries to anticipate what can go wrong in implementing an operation. This is obviously harder at the strategic level and precisely why this can lead to a competitive advantage because so few firms do it.

SECTION 1

DESIGNING STRATEGIES FOR AVOIDING RISK

"A risky situation isn't necessarily profitable. Since the odds are calculable, they are calculable by anyone and so not unique. Profit...is clearly the result of risk, but only of a unique kind of risk, which is not susceptible of measurement."

—Frank H. Knight 1921, Risk, Uncertainty and Profit

Strategy practitioners have spent the last 50 years developing frameworks for strategy, industry, and competitive analysis. However, we keep forgetting one important thing: The whole reason business exists is to take risks; otherwise, we should be keeping our money in treasury bills. Yet most strategy frameworks are focused on analyzing returns or profits and addressing risk only as an afterthought. We are taught to analyze industries to determine whether they are attractive. Attractiveness equates profits. However, using that line of thinking, companies such as JetBlue and Southwest should not exist—they are thriving in an industry where most of the established players are bare-ly getting by, at best, or going in and out of bankruptcy. This book takes a different perspective. Profit is, of course, paramount, but only after adjusting for risk. Simply trying to focus on the ex-ante prof-itable opportunities will not necessarily result in profits ex-post. If an opportunity is profitable, it is because there is an element of risk in it. Profit is the result of a firm's ability to take risks while avoiding the adverse impacts of those risks.

Understanding Risks Leads to More Profits in the Long Run

Throughout the 1990s, we saw an increase in risk taking using busi-ness models that were hailed to be "revolutionary." Yet following the Enron debacle, it suddenly became fashionable to eschew the revo-lutionary approach as being too risky, and there was a swing back to a more incremental approach.[1] This behavior is a classic response firms tend to exhibit when confronted with unexpected risk.[2] It is also exactly the wrong kind of response.

We suggest a different approach. Instead of running away from risk, think of profits as the residual return after avoiding the risk of failure. There are two dimensions for avoiding these risks: clarity and choice. Clarity involves understanding exactly where the risks lie. Choice involves identifying more options than competitors to avoid the risks. The concepts developed in this section allow you to clearly see where the risks are and how to identify more choices than the competition to avoid or lessen the adverse impact of risk. In the long run, this approach will increase your firm's profits by enabling it to select only those risky opportunities where there is less likelihood of negative impacts. If your firm becomes adept of avoiding risks while keeping most of the returns, it ultimately will be more profitable in the long run. Moreover, as your firm begins to understand and avoid the risks in risky opportunities, it will have a much larger palette of opportunities to choose from compared to its competitors, which will pass on many opportunities that look too risky. This is the cornerstone of many successful strategies.

"Where others see risk, he sees gold."[3]

The preceding quotation captures the basic message of this section—companies can use risk as a competitive advantage. If your company embraces risks that others shy away from, you will be operating as a monopoly by default, and the profits will be yours for the taking. You see gold where others see risk.

Business Models Will Be Increasingly More Complex and Risky

A business model captures the logic by which a firm provides value to customers while extracting part of that value for its shareholders. Creating value in business has always been risky, but it will become more risky in the 21st century. Take the issue of technology, which became the panacea for all problems in the 1990s. Firms were increasingly looking to technology as a means to expand the value frontier—more value for price. And therein lies the rub. Technology makes it possible for a firm to become more productive through complex interactions between previously standalone activities. However, firms are quickly learning that this complexity is not easy to manage compared to the simpler business models of the 20th century. By some estimates, 60% of all ERP (enterprise resource planning) implementations fail. In other words, technology that is available to all cannot be a source of competitive advantage. It is the ability to use technology to execute complex business models that distinguishes firms. Trying to take on too much without understanding the risks of these complex interactions is suicidal. Jacques Nasser found this out in his effort to revamp Ford, and Carly Fiorina found out at HP when she tried to change the organization from individual fiefdoms to a common customer interface. On the other hand, going back to 20th century fundamentals, you may boost short-term profits, but that will not on its own enable you to evolve into a 21st century player. Simply speaking, the winners in the 21st century will be firms that are adept at executing complex business models because they can manage complex risks better than others.

Understanding Risk Is the Key To Handling Complexity

While Enron's failure is probably the most publicized, other "revolutionary" firms have also stumbled to various degrees. Case in point: The Cisco Systems $2.2 billion of inventory write-offs in 2001. We submit that the revolutionary strategies developed by firms like Enron, Charles Schwab, Cisco, and so forth are not just fads of the 1990s, but represent models that are absolutely necessary to take advantage of advances in technology and financial techniques. However, by virtue of their path-breaking nature, they also entail more risk—people simply do not know enough about these. In the case of Enron, its initial success in the gas business led to arrogance and underestimating the true risks of its business model, which were made clear when the company tried to apply it to other industries. In the Appendix, we describe how arrogance led to these strategic mistakes and resulted in a fraudulent cover-up. As strategy practitioners, we are more interested in understanding how to create a system that will *prevent* us from ignoring the true risks, irrespective of human failings, and less interested in how arrogance or other factors blind an organization to risk. If you can incorporate systems within the complex business models that give you more clarity about the nature of the business risks, then you are in a much better position to take advantage of new and unproven opportunities.

However, business risk is by no means confined strictly to revolutionary or very complex business models. Even the most mundane businesses carry risks and the opportunity to make profits by avoiding those risks. The concepts developed in this section allow you to frame your profit opportunities using this risk lens, so you can increase the odds of retaining most of your profits while avoiding the associated risks, irrespective of the type of business you are in.

Three Sources of Business Risk

Three basic risks can derail any strategy: *demand risk, competitive risk,* and *capability risk.* Demand risk is the risk that the value proposition a firm is trying to sell will not be accepted by the market. Demand risk may also be caused by demand proving to be *higher* than anticipated. If demand proves to be higher than anticipated, a firm may be vulnerable to competitors capturing its market before it can scale up capacity. In other words, inability to cope with unexpected demand may make a firm vulnerable to competitive risk, which is the risk that competitors will take away its customers. Finally, capability risk is the risk that a firm is not able to deliver the value propositions that customers will pay for or the capabilities cost so much that it is unable to make a satisfactory profit.[4]

At the strategic level, most companies must contain demand risks and competitive risks. Some value propositions, like the Ford Edsel, may never sell. However, others may sell at a lower price point, like the personal computer post-1992, or at a different point in time (the PDA in the early versus mid-1990s) because the market may not be ready for this particular value proposition. Other than demand risk, a strategy must fight through the competition before it can get the customers' dollars. This is true whether a firm is an incumbent or a new entrant. There is only one way to completely avoid competitive risk, if only for a short while—exploit virgin territories (in business parlance, "shaping a market"). Clearly, these situations avoid any immediate competitive risks, but these strategies face demand risk instead. There is no guarantee that the value proposition would sell. It stands to reason that these two risks are somewhat mutually exclusive. In an existing market, it is easier to get a handle on the demand, but the risk from competition determines how much of the demand a particular firm may be able to capture.

Typically, most companies first decide which of these two risks (demand or competitive) they want to contain when developing a new strategy. Irrespective of the choice the firm makes, it will have to contend with capability risk at the tactical or operational level. A major source of execution failure is not having the appropriate capabilities to deliver a value proposition while capturing some of the value for the firm's shareholders. This situation is typically a result of a lack of clarity regarding the objectives of the business model. This has happened to the best of companies, including Dell, IBM, and Rubbermaid. The second half of this section focuses on cabability risks.

In the first chapter of this section, we explore the choice dimension when designing a strategy—how to identify multiple business models. By identifying multiple business models, you will be able to minimize competitive risks by essentially changing the rules of the game.

Endnotes

1 The about-face of the American auto industry, particularly Ford following the Firestone crisis, is a case in point. Ford has abandoned most of the initiatives started by Jacques Nasser and has reverted to a more incremental method for implementing changes to the way cars are manufactured and distributed. Some observers feel that had it not been for the Firestone tire problem, Nasser may have been able to push through some of his initiatives, for better or worse.

2 Considerable empirical evidence suggests that managers are largely loss averse (rather than risk averse) and adjust their risk preferences by framing a problem either in terms of gain or loss. One version of this argument suggests that decision makers generally prefer preserving any anticipated gain in wealth over

maximizing wealth when that option adds the possibility of loss. This leads to an attitude that favors the status quo, especially if the status quo is reasonably profitable, as was the case with IBM and Xerox in the early 1980s. Conversely, decision makers generally prefer riskier options that provide an opportunity to avoid losses over less risky options that don't avoid loss. We think history will show that Enron took on increasingly more risk to make up for some bad bets and to save face rather than cutting its losses. In other words, decision makers have been shown to be conservative when anticipating a gain to wealth and bold when anticipating a loss to wealth. The objective of this book is to alert you to these types of mistakes.

3 Nanette Byrnes et. al. "Is Wilbur Ross Crazy" Business Week 22 December 2003.

4 There will always be risks in the actual execution itself, and there are excellent books that focus strictly on execution. However, the focus of this book is to avoid situations where you have to rely on execution to avoid failure.

1

HOW TO SEE GOLD WHERE OTHERS SEE RISK: IDENTIFY MORE CHOICES TO GET THE GOLD

"Strategy formulation involves the constant search for ways in which the firm's unique resources can be redeployed in changing circumstances."

—Richard Rumelt

In most industries, the major players are well aware of what customers are looking for (generically, more value for money). Yet at any given point in time, many of the customers' desired value propositions (whether price, quality, quantity, and so forth) remain unfulfilled because existing business models are incapable of delivering these values in a manner that is also profitable for the firm. However, if a firm can solve this trade-off, then the profits are almost guaranteed.

Many firms take a linear approach in trying to solve this trade-off—through R&D (research and development) or other resource-intensive processes. Clearly, there is a place for R&D and other forms of capital investments. However, there are several drawbacks in taking a linear, resource-intensive approach. First and foremost, focusing on R&D or capital investments as a solution is inherently more risky simply by virtue of the capital commitment. Second, because this linear approach is the most common, it will most likely force your firm to play in the same playing field as everyone else. Thus, even if your firm develops the capabilities to deliver a value proposition profitably, the differentiating factor amongst competing firms is likely to be execution. This chapter develops a common sense but different way of approaching these issues that should complement the linear approach. Yet, very few firms consciously adopt this approach as part of their strategic planning processes. *The principle underlying this approach is very simple: If your firm can consistently identify more options that can deliver the same value proposition, it will likely be able to reduce the risk of failure by choosing an option where the risk can be managed to practical proportions.* This chapter recommends that the brute-force approach should be adopted only after you have exhausted less resource-intensive options. In the following pages, a framework is developed for identifying multiple options that require much less resource investment.

To Visualize More Options, You Need an Outside-In Perspective

Consider a journey by car to a new city that a traveler is unfamiliar with. The traveler has charted out a route plan but suddenly finds herself at a roadblock. She has to figure out a way to get around the roadblock to reach her destination. Because she is in uncertain territory, her odds of taking a wrong turn are significantly increased. However, if she uses GPS (Global Positioning System) to navigate her to the destination, she will be able to see multiple possibilities and choose the one that best fits her driving style and allows her to reach her destination on time. The framework developed in this chapter first considers the big picture (in this case, GPS), which allows your firm to see many possible routes to its ultimate objective, understand the risks inherent in each route, and then work back to the set of capabilities that can minimize the risks while still reaching the destination. With this approach, your firm considers its own capabilities only in the context of the capabilities identified for the different routes. This process highlights the key difference from traditional frameworks, such as SWOT (Strengths, Weakness, Opportunities, and Threats). Traditional frameworks are intuitive and appealing because of their simplicity—concentrate on your strengths or core competencies and identify a strategy that fits with your strengths. In other words, most firms utilizing traditional frameworks first focus on their core competencies and then try to see if these competencies can be used to reach the destination. You will soon see why it is virtually impossible to see multiple options with this traditional approach. Moreover, there is a real danger that the traditional approaches may very likely blindside a firm from the true risks of the business because it almost always results in an inside-out perspective.

The Traditional Frameworks Lead To an Inside-Out Perspective

Case 1: The Space Pen

When NASA first started sending up astronauts, it quickly discovered that ballpoint pens would not work in zero gravity. To combat the problem, NASA commissioned Fisher to develop a (space) pen that would write in zero gravity, upside down, underwater, on almost any surface, including glass, and at temperatures ranging from below freezing to 300C.

The Soviets used a pencil!

This is a classic illustration of the inherent risks in being focused on your existing competencies. It leads to an inside-out view of strategy. It precludes other options that can deliver the desired goal more efficiently. Typically, this perspective is characterized by the following:

- Alternatives are defined by the problem.

- Focusing on existing competencies/strengths/resources to solve the problem.

- Managers quickly get locked into one option.

The lesson from the NASA story is that just because you have the resources available to develop a space pen does not mean that it is the optimal strategy (see Figure 1.1). Unfortunately, companies do this all the time.

Case 2: Anticipating Competitive Risks

A business equipment firm (such as Xerox) knows that its good service network allows it to enjoy competitive advantage. Xerox has determined that it is difficult for new entrants to develop a comparable service network. How would Xerox determine whether this competitive advantage is sustainable?

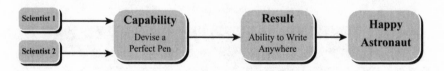

"Inside Out": Based on Resources Already Controlled

FIGURE 1.1   Inside-out focuses on the problem at hand.

In this case, if you focus on studying how your existing service network compares to the competition, you are likely to get blind-sided. This may happen even if you are making every effort to continually improve your service network. You may think you are focusing on your unique resources or competencies and making them even stronger will keep competitors at bay. Perhaps, but you are not asking whether these are the *relevant* strengths to protect you in the future or if there other ways competitors can undermine your advantage. This is the trap of inside-out thinking—focusing on what you do best and not if this is something that you *should* be thinking about.

> **"This internal focus has wasted our time, wasted our energy, frustrated us, made us so mad some nights over some bureaucratic jackass boss that we'd punch a hole in the wall."**
>
> —Jack Welch[1]

Basically, inside-out is the wrong way to think about strategy.

Focus on Desired Outcomes to Identify Multiple Options

Just about everyone these days talks about starting with the customers' needs first. However, if you and your competitors all start with customers' needs, it is highly likely that you all visualize the same value chain. Following through, if you and your competitors basically work from the same value chain, it will come down to an execution battle fought with the same business model. On the other hand, after you have identified multiple value chains, you can use frameworks such as SWOT or core competencies to pick the one that plays to your strengths. In other words, you have reduced the competitive risk by not only choosing a business model that is different from your competitors, but also execution risk because the business model matches either your existing capabilities or capabilities that you can acquire inexpensively. Unfortunately, focusing on customer needs is of little help in visualizing multiple business models.

Simply asking customers about their needs cannot start this process. Customers are unable to phrase their needs in a way that lends itself to multiple business models. Of course, you need to talk to your customers, but to identify multiple business models, you have to *rephrase* the needs and priorities. As an aside, this is one reason why we do not recommend using focus groups when designing a new strategy. Focus-group participants invariably translate their needs into existing products or services. The moment you start thinking in terms of concrete products or services, you have lost your edge by way of your competitors.

To get away from the customer needs-driven mindset, you need to spend more time thinking, "What is the ultimate outcome the customer is looking for?" Customers have needs, but what they are really paying for are outcomes. You will find that by focusing on the outcomes, you are able to identify multiple business models and increase the odds that you can come up with a solution that is simpler, more efficient, and less risky to implement. Traditional market research and focus groups are not very useful in identifying outcomes. You are much better off observing customer behavior and rephrasing their needs in terms of outcomes.

Case 3: Multiple Options for Developing Stents

Stents are one of the major medical innovations of the 1980s. They are used to prop open blocked coronary arteries to prevent heart attacks. However, stents quite often had to be replaced because of scar tissues that form around it, increasing the risk of reblockage. In March 2004, Boston Scientific Corp. of Natick, Mass., won Food and Drug Administration approval for a coronary stent coated with the cancer drug Paclitaxel. Paclitaxel prevents tumor growth and thus prevents scar tissue from developing around the stent. Angiotech holds the patent for this coated stent and licenses the product to Boston Scientific.

Dr. Hunter, the CEO of Angiotech, traced the innovation of the coated stent from the manner in which his company asked doctors about their needs regarding stents.[2]

> "Medical equipment makers typically ask surgeons, 'How can we build a better stent?' and then get the answer, 'You should make it more flexible, easier to see and stronger,'" Dr. Hunter notes. "But we've been asking, 'What does the body do to these stents and why do they fail?' When you ask that, you get to the scar-tissue problem."

Outcome To (Competitive) Objective

Even though Angiotech did not call it as such, in effect, the company was asking the doctors what the ultimate outcome was they were looking for. By asking the customers (users in this case) about the current product, it is usually impossible to get ideas for new products that will satisfy the customers' needs when they see it. Most companies try to focus on marginally improving the existing internal outputs (which lead to the current products or services) by investing in new capabilities. However, if you do this, you are invariably taken to the same playing field as your competitors, and you become vulnerable to competitive risks. You want to deliver what the customer truly wants by using a product or service configuration that is different from existing competitors. This reduces competitive risk without being vulnerable to demand risk. By considering outcomes instead of outputs (products or services), you increase your odds of visualizing multiple internal outputs that lead to new, sometimes radically new, product or service configurations that other competitors are not considering. To design a low-risk strategy, simply select the output that *you* can deliver with the lowest risk.

Case 4: Multiple Options for Developing a Longer-Lasting Hearing-Aid Battery

A battery manufacturer was considering investing in a major research effort for a longer-lasting hearing-aid battery. It assembled a focus group of older people to find out about the size or shape of the battery that would most likely appeal to them. The company's real insight did not come from what the focus group told them but from observing the process by which the participants went about replacing their batteries. The company realized it is very difficult for older people to replace a small hearing-aid battery. Of course, one solution to the problem is spending research dollars to come up with a battery that is longer-lasting. However, the outcome that hearing-aid users really wanted was simply to have a hearing aid with a working battery all the time. The battery manufacturer decided to develop a package that made *replacing* the battery foolproof. Not only did they save the research dollars, but they were selling more batteries in larger packets.

The basic difference between the inside-out/core competency view and an outcome-focused view is the starting point. In the outcome-objective view:

- Alternatives are defined by the desired outcomes.

- It is easier to identify multiple fronts on which you can compete.

- Competitive objectives (this includes your outputs that satisfy the customers' desired outcomes) are stated with greater clarity. (This is the kernel of your business model.)

- Focusing on outcomes makes it easier to identify multiple competitive objectives.

Consider the NASA example again. Instead of *devising a perfect pen*, NASA could have rephrased the desired outcome as *recording information*. This leads to the objective indicated in Figure 1.2. Now you can deliver the outcome without undertaking costly investments, such as the space pen. You can use off-the-shelf products like a pencil or a cassette tape recorder to deliver the desired outcome.

Outcome-   Begins with Customer Outcome—Presumes Necessary
Objectives: Capabilities Can Be Obtained or Developed

FIGURE 1.2   Outcome to objectives framing of a market opportunity.

Case 5: Multiple Options for Competitive Risks— Branded Home-Maintenance Products

In the late 1990s, two branded home-maintenance products produced by Company X and Company Y were vying for shelf space with Home Depot and Lowe's Corporation. Company Y had recently started airing a series of ads with a prominent Cincinnati Reds baseball player. Company Y expected the ads to produce a brand awareness that would give it some leverage over Home Depot. Company X, which was recently acquired by a holding company, did not have the marketing dollars to respond.

Company X's product has been around for a long time and is well-known to the public, whereas Company Y was trying to build awareness for its relatively new product. Home Depot wanted to carry Company Y's products given its recent ads. Further, Home Depot wanted to have more than one vendor of the same product to increase its leverage.

Company X noticed that Home Depot tended to organize its shelves by brand name in long, 18-foot shelves. Company X

continues

Case 5: Multiple Options for Competitive Risks—Branded Home-Maintenance Products (Continued)

suggested to Home Depot that it reorganize their stores by categories instead of brand names. Company X suggested that keeping similar products in one area will facilitate the end-consumer's shopping experience. Home Depot had always distinguished itself by being extremely user-friendly for the do-it-yourself consumer and, therefore, this suggestion was quickly implemented.

After Home Depot went into the shelf arrangement by category type, it quickly realized Company X was selling more, and economics justified carrying only one product, so Company Y was dropped by Home Depot.

Clearly, the goal of Company X was to be the sole supplier to Home Depot. The problem that Company X was facing was simply competitive risk from a well-financed new entrant to a space that Company X had basically owned for a long time. If Company X had the financial wherewithal, it might have launched a counter advertising blitz. However, the company did not have the money and had to identify a different way of reaching its goal. Of course, Company X could have tried to use the franchise value of its product to convince Home Depot not to carry Company Y's product. More than likely, such an approach would have been seen by Home Depot as a way of regaining supplier power that Company X had lost because of the new brand introduced by Company Y. Therefore, Company X had to figure out other options to reach the same goal.

Let us analyze this situation through the lens of the outcome-to-objective framework. Company X decided to leverage the outcomes desired by Home Depot—reduce its inventory and improve inventory turnover—to its advantage. However, if Company X simply offered Home Depot its services in managing Home Depot's inventory, Company X might have been sidetracked by standard supply-chain issues of delivering its product just-in-time or helping with store display. The business model that Company X had to develop was delivering this inventory management outcome in a manner that *also promoted the sale of Company X's product.*

To develop the business model, Company X focused on a second outcome desired, not by Home Depot, but by the end-consumer. In simple terms, Company X wanted to make it easy for the end-consumer to buy what he or she needed quickly and with confidence. This outcome for the end-consumer was also an important internal objective for Home Depot, so this suggestion was well-received. Company X then went about operationalizing this suggestion using its store display strategy described in the sidebar. Instead of trying to convince Home Depot to not carry Company Y's product, Company X reformulated its competitive objective by developing a store display strategy that (a) satisfied the desired outcome of the end-consumer, and (b) made it obvious to Home Depot that it wasn't economical to carry two brands. Thus, by focusing on two outcomes—purchase flexibility for the end-consumer and inventory rationalization for Home Depot—Company X managed to become the sole supplier to the largest do-it-yourself store in the country[3] without countering Company Y's ads.

Even though the story ended to the satisfaction of Company X, this strategy was not without risks. Company X made some critical assumptions before it formulated the design of the business model. Company X strongly believed that its product had a better brand-name than its competitor, Company Y, despite its recent ads. Company X believed that if the end-consumer saw the two products side-by-side, then the end-consumer would choose Company X's product. If this assumption were incorrect, placing its products alongside competitors' products at Home Depot would be a grave logical error. The category management strategy is a low-risk option only if the franchise value of Company X's product overcame the recent advertising by Company Y.

There is a postscript to the story. The competing brand, Company Y, went to Lowe's Corporation and persuaded Lowe's to carry its products as sole supplier as a buffer against Home Depot. Unfortunately, Lowe's soon found out that Home Depot was cornering most of the sales in this product category. This resulted in Company Y's product being removed from Lowe's, and Company X became the sole supplier to both Home Depot and Lowe's. Clearly, the objective of Company X was to increase its market share with Home Depot and Lowe's. There were many ways that it could have tried to achieve this. The more expensive and risky options would have been to get into an advertising battle. Equally expensive would be to cut prices or take over the inventory management function of Home Depot and Lowe's by integrating with their supply chains. Both of these choices are risky because they either jeopardize the financial viability of the company or require additional investment. What Company X did was very similar to our outcome-to-objective process (of course, it did not call it as such). Company X managed not only to attain its objective, but it did so without investment in new capabilities.

We Can Anticipate Competitive Risks Better by Focusing on Outcomes

Consider the service network case (Case 2) once more. It is not enough to analyze the difficulty of a competitor imitating the service network. Rather, it is necessary to figure out whether the service network is the only way a new competitor can match the incumbent's competitive advantage. Using either SWOT or a core competency framework, this becomes a completely open-ended question.

However, if you move away from viewing the competency (the service network) as the basis of the competitive advantage, and instead look at how you can deliver the outcome that customers desire, the vulnerabilities of the current strategy are easy to understand. In this case, customers would be loyal to Xerox not because of its service network per se, but because the service network prevents downtime. If you start the analysis by questioning whether others can deliver the same "uptime" outcome, possibilities beyond mere imitation of the service network open up (see Figure 1.3). A competitor may be able to deliver the same outcome of reduced downtime through a different resource, such as by manufacturing excellence (so that a machine needs few repairs) or by designing a machine that customers can service easily by themselves. Canon's entry into the personal copier market and the office equipment market utilized both design and manufacturing strategies to get around its lack of service and other infrastructures in the copier market (see Chapter 4 on Canon's actual implementation).

The outcome-to-objective framework is a thinking style that can be applied in just about any situation where you can benefit from identifying multiple options. In the following case, this framework illustrates how operational efficiency can be attained by avoiding resource-intensive solutions.

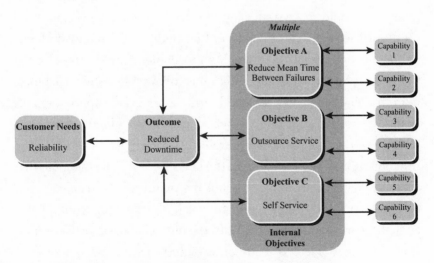

An Outside-In Approach Opens the Door to Develop Multiple Alternatives Objectives for Delivering Value to Customers.

FIGURE 1.3 The outcome-to-objectives approach.

Case 6: Rephrasing Outcomes of an Operational Problem

Large efficiency costs result when an assembly line has to be stopped for any reason. Crown Cork and Seal ran into this problem when it found its assembly-line supervisors had to run from the can seamer end to solve problems at the labeling end because of problems with the labeling machine that the labeling-end worker was not trained to solve. The minute or two that it took the supervisor to reach the other end of the assembly line was enough to cause a blockage and, therefore, the line had to be stopped even though the problem itself could be resolved in a few seconds. How can you try to solve this problem most efficiently, so the line does not have to be stopped?

You can identify solutions that involve training the assembly-line worker, hiring a new supervisor for the labeling end, or buying a more robust labeling machine. However, then you have basically applied a competency-based solution to the problem: acquire competencies to develop competitive advantage, in this case, by reducing downtime costs. In terms of SWOT, managers have identified a weakness in their value delivery system, and they get rid of the weakness by acquiring the skills. The SWOT or other traditional frameworks focus on the current output—keeping both machines running 100% of the time. Therefore, the obvious solution is to invest in better machines, more training for its workers, and perhaps a second supervisor. This is an inside-out approach, which would have added other risks because of the increased commitment. However, let us consider the situation by isolating the cause of the line stoppage. The outcome that actually triggers the stoppage is not the failure of the machines but the inability of the supervisor to reach the labeling end quickly enough to prevent a blockage. With the outcome–to-objective framework, you now need to focus on avoiding the adverse outcome of the supervisor's inability to have access to both ends quickly. The objective that follows from this desired outcome is an assembly-line configuration where both ends can be accessed simultaneously *without costly investments*. Considering this desired outcome, it is easy to visualize the unorthodox, creative, and inexpensive solution that Crown Cork and Seal came up with. They made the assembly-line U shaped. This does not mean the U-shaped option is the optimal one. It is only optimal if this is the least expensive option without any adverse consequences in the desired outcome. All we are saying is that if you focus on outcomes, such as lack of downtime, instead of the means to deliver it, such as a service network, you will be able to visualize multiple business options and, by extension, multiple business models. This ability is the first step in avoiding unnecessary business risks.

An Aside on Creativity and Choice

You may feel that the concepts here are similar to creative thinking, and there is some truth to this. Creativity occasionally leads to breakthrough innovation, but the bulk of creative business models usually just uses existing ideas in a different context. For example, a design group in IDEO saw the possibility of using the heart valve used in medical products to design a "slit valve" for a bicycle water bottle. To see the possibilities, however, you have to ask the questions that can lead you to see the choices. This is exactly the approach that Dr. William Hunter, CEO of Vancouver-based Angiotech Pharmaceuticals, wants his employees to take. According to Doctor Hunter, "The difference between good science and great science is the quality of the questions posed."[4] By focusing on outcomes, you can improve the quality of the questions you ask as you design a strategy.

Decide on Objectives Based on How Your Firm Wants To Compete

To summarize, the notion of competitive objective allows us to understand the logic of the output that we can deliver (different from our competitors) in order to satisfy the customer-desired outcomes. But how do you decide which objectives to focus on? In Chapter 2, "Three Steps to Design a Low Risk Strategy," you will consider a three-step methodology that distills the essential logic of how you are going to compete. However, this is not necessarily a linear process. By using the outcome-to-objective framework, you are able to identify multiple internal outputs that reduce competitive risks. However, you still may not be able to deliver the new output with capabilities you possess or can acquire at a cost that allows you to make a profit. The competitive objective should be designed not only to ensure that your outputs can deliver the customer outcomes, but also to avoid any increased risk of loss. This is an iterative process that leads to the final competitive objective that you should settle on and clearly articulate when designing a strategy.

In the case of the hearing-aid battery maker, the company finally decided to compete on the basis of packages and not product. The battery company clearly understood the logic of why packages can allow it to deliver the same desired outcome instead of creating a new product. Compared to the uncertainties involved in developing a new product the option of focusing on a competitive objective by developing a package has tremendous appeal. This objective avoids competitive risks (no one else has thought of it yet) and has a higher probability of being developed (they are more likely to come up with a packaging innovation than a new product) without costly and uncertain R&D investments. In the case of the coated stent, the company decided to compete on existing coating technology with an existing drug rather than new mechanical engineering. The competitive objective for Company X was to persuade Home Depot to adopt category management. Persuading Home Depot to adopt category management is a much lower risk than investing in expensive advertising or a supply-chain management capability. Basically, all of these examples repeat a theme you shall see used by many low-risk strategies that we use as examples in this book. In all of these cases, the companies might have considered other product or service configurations, but the option of using existing or off-the-shelf capabilities swayed the final decision.[5]

This brings us to the final concept, which you will explore further in Chapter 2. Even if you manage to reduce competitive risks by identifying a competitive logic that is distinctly different from competitors, you are still vulnerable to capability risks. Do you really have the capabilities needed to deliver the outputs dictated by this logic? This is where many strategies sow the seeds of failure. They do not simply take the time to think through what the firm has to do to make its business model work, and in failing to do so, they implement a strategy that is difficult to execute. To mitigate execution risk, you need a dashboard that alerts you to the failure of critical components of your business model in real-time. This dashboard, in conjunction with the outcome-to-objective framework, allows you to seek out gold where others see risk.

Endnotes

1   Stratford P Sherman. "Inside the Mind of Jack Welch." *Fortune* 27 Mar. 1989: 38.

2   Carol Hymowitz . "The Best Innovations Are Those That Come From Smart Questions." *The Wall Street Journal* April 13, 2004; Page B1.

3   This example also illustrates the power of creating value by making the attributes of your product or service visible to the customer. This framework is developed in Chapter 5.

4   Hymowitz. Op. Cit.

5   We need to emphasize the difference between the outcome-to-objective framework and the traditional core competency frameworks. Our framework considers a firm's core competency, but only after identifying multiple objectives using an outside-in process that starts with customer-desired outcomes.

2

THREE STEPS TO DESIGN A LOW-RISK STRATEGY

"If you do not know where you are going, any road will lead you there."

—Anonymous

To avoid risks, you need to understand where the risks are, their exact nature, and what you can do to control them. Reviewing our three risk categories, *demand risk* represents the risk that customers will not buy the firm's product or service at the expected level.[1] *Competitive risk* represents the risk that competitors can imitate what your firm does and take your customers away. *Capability risk* represents the risk that your firm may not be able to deliver the value to your customers and capture some of the value for your shareholders.

We recommend a three-step process to identify and mitigate these three risks when designing a strategy. First, in order to sell what your firm makes, you must ensure that whatever your firm is doing internally (internal objectives) results in delivering the outcomes that your firm's customers are willing to pay for. The outcome that Home Depot's customers were looking for was help that allowed them to quickly finish their home-improvement projects. Thus, a store display that allows a customer to buy what he or she needs quickly and with confidence is *one* possible important internal objective for Home Depot. The next step is the critical step that dictates the success or failure of the business model. Using the outcome-to-objective framework developed in Chapter 1, managers are able to identify many different internal objectives. At this point, it is necessary to focus on the most promising objective(s) and articulate the objective in a manner that captures how the strategy will make money. This is the core logic of the business model. Before implementing the category management objective described in Chapter 1, Company X had to make sure that not only was it satisfying Home Depot's desired outcomes, but it was also allowing Company X to make money (in that case, by eliminating competitive risks).

Basically, at this step, you are choosing between a differentiation (avoid competitive risks) or low-price (avoid demand risk) strategy to capture some of the value that you are giving to your customers. Company X chose to emphasize its differentiation without resorting to costly advertising. This ended up being more profitable than either spending money on ads or giving a price discount to Home Depot or the end-consumer. Starting from one of these high-level competitive objectives, you need to develop a focused set of core (operational-level) objectives that can be calibrated and tracked in real-time (a dashboard for the business model). For example, go back to Company X's strategy; it had to closely monitor the sales of its products versus Company Y's. If Company X's assumption about the franchise value of its products was incorrect, it would not see any reduction in Company Y's sales, and then Company X would have to re-think its strategy and perhaps raise funds for an advertising battle. However, if Company X did not have a dashboard that alerted it to the failure of its strategy, it may allow Company Y to develop a stronger position that would be more difficult to counter later on. In summary, Company X embarked on a risky strategy that invited direct comparison of its products with the competitors. If it did not have a metric to track and manage this risk, then it would have been relying on luck and not a framework for its ultimate success. This is very dangerous. The dashboard concept reduces the adverse impact from the element of chance.

Finally, the strategy may fail because Company X's sales force was not capable of implementing the new category management system to the satisfaction of Home Depot. This is a capability risk. The clarity with which managers can state the core objectives dictates the clarity with which they can identify the mission-critical capabilities needed to make the business model work. At that point, managers may realize that the starting objectives cannot be delivered by the capabilities they have or can acquire. If so, the strategy designers need to repeat the process by selecting a second set of objectives until they are comfortable with the risks at each stage. This is the third step in designing a low-risk strategy.

There is another issue regarding capability risk that you will encounter in Chapter 6, *Organizations That Can Benefit from the Outcome-to-Objectives Framework*, based on the concepts discussed in the third step. You must make sure that your organization understands the core objectives and the capability requirements. Basically, the objectives and capabilities must be stated using words that put everyone on the same page, and everyone realizes what they have to accomplish individually and collectively to deliver the objectives. This will mitigate much of the execution risk.

Step 1. Demand Risks: Broad Competitive Objectives Must Deliver the Core Customer Outcomes

The broad competitive objectives should clearly explain how the strategy will deliver the outcomes that *your firm's* customers desire. These broad competitive objectives should also clearly demonstrate how the firm can simultaneously capture part of the value for its shareholders. To illustrate this process, consider the strategies of some world-class companies.

Case 1: Southwest Airlines

Southwest is a short-haul, low-price airline with a unique corporate culture and an original approach to day-to-day operations. Even though Southwest employees are unionized, they are very flexible in terms of their day-to-day duties. For example, it is not unusual for pilots to check tickets if this can avoid a delayed departure. The airline flies only one type of aircraft, the Boeing 737. Unlike most airlines, Southwest historically keeps their planes longer than other airlines, which they service through their in-house maintenance facility. Southwest flies short hops (on average 375 miles) between city pairs and favors secondary airports, such as Dallas Love Field, Chicago's Midway, and Houston Hobby.

Based on the outcome-to-objective framework, we start with the customer outcomes and work back to the objectives. The important thing to note here is not just what outcomes customers seek out, but also what they *do not*. In other words, customers have to be identified at a suitably *granular* level for this process to be successful. In the case of Southwest, it primarily targets leisure travelers or the business traveler who is willing to substitute an airplane ride for car travel or other short-haul transportation. Unlike traditional business passengers who prefer and are willing to pay for the flexibility of complicated schedules, Southwest's passengers are looking for low-prices, the ability to fly whenever they choose, and on-time arrival. Obviously, to deliver the low price and capture some of the value for its shareholders, Southwest has to have a low cost-structure.

To have a low-cost structure, a firm must have a combination of higher fixed-asset utilization, higher labor productivity, and lower variable costs. Higher asset utilization by itself is not specific to Southwest; all airlines and, indeed, all companies strive for this. For most airlines, however, asset utilization implies selling out all their available seats (100 percent load factor). This automatically lowers the cost-per-average seat mile (CASM)—the ubiquitous formula used to measure cost structure across airlines. However, to understand how Southwest manages to have lower CASM, even if it has the same load factor as others (Southwest's is usually much higher), we need to define what asset utilization specifically means for a point-to-point airline, such as Southwest. Note that Southwest has two things working against it in terms of variable cost. First, Southwest normally flies a much older fleet than the major airlines, leading to increased fuel and maintenance costs. Second, the cost of flying short hauls is usually much higher than long hauls. These factors adversely affect the CASM.

Many in the business press suggest that the key to Southwest's success is having full and frequent flights. A little later in this chapter, we explain why these broad competitive objectives do not really help us understand why competitors have found it so difficult to imitate Southwest's strategy. But first, we must address a very important point that has a direct bearing on demand risk. Whatever final competitive objectives any firm settles on, these objectives must be able to deliver the outcomes *its* customers desire. Absent this link, Southwest will never be able to achieve at least one of its broad objectives—fuller flights—falling victim to demand risk. This link is the foundation of all successful business models. We will see later how competitors who tried to imitate Southwest and failed did not take the time to develop this link.

Note that to identify its broad competitive objectives, Southwest has to focus on the outcomes that are critical to *its* customers. These customers are first looking for a cheap airfare and, second, the option to travel at a time of their choosing. To provide cheap airfare, Southwest has to have a lower CASM than other airlines. However, to provide the flexibility to travel any time of the day, Southwest has to provide many flights. Of course, if these flights are full, then Southwest may not have a problem reducing its CASM. However, to deliver this outcome, any airline, including Southwest, is taking the risk that the flights may not be full. This is a critical point where Southwest has an advantage over its competitors, which we elaborate on later in this chapter.

Let us now consider other ways Southwest can reduce its cost structure. By not providing services such as on-board meals, luggage checking, and different classes of service, Southwest is reducing its variable costs. However, in so doing, is Southwest taking on the risk of reducing demand for its flights? There is no doubt that if Southwest were to offer these services, its customers would like it. However, because Southwest's passengers are not looking for a complicated schedule, luggage check-in is not that high a priority for them, unlike traditional business fliers. Likewise, given the short duration of the flights, food service is also not critical. Finally, there is probably no need for different classes of service. This is the first of many trade-offs that we discuss throughout this book. Managers must be able to identify trade-offs that do not risk losing customers (demand risks) when developing their competitive objectives. The key takeaway from this discussion is that to identify these trade-offs precisely, managers have to define their customers at a level of *granularity* that many companies do not. For example, Southwest's objectives are completely unsuitable for business passengers needing very flexible routes covering many cities and schedules. The process by which Southwest can identify its broad competitive objectives is graphically represented in Figure 2.1.

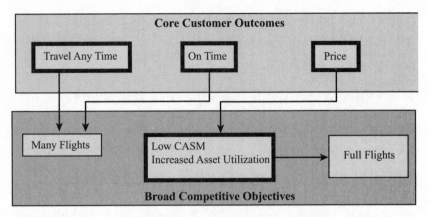

FIGURE 2.1   How to identify broad competitive objectives—Southwest.

Step 2. Competitive Risks: Identify the Core Competitive Objectives That Cannot Be Imitated by Competitors

The business press believes that the key to Southwest's success is fuller and more frequent flights. If Southwest can beat other airlines on *both* of these objectives—have more flights between two points as well as fuller flights—it will have a lower cost structure. Therefore, the core business logic of Southwest (or any other airline that wants to imitate Southwest) may be plausibly captured by these two broad competitive objectives—frequent and fuller flights. At such a high level, these objectives will not give you much insight into Southwest's capabilities or the engine of its business model, which delivers these objectives. Further, these high-level objectives also do not allow real-time tracking of its business model's performance. You need to identify the components of the broad competitive objectives with a degree of specificity that precisely captures what its competitive advantage is—the exact performance parameters of the engine or the critical outputs of its capabilities. Additionally, the components must be defined such that Southwest's output can be measured in real time. At the end of this process, you will have identified what we call "core competitive objectives." These core objectives are specific to a business and precisely measurable because their outputs are the dashboard of the business model.

Core Objectives Must Be Specific and Measurable

Let us now revisit the issue of the customers' desired outcome to be able to fly anytime during the day. In order to deliver this outcome, it is necessary, as stated, for an airline to schedule frequent flights. Two risks are involved in doing this. First, to schedule many flights, an airline has to buy more planes. Second, if for any reason the airline has to reduce the number of flights, its asset utilization will suffer. This is where Southwest puts space between itself and competitors. Southwest can offer the same number of flights but with *fewer* planes. Southwest does this by ensuring that its planes spend more time flying than on the ground.

Consider all the factors that might lead to a flight between two points taking longer than usual. This can be broken down broadly into delays at the gate, delays in takeoff and landing, and the actual flight itself. The actual flight is a function of aircraft and weather that is unlikely to be any different from one airline to the other. Southwest, therefore, has focused on minimizing the other two factors. This creates more clear-cut objectives that can be observed in *real time,* leading to corrective actions if a negative variation is observed. As shown in Figure 2.2, maximizing flights can be achieved by a set of three specific and measurable core objectives. These are proper route selection, quick turnaround at the gate, and no takeoff or landing delays. Suggested[2] metrics for each of these components are also included in the figure. Of course, Southwest does not use these specific metrics (except the turnaround time), but it does have a process such that, if a plane gets delayed at the gate, it will be observed by the employees immediately so corrective action can be taken.[3] The same is true for idiosyncratic events that may lead to takeoff or landing delays. This precise articulation leads to the first principle of how core objectives can reduce the risk of failure.

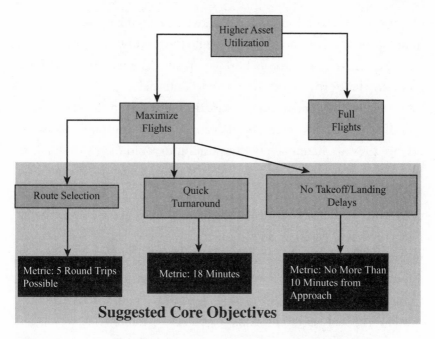

FIGURE 2.2   Identifying specific and measurable core objectives.

Core Objectives Must Be Leading or Contemporaneous Indicators

Southwest knows that its ability to offer frequent flights is suffering as it is happening and not at the end of the week. In fact, Southwest's employees have contingency plans to speed up gate operations in case a plane is delayed for whatever reason. This ensures that the plane can depart on time. If the plane is delayed at the gate beyond acceptable norms, a written explanation has to be offered by the involved parties. Basically, core objectives force a firm to track the few things it must do to succeed. If a firm is hitting the targets set by properly specified core objectives, it is very likely that it is enjoying the expected returns from its business model while avoiding the risks of failure.

A study by Hackett Benchmarking (in 2001) compared the planning and control practices of world-class companies with other businesses. One of its key findings underscores the importance of core objectives. Hackett found that the average company has 372 line items at the level of budget detail, while the world-class company has only 21. To emulate these best companies, managers must have absolute clarity regarding the few core internal objectives that they must deliver to maintain their competitive advantage. The process of identifying these few core objectives is not easy, but once managers do this, they are in a much better position to avoid the risks of failure than the average company. Why? Very simply, managers do not suffer from information overload and instead can focus their resources on delivering the mission-critical objectives. If an objective is not being met, it is much easier to spot it among 21 items than 372. However, to reduce the many things a firm must do on a day-to-day basis to a few core objectives, it is critical to have almost complete clarity as to how the firm's business model is expected to work. Absent a framework, such as the outcome-to-objective framework, we do not recommend relying on a small set of metrics. Without the clarity of a framework such as ours, relying on a few metrics actually would be riskier.

Most businesses believe they already have metrics for their core objectives. However, when we ask them what these are, they come back with broad metrics, such as returns on investments (ROI), market share, or profit margins. *These broad metrics are practically useless in tracking the true risks of the business.* Why? Because these measures are at best symptoms of what has already happened within the company—they are *lagging* indicators. The measurement of core objectives must be precise and use a metric that unambiguously alerts the firm if the business model is not working *before* it shows up in broader measures, such as profitability. The metric for a core objective, such as time spent at the gate, must allow managers to get the pulse of the business at a glance in real-time. Using this criterion, the frequent flights and full flights are not sufficient for Southwest to manage the risks of its business in real-time. These are not indicators that tell Southwest whether or not something is going properly.

However, even if Southwest identified quick turnaround times as a core objective, which would allow it to track its execution in real-time, it still has not avoided all risks. Quick turnaround times give Southwest an option of what they need to do to beat the competition. Now they have to decide whether they *can* do it. Basically, up to this point, the risk is theoretical. Only when Southwest implements the quick turnarounds option does the risk become a reality. To do this, Southwest has to delve into the capabilities that allow it to achieve the frequent flights.

While tracking and measuring the core objectives gives managers a heads-up regarding the risks that matter, the *source* of those risks is in the many interdependent activities (and supporting resources) a firm carries out to deliver the core objectives. Thus, for an automobile, a number of components such as tires, suspension, and body integrity collectively determine acceptable ride quality and noise levels. For a business model, the analogous factors are the many interdependent activities and resources that we call the "capability set" needed to deliver a particular core objective. Very few businesses take the time to isolate the critical components of their capabilities, and even if they have an idea, few take the time to understand the nature of the trade-offs that can lead to increasing the efficiency of the capabilities. The framework presented in step 3 puts you in the right direction toward understanding capability risks.

Step 3. Capability Risks: Using Core Objectives to Reduce Capability Risks

Defining the core objectives is absolutely critical to understand the capability risks of the business model. Without this precision, managers will not know what the capabilities they invest in have to deliver. You may also endanger your business by investing in the wrong capability or trying to force your existing competencies to deliver the wrong objective. Later in this chapter, we will consider how both of these risks manifest due to a lack of clarity in defining the core objectives.

Major risks always exists when acquiring the capabilities to deliver your objective, and this is where many business models fail during execution. You have to be brutally honest with yourself to determine whether you can truly deliver the core objectives. The first step to reduce the risk is to have complete clarity regarding the components of the engine of your business model—the activities and resources that comprise the capabilities. In some instances, you have to bite the bullet and invest in these capabilities and accept the risk of failure, and there is no doubt you will fail in some instances. The difference in this approach is that you clearly knew the risks going in and can potentially learn from the experience. However, as we have indicated several times, capability risks are not just an execution issue. You can do many things to significantly reduce capability risks by using the clarity and choice dimensions at the capability level. We start with the clarity dimension.

Core Objectives Lead to Clarity in Capabilities: Capability Maps

Capabilities are the interlinked set of activities that deliver a particular core objective. In the case of Southwest, quick turnaround of its planes is one of the core objectives. In Figure 2.3, we map the activities of maintenance, gate operations, and flight operations that make this possible. This kind of mapping where the components of a capability are clearly linked to the core objective pays very high dividends in terms of reducing capability risks. This mapping provides complete clarity about what needs to be done to deliver the core objective. By studying such a map, functional-level employees would be able to give early warnings about the feasibility of the business model. This basically lets the strategy designers know what they can

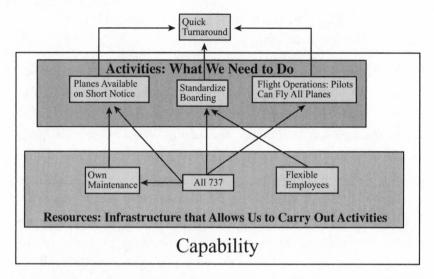

FIGURE 2.3   Identifying capabilities—activities and resources needed to deliver the core objectives.

or cannot do before they implement the strategy. By explicitly considering what they can do, the managers are able to anticipate and avoid risks irrespective of the capability configuration they choose to adopt. To illustrate this point, consider Southwest's gate operations.

From the moment a plane arrives at the gate, every single Southwest employee knows the role he or she has to play to ensure that the plane leaves the gate within the allotted time. This clarity comes from drilling down the core objectives of quick turnaround (this process needs to be repeated for each core objective) to the functional-level employees, which makes it possible for them to carry out the activities needed to accomplish the objective. Going back to the engine analogy, a capability map displays the components of the engine of a business model. The mapping (or similar) process contributes to risk reduction in other ways. Because the map is vetted by functional-level employees, it provides a shared framework where all employees know their roles and reduces the risk of things not going smoothly during execution.

Capability Maps Provide a Shared Framework for Making Business Decisions

Using the core objective lens, the wisdom of Southwest's other decisions begins to become crystal clear for the rank and file. The in-house maintenance facility may not be as cost-effective as outsourcing maintenance, but because of the core objective of quick turnaround, the trade-off is clear to everyone. Given the single-minded focus on quick turnaround as the basis of its competitive advantage, it is actually riskier for Southwest to try to save money by outsourcing maintenance because it would lose control over the availability of a replacement plane—a critical activity for delivering its core objective. Likewise, having the same planes (Boeing 737s) allows a seamless transfer of passengers in case of a maintenance problem with one plane. Without a shared framework, as illustrated earlier in Figure 2.3, it is extremely difficult for employees to accurately understand their roles in making the company's businesses function smoothly. This shared understanding reduces the risk of failure in four important ways. First, the employee knows exactly what he or she has to accomplish. Second, the employee does not feel like a cog in the wheel but an important component of the business— execution risk is much lower with a motivated employee. Third, this shared framework allows the employee to experiment within the boundaries set by the core objectives to help expand the value frontier. Finally, as we have seen before, core objectives allow employees to take corrective actions before things get out of hand because it is observable as it is happening. Many prominent companies are beginning to use variations of capability maps in their decision-making. For example, Figure 2.4 illustrates the architecture that IBM uses in its Enterprise Web Management group that is very similar to the capability map illustrated earlier in Figure 2.3.

**EWM Defined Five Primary Functions That Aligned with the
Mission's Three Objectives**

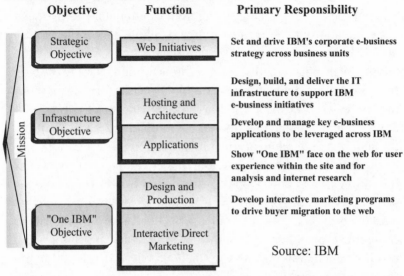

FIGURE 2.4   A similar framework that is used by IBM Enterprise Web
Management group.

Lack of a Shared Framework Increases Capability Risks

Let us now consider the capability risks of not having clarity regarding the core objectives of the company.

Case 2: Continental Copies Southwest

Continental was the first of the major airlines to try to copy Southwest's point-to-point, low-cost strategy. At the time, Continental had the lowest labor costs among the major carriers. Continental felt it could leverage this into a low-priced Southwest imitation in the South-Eastern U.S., which had the advantages of a large market and a weak competitor in money-losing USAir. Continental named its newest service CALite to differentiate it from Continental's longer routes.

continues

Case 2: Continental Copies Southwest (Continued)

The impetus for this strategy came from Continental's desire to get out of its unprofitable Denver hub and culminated in the moving of nearly 80 planes and 200 plus flights from Denver to the Southeast in nine months. As a reference point, Southwest took five years to implement a comparable expansion. However, after the strategy was explained to top management, there was considerable doubt among the operations people. Instead of sorting through this disagreement, the CEO, Mr. Ferguson, fired the airline's president and chief operating officer within a few months of the move. In addition, Donald Valentine, a Southwest marketing executive with little operational experience, was hired as the chief marketing officer. Valentine, of course, was aware of the broad competitive objectives of Southwest—frequency and price—and was instrumental in making Continental believe that it had found the secret to matching Southwest.

Unfortunately, Continental did not understand the core objectives. For example, Continental did not understand the difference between secondary airports that are close to large cities and smaller airports with less demand. Thus, Greenville/Spartanburg, South Carolina, got 17 daily jet flights and Dayton, Ohio, a hub abandoned by other carriers for lack of demand, received 20 extra flights. Next, Continental used its fleet of jets to replace smaller airplanes on routes that simply could not absorb the extra capacity. Finally, its marketing and promotional strategies led to absurd situations. Travelers standing in line to buy tickets shared itineraries with strangers and took advantage of the "Add a Penny, Add a Pal" fares.

As a result of not delivering the core objectives, Continental failed to achieve the kind of utilization from its airplanes that led to Southwest's low-cost structures. For example, Continental was unable to replace a canceled flight with another plane because, unlike Southwest's Boeing 737 fleet, Continental had 16 different types of planes. Furthermore, Continental's maintenance staff did not have the in-depth expertise of Southwest's because Continental's staff had to understand the mechanical problems and spare parts requirements of 16 different airplanes. Also, Continental had its maintenance facilities in its main hubs as opposed to localized maintenance by Southwest. Thus, any maintenance-related problems that occurred at an airport without a major maintenance facility had a domino effect leading to delays all through the system. These delays and flight cancellations led to passenger frustrations and deteriorating employee morale. Oblivious to all of these problems, Continental increased its daily flights to 875 to pursue its goal of frequent flights.

However, the losses quickly began to mount and Continental took desperate steps to cut operating costs, such as ending meals on shorter flights and reneging on its commitment to issue credit for its frequent-flyer program to CALite passengers. Travel agents' commissions were also cut and overrides ended.

The Continental situation is a classic example of the risks of not clearly defining and calibrating the core objectives of the business model—its managers simply did not know what their capabilities should be. Continental knew it had to increase the frequency of its flights—a broad competitive objective—but did not or could not deliver the core objective of quick turnaround. In fact, Continental's executive hiring and firing decisions suggest the company was more focused on marketing (promoting price and frequency) and less on operations (quick turnaround). The fact that the chief operating officer was fired is testament to the company's lack of understanding of the capability that is central to making Southwest's strategy work. If Continental had calibrated its broad competitive objectives of price and frequency by focusing on the core objective of quick turnaround, it probably would have quickly realized the importance of having one type of plane and maintenance facilities near all originating airports. Then Continental might also have refrained from firing the chief operating officer. Of course, the desire to use existing planes underscores the danger of leveraging current competencies. This invariably leads to an inside-out perspective, which is precisely what makes it impossible to define the core objectives of a new business model.

The point of the Continental story should be clear. If you define and calibrate your core objectives with clarity, you will have a clear understanding of the capabilities you require to deliver these objectives. If you try to superficially copy another strategy and do not develop your own core objectives, you are overlooking the risks of failure.

Likewise, e-Commerce firms, such as Value America and eToys, failed because they did not establish core objectives to monitor the risks of implementing a zero-inventory model (contrast this with Dell and Wal-Mart, which are discussed in Chapter 6). Take the case of Value America. Its vision was that customers could order anything they wanted, in any quantity they wanted, any time they wanted. The company envisioned a fully digital business model with zero inventory by outsourcing the fulfillment and returns. "It would pick up orders from consumers and immediately transmit them to manufacturers that would ship IBM computers and Knorr soups, Panasonic televisions and Vicks VapoRub, direct to customers. It featured more than 1,000 brand names, many in multimedia presentations online.[4]" In reality, Value America did not set up the digital infrastructure before opening for business. The result was that many orders were transmitted to vendors by fax or e-mail. Value America was completely dependent on its vendors for fulfillment and, unfortunately, companies such as Proctor & Gamble, which were used to shipping in palettes, were incapable of shipping a single box of Tide or a bottle of Advil. A core objective for Value America should have been to monitor the vendors' "pick-and-pack" capability. The end result of all this was that products were not shipped properly or on time, computers crashed, and orders took forever to get filled. Value America did not anticipate the risks in executing its business model.

Now suppose that Value America had defined its core objective not as "having zero inventory" but instead something like "98% pick-and-pack accuracy from its vendor." Value America would have immediately known that Procter & Gamble would not have the capability to deliver this objective, whereas a company like Walgreens, with strong pick-and-pack expertise, possibly could. We are not claiming that the Value America business model would have worked in any case, but if it had partnered with Walgreens, it could have avoided a key capability shortcoming that derailed the business model.

Now contrast Value America with Amazon.com. Like Value America, Amazon also started with a zero-inventory model. However, Amazon focused on books and CDs and did not try to become the Wal-Mart of the Internet, at least not initially. Moreover, Amazon made an extremely critical decision very early. It moved to Seattle to be close to its primary distributor, Ingram, which would be handling its drop shipments. In other words, Amazon correctly identified near-perfect fulfillment as a core objective and developed a business model around the capability to monitor this function.[5] Amazon outsourced the pick-and-pack capability to a firm with the proven ability to do this consistently. Further, by moving to Seattle, Amazon was on-hand to supervise the fulfillment process. In contrast, Value America was based in Charlottesville, Virginia, and was hundreds—if not thousands—of miles from its vendors' establishments.

Improper core objectives may also have contributed to Ford's problems with the Explorer in connection with the Firestone tire problems. According to published reports, Ford chose ride quality, noise, and vibration levels as the core objectives when sourcing the tires for the Ford Explorer. However, if Ford had used the likelihood of rollover as a core objective (with safety being the broad competitive objective), then the company might have been able to avoid the Firestone-related disasters. To accommodate Ford, Firestone compromised on the recommended tire pressures to improve ride quality with disastrous results. The Ford decision process also highlights the importance of identifying its customers at a suitably granular level. It seems that Ford and other SUV makers were confused about what their customers really wanted. Did they want a vehicle that basically drove like a car but had superior traction, or did they really want a vehicle with off-road capabilities? The majority of SUVs are never used off-road.

How To Lower Capability Risks with Alternate Configurations

Up to this point, you have explored the choice dimension in identifying multiple competitive objectives and the clarity dimension in specifying the capabilities needed to deliver a specific set of core objectives. In Chapter 3, *Identifying Multiple Capability Configurations*, we revisit the choice dimension that allows you to consider different capability configurations that can deliver the same core objectives without making the mistakes made by Continental CALite. This will help you understand how elements of a successful strategy from one business can be applied to just about any business without undue capability risks.

Endnotes

1 Note that demand that is higher than expected can also be a risk, as we shall see in the case of EMI in Chapter 9.

2 These are for illustration purposes only.

3 As an aside, this focus on turnaround time was not by design, as suggested by academic case studies, but out of necessity. When Southwest started its operations, it had purchased four planes and had scheduled flights based on this number. However, because of a lack of profits initially, it had to return the fourth plane. It is at this point, Southwest decided to keep the same schedule with three planes. This was the genesis of the quick turnaround time "core objective" as a way of implementing the strategy.

4 John A. Byrne. "The Fall of a Dot-Com" *Business Week* (2000) 1 May 2000 (http://www.businessweek.com).

5 It is interesting to note that Amazon ran into problems when it deviated from this model by going beyond books and CDs.

3

IDENTIFYING MULTIPLE CAPABILITY CONFIGURATIONS

Deliver the Same Core Objective with Different Capabilities

It is not imperative that a new entrant copy the strategies of the dominant incumbent verbatim, but it is necessary to have an alternate configuration of core objectives that can deliver the same outcome to the customer.

Case 1: JetBlue

JetBlue commenced operations on February 11, 2000, with two planes out of John F. Kennedy Airport in New York City. Within one year of operation, JetBlue was voted #2 Domestic Airline in the 2001 Zagat survey and posted a profit of $38.5 million in less than two years of operation. Part of JetBlue's success so far can be credited to CEO David Neeleman's unconventional emphasis on using IT in an industry where all major players have only dreamt

continues

Case 1: JetBlue (Continued)

of automating operations. All JetBlue pilots are provided with HP laptops to calculate the load and balance of their planes before take-off, which eliminates the dependence on dispatchers to crunch the numbers for them, as with other major carriers, and shaves off 15 minutes from their ground time. Ticket reservations are done electronically through its web site www.jetblue.com, or through its reservation agents who work from home in Utah; no paper tickets are issued. All travel is ticketless, all fares are one-way, no Saturday stay is required, and all seats are pre-assigned. Only one class of seats is offered, and passengers can check-in through electronic touch screens located at flight counters. JetBlue isn't even at maximum efficiency. By summer 2004, JetBlue will have begun its plans to move to all electronic check-in without ticket agents by installing kiosks at the airport that will even dispense luggage tags—something that no airline has done at this time.

JetBlue has a policy of not overbooking its flights, and passengers are encouraged to book tickets in advance as seats are limited. A discount of $5 is awarded for booking tickets online as a tactic to promote online ticket reservations. As a result, 63% of the tickets were booked online in 2002, which is also JetBlue's cheapest form of distribution. The ticketless travel system saves paper costs, postage, employee time, and back-office processing expenses. Its registration agents work from home using a VoIP line exclusively maintained by JetBlue for ticket reservations. All this contributes to its industry-wide lowest CASM (cost per average seat mile) of $6.43.

High-level capitalization was part of JetBlue's strategy to aid in the purchase of new technologically advanced Airbus A320s. By 2004, it had 42 aircrafts in operation, 132 new A320s on firm order, and new aircrafts being added to the fleet at the rate of one every week. These aircrafts are also the quietest and most fuel-efficient jets in the air. The greater reliability of the new aircrafts allows JetBlue to schedule them to fly more hours each day and achieve higher capacity utilization. It also operates a number of "red-eye" flights, which enables a portion of its fleet to remain productive through the night. To avoid weather-related congestion in the North East, aircrafts are equipped with life rafts, life vests, and high-frequency radios to enable flying farther out over the Atlantic ocean between New York and Florida, thus maintaining its on-time performance and completion factors.

JetBlue's strategy is fundamentally similar to that of Southwest's in terms of the broad competitive objectives. However, it has an additional core objective that Southwest does not. Like Southwest, JetBlue also relies on quick turnarounds, selects routes that can generate maximum number of flights, and avoids takeoff and landing delays. However, one of JetBlue's core objectives is avoiding any in-flight delays due to weather. Southwest is simply not equipped to do this. JetBlue's core objectives are illustrated in Figure 3.1.

Now let us consider the capabilities. Like Southwest, JetBlue also relies on quick turnarounds, but it does so by a heavy investment in

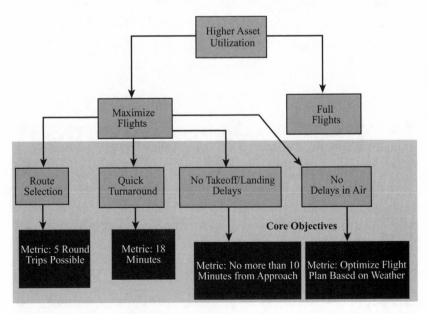

FIGURE 3.1   Core objectives for JetBlue.

IT rather than by the flexibility of its workforce (see Figure 3.2). For example, pilots can perform pre-flight checks on their laptops, which saves them 15 minutes compared to other airlines. Unlike Southwest, JetBlue uses brand-new Airbus A320 airplanes, which require much less maintenance and reduce delays due to breakdowns. Additionally, because of its computerized check-in procedures and pre-assigned seats, there are hardly any gate delays for passengers. In contrast, Southwest passengers who want to be seated in the front rows of the aircraft have to come in well ahead of the departure time or be relegated to the back rows.[1]

JetBlue also gets better utilization out of its aircrafts than Southwest because they are new—they can be run for longer hours and are more fuel-efficient. Finally, one of JetBlue's core objectives is avoiding any in-flight delays due to weather. In other words, JetBlue has consciously considered the risk of weather-related delays to its broad competitive objective of frequent flights and has designed a core objective (let's call it flexible flight plans on the fly—no pun intended) to counter this. Thus, JetBlue has made sure it has the capability to fly over the Atlantic and around any severe weather because its planes are certified for such flight plans. Note that Southwest does not have this flexibility.

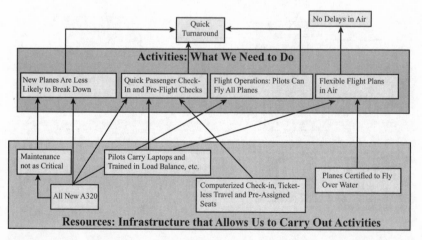

FIGURE 3.2 Core objectives and capability mapping for JetBlue.

Outsourcing Core Capabilities

A common theme across all the low-risk strategies you have seen so far is the ability to get the same or higher output with a lower fixed-asset base and lower investment in general. In effect, this leads to higher asset turnover (for the same level of demand as competitors), but it also lowers the capability risk (reduced investment in fixed assets) because the breakeven point is much lower. A smaller fixed asset allows a firm the luxury of cutting back at times of reduced demand with a less adverse cost impact compared to its competitors. At the same time, a firm can scale up to take advantage of increased demand because it can service more demand than competitors with the same asset base.

However, to achieve the broad objective of higher fixed asset turnover, most of these firms had to invest in some other capabilities, be it a unique company culture (Southwest) or IT (JetBlue). In contrast, consider the strategies of four companies in four completely different industries that achieved the same broad objective by outsourcing the capital-intensive part of their value chain. The companies are Cisco Systems, FedEx Custom Critical, Eli Lily, and Sony PlayStation. The difference between these strategies and the garden-variety outsourcing carried out by most companies is that these companies chose to outsource their *core* activities, contrary to conventional wisdom. The conventional wisdom is right in that it is very risky to outsource core activities because those constitute the source of a firm's competitive advantage. The common theme in the strategies of these companies is how these firms managed to avoid this risk. However, after they figured out a way to avoid the adverse consequences of relying on outsourcing to carry out a core activity, these companies began to get an unprecedented advantage of scalability that became the basis of their competitive advantages.

Case 2: Cisco: Scalability in Manufacturing

Cisco has integrated its suppliers through a virtual network called the *Manufacturing Connection Online (MCO)*. Cisco's core products—networking devices and software—are more or less mass-produced. Cisco owns just two of the 38 plants that assemble its products. Beginning in 1992, Cisco outsourced the manufacturing responsibilities for its products to partner firms, like Solectron and Celestica. Its partners perform nearly all of the complicated manufacturing, assembly, product configuration, and distribution activities. The shared core objective is customer satisfaction that obviates the need for direct control or micro-management. However, Cisco maintained quality control through proprietary procedures. It identified and standardized testing procedures that could be automated but would not require the involvement of a live Cisco representative. After Cisco tested the quality-control procedures internally so they were virtually infallible, it handed over these procedures to its partners, so they could carry out the quality control themselves at their manufacturing facilities. Moreover, the output of the testing results could be accessed remotely by Cisco in a second if Cisco's intervention was called for. If a quality problem arose beyond the set limits, an alert would go off at Cisco's headquarters allowing Cisco to intervene with the outsourced manufacturing process before the product got shipped to the customer. Thus, Cisco suppliers, in effect, took over the responsibility of quality assurance without sacrificing the high standards required by Cisco. Cisco, however, retained the intellectual property of this monitoring procedure, which was named "Autotest."

After Cisco trained its selected vendors to incorporate Autotest in its manufacturing processes, it had tremendous flexibility to respond to customer requests without sacrificing quality. Cisco can monitor manufacturing quality in real-time, while its partners take on the investment risks. This scalability objective also gave Cisco tremendous leverage in the ability to buy a new technology and quickly put it into large-scale production. This capability was an integral part of

Cisco's acquisition strategy in the 1990s. Cisco had a much lower risk that its acquisitions would fail compared to other acquirers because of its ability to swiftly generate top-line growth using the acquired company's technology. This was a capability that Cisco's competitors were simply unable to match.[2]

The exact same core objective of scalability can be used to understand how FedEx Custom Critical came to dominate the urgent delivery market niche, even with the entry of new competitors. How has it managed to reduce competitive risks? FedEx has done so by focusing on the core objectives that really make a difference to the customers, while not allowing competitors to reduce their profits by shifting the competitive basis to price.

Case 3: FedEx Custom Critical: Scalability in Urgent Delivery

FedEx's Custom Critical business model is based on speed, customization, and reliability. FedEx Custom Critical uses five types of vehicles to cover all possible services. In addition, the customer's cargo is the only cargo carried in the truck, and some hauls are delivered the same day as pick up. Urgency is a transcendental issue in this type of service, which turns the extremely fast delivery of FedEx Custom Critical into its most critical activity. At the present time, FedEx Custom Critical picks up most of its shipments within 90 minutes of receiving a customer's order and delivers faster than air freight.

About 96% of the time, FedEx Custom Critical delivers on time. This percentage is closely monitored by the company to meet the demanding customers' expectations. As one of the dispatchers once recalled, "When customers call FedEx Custom Critical, it is because they have a problem. Something went wrong, and they need a fast and efficient solution for it." Therefore, the company has to be flexible enough to adjust their resources to any type of customer request. To that extent, availability of the fleet of trucks is a decisive issue.

continues

Case 3: FedEx Custom Critical: Scalability in Urgent Delivery (Continued)

The surprising element of this strategy is that FedEx Custom Critical has no control over the delivery. The trucks are owned by independent owner-drivers who are contracted on demand. Each driver is contacted by a dispatcher depending on his location. They can accept or reject a haul depending on their own convenience (long hauls are preferred because they involve more money). FedEx Custom Critical pays its contractors 58% of the shipping costs, but the drivers have to pay for the fuel.

The dispatchers at FedEx Custom Critical play a crucial role in the company's ability to compete. They have to make quick decisions and make them correctly. There is no doubt their jobs are stressful; however, the company does all it can to minimize the burden placed on these vital individuals.

On the other hand, the relationships with the drivers are another tricky issue. The drivers are closely monitored by the company as to how many and what kind of hauls they accept, and dispatchers and drivers help and trust each other to meet each other's needs. As part of this culture, the dispatchers try to understand the issues faced by drivers in "ride-alongs," where a dispatcher goes on a ride with a trucker. The bottom line is always the same: "They just do not want to disappoint the customer."

Cutting-edge technology has been implemented in the company to shorten the delivery times at all levels. When an incoming call is received, a complex system is able to immediately recognize the caller and pull up its complete information from the database to the computer screen. Also, *OmniTRACS*, a two-way satellite communications system, is used to instantly locate any of the trucks in the fleet. This amazing and powerful software, named *Dynamic Vehicle Allocation,* determines which trucks the dispatcher should send and where. Finally, a system of *IBM network* computers is used to immediately alert the drivers if they fall 15-minutes behind on their schedule.

From an external point of view, FedEx Custom Critical tries to keep the company small. It relies on the customer's assumption that small companies provide a more personalized service than larger ones. That is why FedEx broke the company up into CATs (Customer Assistance Teams), each of which always deal with the customers of the same area.

FedEx Custom Critical's customers are looking for just one outcome. They need to have a parcel or package delivered very quickly. Under this circumstance, price is not an issue. Total reliability is. Let us now consider what this means for FedEx Custom Critical's capabilities. They need to have complete flexibility in terms of the size of the vehicles and the availability of vehicles in their area of operation, which is national in scope. To avoid the capital risk and yet achieve this sort of scale, FedEx has to outsource the actual deliveries without compromising reliability. The risk to FedEx Custom Critical is, therefore, very similar to the risk to Cisco when it outsources all its manufacturing to obtain scalability. FedEx has to constantly monitor the performance of its drivers, much like Cisco does with its Autotest, to reduce the risk of a late delivery (analogous to quality for Cisco). However, FedEx Custom Critical has to go beyond a real-time quality measure. Unlike Cisco, with a very limited number of outsourced manufacturing partners, FedEx Custom Critical has hundreds of owner-drivers that it has to keep track of. Finally, there is the risk of a misunderstanding or even poor chemistry between the highly stressed dispatcher and the driver. FedEx Custom Critical's risk-management solution: Get the dispatcher and the driver to know each other in a real-time working environment, such as the ride-along. In other words, both Cisco and FedEx Custom Critical have scalability as a competitive business objective. For Cisco, the risk-management capability is monitoring, whereas for FedEx Custom Critical, monitoring as well as motivational compliance are the capabilities it had to develop to manage the risks.

Properly specified core objectives can help you tackle risks that have some of the highest failure rates. These are the strategies that depend on a constant flow of innovation. You will look at this strategy by studying firms in two different industries. The common theme is how both firms have scaled up their innovation capabilities.

Case 4: Eli Lilly: Scalability in R&D

The lifeblood of the pharmaceutical industry is to develop new drugs and have them approved by the FDA. Both the development of new drugs and their approval are usually few and far between. If a pharmaceutical company has two drugs approved by the FDA in one year, then its ready to break open the champagne. Between January 2003 and April 2004, Eli Lilly received approval for six drugs. This is the story of how Eli Lilly developed a novel approach to scale up its R&D (research and development).

In the late 1990s, Eli Lilly had to ramp up its R&D strategy when faced with the prospect of the patent expiration of Prozac in 2001. In 1998, Lilly created a company called InnoCentive LLC to tap a global community of scientists to solve critical "intermediate" problems (a substance formed in the middle stage of a series of chemical reactions) of a new drug that chemistry-driven companies want to crack but can't. InnoCentive awards of as much as $100,000 are offered to scientists who can unravel a problem. In return, companies get the intellectual-property rights to the solution of the intermediate. These problems are described on the InnoCentive web site.

Clearly, Lilly feels that it can reduce the risk of research output by tapping into a wider community—sort of like open source software. In exchange, Lilly is taking the risk that other pharmaceutical companies would find out about the drugs they are working on if they exposed mission-critical problems to the outside world. So, how does Lilly manage this risk? Basically, Lilly ensures that there are enough missing pieces that others will not be able to come up with the drug, even if the chemical composition of a few intermediates are known. Further, Lilly has become an expert in finding multiple uses for the same compound that others have given up on, as illustrated in

Table 3.1. The early results seem to be promising, even though Lilly's stock price is lagging due to factors unrelated to its research output.

Table 3.1   Lily's Revised Use for Certain Drugs

Drug	Status	History
Strattera studies	Marketed for ADHD treatment	Failed in depression
Evista	Marketed for osteoporosis	Failed for birth control
Alimta	Marketed for mesothelioma	Trial had been stopped
Cymbalta	Reviewed by FDA for depression	Failed at lower dose
MEPM	In trials for cancer	Failed for psoriasis
Gemzar	Marketed for cancer	Failed as antiviral agent
PPAR-alpha agonist	In trials for cardiovascular disease	Failed asthma trial
Ghrelin blocker	In preclinical trials for obesity	Failed frailty study

Source: Wall Street Journal April 21, 2004[3]

Capability Options for Reducing Demand Risks

All three industry situations you have seen so far do not really have a major demand uncertainty. To avoid competitive risks, Southwest and JetBlue chose to compete in an underserved market. However, both of these airlines are quite sure of the demand potential in markets that they chose to enter. Cisco and FedEx Custom Critical have a fairly reliable demand for their well-established products and service. Even Eli Lilly is fairly sure of the demand after it develops a drug, even though it may face some competitive risks.

Some strategies have to contend with a different type of demand risk. This is demand risk in a brand new market segment ("market shaping", which is covered in Chapter 9, *Strategies to Shape Markets: Products, Process, and Platform*). The difference between the strategies for firms acting as market pioneers versus firms operating in already-established markets is that the pioneering firms have very little idea of what is going to sell. Very often, these firms have to get lucky to succeed. This space is usually occupied by entrepreneurs, and their high failure rate is testament to the risk of such strategies. This space is also populated by toy makers, which have routinely gone bankrupt. Of course, you can try to reduce demand risk by sophisticated market research or even through the extensive use of focus groups subject to the reservations expressed in Chapter 1.

It is also possible to reduce the likelihood of demand risk by incorporating it into the core objective and investing in risk-reducing capabilities. The master of this craft is Sony—maker of everything from the Walkman to videogames.

Case 5: Sony PlayStation: Scalability in Innovation

Sony targeted the older generation of gamers who grew up playing with Nintendo's Super Mario since the 1980s, but had stopped playing and had developed a different interest in the themes they wanted their games to revolve around. Their tastes were anything but uniform, and to develop games to cater to this audience required a deep understanding of their preferences. For example, they typically enjoyed a more challenging and sophisticated gaming experience that differentiated them from younger gamers. Finally, there were potential gamers who had never really participated in videogames, but were interested in a new form of entertainment.

It was a tough challenge to try to exploit this market because no one knew what sort of videogames would spark the interest of college grads and even young parents. Andrew House, the 32-year-old Vice President for Marketing, puts it this way: "If Nintendo owns *fun*, then we own *cool*."[4] Sony further designed the PlayStation console to look less like a toy and more like a trendy gadget. Indeed, PlayStation soon turned out to be a pop-culture phenomenon.

Sony also broke with tradition in its media choice for distributing its games. Sony chose CDs instead of the cartridge technology used by Nintendo. This choice had profound implications on both the market presence as well as the agility of the internal software development and commercialization processes for game titles.

Taking on Nintendo, the 500-pound gorilla in the videogame business, head on was risky even for Sony. As a result, Sony decided to substitute demand risk to avoid competitive risk. Sony went after an entirely untapped segment that Nintendo and Sega were not targeting, but there was still a complete lack of information to identify what the tastes of this new target group actually were. How did Sony reduce this risk? In terms of our framework, Sony defined the broad competitive objective as "maximize variety."

Let us think this through. If Sony can try out many games and get the few that cause a stir quickly to market, Sony does not have to be exceptionally creative, or lucky, to come up with a hit game. Sony's solution: Change the platform for developing games from the industry-standard cartridges to CDs. By choosing the CD ROM technology, Sony gained a tremendous advantage in customizing its offerings to what its target gamers wanted. The CDs were not only much cheaper ($5–10 for a blank) than the cartridges, encouraging developers to experiment with new ideas and generate wider variety, they also had a much larger data storage capacity (650 MB versus 16 MB for the cartridges), allowing more graphics (realism), animation, and levels of difficulty to be incorporated into the new games.

Nintendo and Sega had boxed themselves into a strategy that made it actually quite risky for them and their partners to increase the variety of their games. Nintendo and Sega had unsuccessfully tried to develop second generation (realistic, 3-D sophisticated simulation) console games since the early 1990s. They faced the obstacle of the high, upfront investments in both developing the software and loading it onto expensive cartridges ($35 for a blank at 1996 prices), facing a high risk if the title was not successful with the gamers. And if it was a hit and the retail shelves were raided by lusty gamers, it was highly likely that disappointed customers who arrived too late would have to wait three more months to get their copies—the typical lead time for cartridges manufactured and shipped from Japan. At the end of the chain, retailers faced the same risks, and many of them were unwilling to place orders for expensive new titles that might flop. This meant retailers were stuck giving their shelf space to a limited assortment of "tried & proven" game titles and sequels. This conservatism is what Sony exploited by focusing on a core objective that can be described as "maximize variety inexpensively."

Sony not only reduced its own risks but exploited the fact that Nintendo's developer community had also become risk-averse. Nintendo requested third-party developers to pay all of its proprietary cartridge costs as well as manufacturing fees and royalties upfront, meaning the software developer bore the entire commercialization risk. This proposition was not very attractive for most third-party developers, especially when it came to experimenting with new themes or game genres. Sony's choice of CDs translated into an ability to form partnerships with a large pool of talented third-party developers who were willing to take the lower risks of writing new games that could be distributed on the CD platform. Hundreds of ideas and development projects now seemed more attractive for third-party developers (such as Electronic Arts, Lucas Arts, Crystal Dynamics) both because the upfront cost was much lower, and because Sony had more lenient terms for licensing. This leniency was especially attractive because of the increased margins achieved by beating the cartridge retail prices. These partnerships were a critical component of gaining an advantage in the industry and were leveraged by Sony to the extent that its in-house development accounted for only about 15% of the games playable on its console. In sum, Sony had reduced the risk of creating variety by making it very cheap to produce new games.

The CDs were also much faster to source, which reduced the market demand risk—whether too much or too little. Sony manufactured the discs in three locations in the U.S. and needed a lead time of only three weeks to respond to hit titles. Both Sony and third-party developers could easily produce a batch of a new title, say 5,000 copies, and test it in the market. This ability to quickly manufacture in small batches was especially handy when it came to a global roll-out for a new title because many hits in Japan could bomb in the U.S. or Europe and vice versa. For a title that could potentially sell 2 million copies at $50 retail, the cost of testing was not that significant compared to the cartridge technology. Depending on the (almost real-time) response, a more intelligent estimate of demand and shipping plans could be developed.

Several takeaways from the Sony PlayStation strategy can be generalized to other companies. Sony's first priority was to avoid competitive risk by not going after the same customers as Nintendo. This meant that Sony had to take on demand risk because demand from this new gamer segment was unknown. Sony had a two-pronged core objective to reduce the demand risk. First, it decided to have a core objective of being able to maximize the variety of games at a low-cost, which led to the investment in the CD platform. Second, Sony had a core objective of allowing outside developers to absorb the risk of innovating new games. In order to do that, Sony had to reduce the risk that the outside developers were exposed to under the Nintendo business model. Once again, the investment in the CD platform was the key decision that made this possible.

How to Apply This Framework to Any Business

Analysis of strategies of different companies may be interesting, but the details may not be applicable to all businesses. To get the most from this analysis, you need to recognize the high-level themes that cut across all the strategies. The outcome-to-objective framework makes it easy to identify these themes across seemingly disparate strategies. Some of these themes may apply to the business you are interested in. To do this, you need to work through the logic the companies described in this chapter used to arrive at the core objectives and the configuration of capabilities that led to their competitive advantage.

Case 6: Little Tikes

Little Tikes, based in Hudson, Ohio, was a toy company that made developmental toys for pre-schoolers. It was started in 1969 by Thomas Murdough in his garage. It was a successful small company, catering to specialty toy stores.

Product Innovation

Little Tikes' main strengths were in customer service, established distribution networks, and innovative products. The company operated its own day-care center in the facility, caring for up to 30 children from ages 3 to 6. Twice each day, the children were decked out in Little Tikes' hard hats and taken to visit their parents. Parents could also spend their lunch hour with their children in the day-care center. The facility was equipped with several two-way mirrors. When Tikes had a new product idea, they placed the product in the day-care facility, sat in rooms on the other side of the two-way mirrors, and watched how the children played with the product. This proved to be a very effective way to test products. Little Tikes also relied on consumer input. Consumers were encouraged to suggest new product ideas through the 1-800 number. Little Tikes felt that product innovation was a must in this business, and the company pursued heavy new product introduction to keep its major competitors off-balance. Updated and sophisticated CAD (computer-aided design) systems were designed to take rough sketches to finished goods in weeks instead of months. The quicker a new product could go from the drawing board to reality, the better. Little Tikes, with its unique manufacturing process (described next), could easily and inexpensively change molds to produce a potential new product for trial.

The Manufacturing Process

Little Tikes used a process called *rotational molding*, which forged plastic pellets into toys. Rotational molding requires heavy capital investment. For example, a $115 plastic kitchen requires an investment of about $850,000, including the cavity and spider molds.

Once the initial investment is made for the spider, the molds within the spider can be changed at a much smaller expenditure of approximately $30,000. Each cavity makes one piece of the product. The kitchen, for example, has a dozen component parts. The Tuggy Sandbox has two. "The beauty of rotational molding is that it enables us to quickly change the molds in the spider, which we may do weekly if we wish," Brian Howard, Purchase Director, stated. "The costs of the molds within the spider are only about $25,000 to $30,000, so we could test a new product idea rather cheaply, as well as quickly (or slowly). In effect, we can test a product even as we prepare to launch it." Rotational molded plastics have increasingly displaced materials such as wood, aluminum, and steel. While the rotational molding allows a firm to try out new molds relatively inexpensively, it is not as cost-effective as standard high-volume injection molding.

You probably recognize that the core competitive objective of Little Tikes is almost exactly the same as Sony PlayStation—maximize new innovation inexpensively. The investment in the rotational molding process is analogous to the CD technology for Sony. In both cases, the objective was to minimize demand risks.

Managing Capability Risks

In Chapter 4, *Designing Strategies with Low Capability Risks*, we will review the different options to reduce capability risks that we have seen so far with some more examples. These options are using an existing or off-the-shelf capability and investment in capabilities that affect part of the value chain, sometimes in order to outsource the risky capabilities. Thus Lilly, Cisco, FedEx Custom Critical, and Sony PlayStation have outsourced the critical parts of their value chains contrary to conventional wisdom. These parts of the value chains are also the most capital-intensive for all these companies.

Further, all these companies had to make investment in another capability that allows them to manage the risks of outsourcing critical parts of their value chains without compromising the quality of the output that satisfies the desired outcomes of the customers. Finally, in Chapter 4, we will also consider the risks in investing in all the capabilities for an entirely new business model.

Endnotes

1 This has since changed, somewhat. Southwest passengers can check in at Southwest's website. However, it is still first-come, first-served.

2 Autotest is an important, but by no means the only, part of the total package that enabled Cisco to have that much confidence with its suppliers. The manner in which Cisco treated its suppliers (often taking equity positions) is also worthy of studying. However, Autotest is a unique component because, unlike Dell Computer, Cisco does not even manufacture (assemble) its products, which are mission-critical components of corporate networks.

3 Thomas M. Burton. "By Learning From Failures, Lilly Keeps Drug Pipeline Full" *Wall Street Journal* 21 April 2004.

4 Michael Grecco. "Different Market, New Message" *Fast Company* issue 10 (1997).

4

DESIGNING
STRATEGIES WITH LOW
CAPABILITY RISKS

A strategy ultimately succeeds or fails based on whether the capabilities are appropriate for the business model. By now, you have seen how firms run into execution problems, not because of poor execution, but because they did not anticipate the risks in the capabilities needed to execute the strategy. These risks can be traced to three basic sources. There can be a mismatch between the core objectives and the capabilities as we saw in the Continental case in Chapter 2, *Three Steps to Design a Low-Risk Strategy*. The risks can come from not understanding the complexity in the capability. The risks also may come from the investment needed to acquire the capability.

In this chapter, we primarily focus on some ideas for reducing the risks in capability investments—how to avoid major investments and when investments are more likely to pay off. However, we start with the issue of the risk in building complex capabilities. Not all capabilities are difficult to imitate, and after a firm has shown its competitors the new business model, it may be vulnerable to competitive risks.

This leads to two basic choices. A firm may decide to build a complex capability (Southwest). Alternately, a firm relies on identifying new business models as it is imitated in the previous one. Examples are Capital One and Sony. The first choice may lead to a temporally longer stream of profits, but investment in complex capabilities carries its own set of uncertainties, especially if the capability is far removed from what a firm is used to doing. The second choice typically leads to a short-lived profit advantage. Table 4.1 gives an overview of the options presented in this chapter to give managers more choices in reducing capability risks.

Table 4.1   Nature of Capability

		Complex	Imitable
Capital Investment	High	Reduces competitive risks. However, demand risk must be managed to justify investment.	Avoid. High risk in all three categories.
	Low	Ideal.	Must have exit strategy.

Complex Capabilities

By looking at the internal components of Southwest's capabilities, it is easy to see why it is so difficult for other airlines to imitate Southwest's strategy. The activities that support its unique ability to get an airplane to the gate, load the passengers and baggage, and take off on time (quick turns) are not individually unique, but collectively they are very difficult to imitate. Southwest is a perfect example of capabilities that are centered on tacit knowledge often being more difficult to imitate than those that need heavy capital investment. Further, Southwest was not really taking on major demand risks as it was developing its capabilities. It had strong demand in the limited routes that it had selected. Finally, the development of these complex capabilities actually allowed Southwest to scale back its fixed asset investments (fewer planes). Southwest is admittedly a unique case in that it has developed a set of inimitable capabilities without heavy upfront investments and low risk across all three categories. However, not all business models allow a firm the luxury of developing complex capabilities without major capital commitments (see the following Lexus example). There is a second risk. Complex capabilities often need a long gestation period, and this can not be hurried.

Devote Sufficient Time to Develop Complex Capabilities

In the early 1990s, U.S companies became aware of the need for speed. However, when it comes to developing complex business models, it is more important to be deliberate when developing the capability. The more complex the engine is, the slower managers should go to make sure all the parts work together. This includes cloning a successful business model in a different market. This may go against common wisdom, but when it comes to developing complex capabilities, a firm has to go slow to go faster. "Make haste slowly" was the motto of the printer Aldus, arguably the father of publishing.

If you are developing your business model based on a complex capability, you must absolutely slow down in the building stages of the model. For example, it took Southwest more than five years before it felt comfortable to move out of its original routes to other parts of the country. Saturn was very deliberate in starting a second plant after its initial success. Part of the problem that Continental faced in trying to imitate Southwest was that it tried to imitate Southwest's strategy in nine months. This would be an uphill task even for Southwest, let alone a newcomer to this field. Likewise, it was unwise for GM to try to replicate the Japanese manufacturing process in the 1980s by simply investing in factory automation. GM's workforce simply did not have the skills and the culture to take advantage of automation—skills and culture that took the Japanese decades to perfect.

Even among firms that have been successful with a business model, many still make the mistake of rushing out to replicate their success in other ventures. Enron was extremely successful in the gas and electricity business.[1] It is no coincidence that Enron was very deliberate and painstaking in developing the capabilities for these businesses. Unfortunately, after these two initial successes, Enron rushed into many businesses without giving itself sufficient time to understand or develop the capabilities needed in the new businesses. Enron's current problems stem from its illegal maneuvers to cover up these strategic mistakes (see the Appendix for more detail). While Enron is the extreme, it is by no means the exception among companies that suffered due to overreaching and haste. With this background about complex capabilities, we now consider different options for reducing the inherent risks of investing in new capabilities, complex or otherwise, and the options for reducing these risks.

Investment Risks in Acquiring Capabilities

Lexus' (the luxury car division of Toyota) core objective in competing with Mercedes was to build a luxury car that had an out-of-the-door price tag an order of magnitude below that of Mercedes. Part of the capability that Lexus invested in was to have a manufacturing process that could build luxury cars efficiently using mass manufacturing processes. It had to invest in completely new designs and tools that would make this possible. Lexus left no stone unturned in its effort to reduce the final price for the consumer. An extreme example of this is how Lexus completely redesigned the car at considerable expense, solely to reduce the drag coefficient (air resistance) to beat the gas-guzzler tax to the consumer (a savings of nearly $1500 in 1989 prices). Investment in all of these capabilities allowed Lexus to meet its core objective of the lowest price luxury car that was comparable to a Mercedes. However, by all accounts, these were sizable investments, and there was no guarantee that Lexus would be able to overtake the status symbol represented by the Mercedes brand even if Lexus delivered more value for money. This demand risk is underlined by the fact that Lexus has very little success in Europe where the Mercedes brand has much more value than in the United States.

Now consider a different company, Saturn. Saturn's core objective was to improve productivity through worker empowerment.[2] Saturn has, therefore, invested in a training program where workers are trained to read income statements so they can directly see the link between their wages and the company's cost structure. Worker involvement has led to many innovative processes that both cut the cost of production by reducing tooling and machining costs and reduce the cost of post-purchase repair to the customer. In other words, Saturn also managed to develop a competitive business model, but with a relatively low capital commitment to develop its capability.[3]

The two preceding examples illustrate the principle that the same core objective can be delivered by different capabilities. Some of these involve a high level of capital investment, like that of Lexus. Others involve much less investment in capital goods, like Saturn or the many examples we saw in Chapter 3, *Identifying Multiple Capability Configurations*. By now, you know where our bias is. If a firm can meet the demand without heavy fixed asset investment, that is the lowest risk strategy. However, sometimes that is not possible and, as the Lexus example suggests, the investment may be worth every penny.

Lowest Risk: Use Existing Capabilities for the Current Value Chain

It should be obvious that the acquisition of unfamiliar capabilities will increase the risk of execution, and being able to use existing capabilities will lower it. Sometimes, acquiring unfamiliar capabilities is unavoidable. However, in the previous chapters, we have already seen how managers may be able to identify opportunities for leveraging

existing capabilities using the outcome-to-objective framework.
We summarize some of these previous examples in the following sections and supplement these by other situations where managers can
use off-the-shelf capabilities that also carry very little investment risk.

Reduce Risk Using In-House Capabilities

The outcome-to-objective thinking technique can be applied not just
to the external customers, but also for internal customers of an organization. Recall the Crown Cork and Seal problem in its assembly line
for making cans. We can visualize the same solution that Crown
reached by rephrasing the outcome as reducing the time it took the
supervisor to move between the two machines. Using this outcome,
it is relatively easy to come up with the U-shape reconfiguration of
the assembly line. This was not only an efficient solution, but it did
not add any other risks associated with investment in new capabilities.
Likewise, recall the Xerox service network issue in Chapter 2. Instead
of trying to solve the customer "need" for a service network, what
Canon did was identify the outcome that customers value as "lack of
downtime." Cannon decided to deliver this outcome by designing
parts of the machine (printing drum) that is most susceptible to failure as disposable. For Canon, this output represented the least risk
because it allowed Canon to leverage some of its existing competencies, such as miniaturization and optoelectronics. Thus, Canon
entered the personal copying market without a service network by
developing a disposable print drum that did not need any service.
The disposable drum has now become the industry standard.

Reduce Risks with Off-the-Shelf Technology

Likewise, in the NASA space pen story, there may be no market for
the space pen, but there is always going to be a market for efficiently recording information. Hence, if the astronaut's desired outcome
can be met using an off-the-shelf technology, such an option will

almost always be a low-risk alternative.[4] The pencil is a trivial example of using an off-the-shelf technology. Consider the following somewhat more intricate example. Dairy farmers routinely dry manure to use it as fuel. In early 2000, California dairy farmers stung by high electricity prices were searching for an alternative energy source to dry their manure. Their low-risk solution was to reframe the problem for finding an inexpensive energy source by taking the *moisture out of a waterlogged object*. By focusing on outcomes, they realized there are multiple ways to solve this problem. They ended up using the off-the-shelf technique that transforms orange juice into concentrate by bubbling out the water molecules with the addition of hydrophilic gas. One farm is reportedly building a plant that will use such a gas to dry manure for a fraction of the cost of electric dehydration.

Now consider a commercial high-rise building that has slow elevators, leading to a lot of complaints from visitors. If you asked the visitors, they would have probably recommended an inside-out solution, such as adding faster elevators. However, the outcome that reduced the visitors' complaints was to remove the *perception* of wasted time. The building managers installed mirrors in the lobby and complaints were reduced significantly. A variation of this solution is found in airports with TV monitors displaying news and sports channels. However, consider the following question. Would the same approach work for a residential high-rise building? Unlike an infrequent visitor, who can be distracted with mirrors or TVs, repeated users of the building are likely to see through this tactic. In other words, the solution is more or less risky depending on the context. This example is also useful to reiterate a critical factor in understanding the capability risks in trying to use the off-the-shelf technology. It is very critical to define the customers at a suitably granular level to make sure that managers develop the correct core objectives. In this case, the customers or users of the elevators in a commercial high-rise building require a different set of core objectives than users in the residential high-rise building.

Sherwin-Williams' Dutch Boy division added a screw-on cap (called twist and pour) to paint cans that reduced a major frustration of do-it-yourself painters—opening and closing paint cans. You can conceptualize the twist-and-pour innovation if you focus on the outcome of a painting project undertaken by a do-it-yourself painter—the *time* it takes to paint a room. Of course, there are motorized paint sprayers, such as the Wagner Power Painter, that you can use at a significantly higher cost. However, most people are not uncomfortable with the basic painting task and dread prying open the can and the associated spills or encountering dried paint because of an improperly sealed can. By making it easy to take breaks while painting, Dutch Boy managed to add a feature without much demand risk. Still, the capability underlying this strategy is fairly simple, and there is a good chance that the advantage is likely to be short-lived.

Moderate Risk: Investment in Capabilities to Modify Part of the Value Chain

Businesses are constantly trying to add features to existing products and services in order to attract customers. Businesses are also constantly trying to modify parts of the value chain that cater to internal customers. You have already seen examples of modification of internal components of the value chain, such as the Crown Cork and Seal example. However, some modifications require more significant investments. Such modification to a value chain almost inherently adds demand and capability risks. We recommend investing in such capabilities only if there is minimal demand risk. Focusing on outcomes is, once again, an effective technique in isolating such low demand risk opportunities.

Satisfy a Latent Desired Outcome

After you get comfortable with being able to rephrase customer needs and priorities as desired outcomes, you can try to apply this thinking to new features. Many new features simply represent a deep understanding of what outcomes consumers are willing to pay for and how managers can deliver these without much risk to the firm. By rephrasing needs in terms of outcomes, you may find all that is required is the appropriate message that others may have missed. These are the kinds of low risk opportunities that were exploited by CML's NordicTrack, the George Foreman Grill marketed by Salton, and even successful TV and radio talk shows. Most of these examples did not involve investment in fixed assets. However, sometimes if a firm feels that there is a latent outcome that can be satisfied with minimum demand risk, it may be worthwhile to make the investments to exploit such an outcome.

In the 1980s, Yamaha was looking at a 10 percent annual decline in overall demand for pianos. It is not that people did not like to play the piano or listen to it being played; it took too much time and maintenance (tuning). Consumers were seemingly unwilling to dedicate the time necessary to learn how to play the piano. The traditional strategies of either higher quality or lower costs would do little to reduce the demand risks in these circumstances. Yamaha instead decided to remove the barriers that prevent consumers from enjoying their existing pianos with the expectation that the underlying demand from listening to the piano music is fairly certain and constant.

To accomplish this, Yamaha redefined the customer outcome as music from a piano, rather than a piano to play. Surprisingly, this outcome had previously been served by the player piano, although their poor sound quality had limited their market acceptance. To deliver a high quality player piano, Yamaha grafted the evolving digital and optical technology onto existing pianos. This technology allows piano performances to be recorded on disks and reproduced on pianos with a high degree of accuracy. By recording or purchasing virtuoso piano performances, customers could utilize their piano to enjoy the performance at home. By focusing on the customer outcome, and adding features to deliver this outcome, Yamaha was able to stimulate its sales in an otherwise stagnant industry with relatively low demand risk.[5]

USPS managed to reduce its sorting and delivery costs as well as increase the effectiveness of direct marketers and bulk mailers by its "zip + 4" feature. USPS had to invest in some additional capabilities to handle the zip + 4 feature, but it had carefully studied the outcome that direct marketers were looking for—precision mailing—that was not available prior to this feature. Thus, the demand risk was not very high, which made the investment in the capability a low-risk decision. And, of course, for the USPS, there is no competitive risk. Recall the slow elevators in the high-rise buildings. A perceived waste of time while waiting for an elevator is the numerous stops it makes on the way to the destination floor. Otis has developed elevators where you punch in your destination floor in a control panel that greets you as you enter a high-rise. The panel will guide you to the car that will take you directly to your floor without any stops. In this case, Otis has used an off-the-shelf capability (queuing theory) to deliver an output that provides a real (as opposed to perceived) solution for the desired outcome. Not only are the visitors happy, but architects can have extra space by eliminating a number of elevator shafts.

Add Optional Features to Deliver New Outcomes

The BMW Mini and the Chrysler Crossfire had to have a small trunk to be able to deliver sports-car functionalities. Both of these cars overcame the small luggage space problem by first developing luggage that contoured to the shape of the small trunk—an idea borrowed from the air cargo industry. The luggage came standard with the car.[6] The outcome that the customer wanted was not a large trunk, but the ability to carry a normal load of luggage. By virtually eliminating wasted space in its trunk, BMW managed to solve the trade-off. The basic takeaway from this is very simple. Sometimes, the trade-off seems to be unsolvable because of the conditioning of our thought process, which is usually linear. The outcome-objective thinking style can help reverse this process.

Consider another example. Many of us love chocolate with fruit syrup inside. Most of us have wondered how they get the syrup inside the chocolate coating. The reason for our puzzlement is because we assume that the liquid syrup is somehow injected into a hollow chocolate shell. The answer of course is that the syrup needs to be liquid only when the consumer eats it and not when it's manufactured. Framing the problem in this manner opens up the possibility of freezing the syrup in a desired shape and then coating it with molten chocolate. Both BMW and the first company that manufactured chocolate using the frozen syrup technique had to make some customized investment to deliver these features. However, such an investment is relatively low risk if it allows you to solve a trade-off with a fairly certain demand. Cell phones that can take and transmit pictures are also a good example.

Let us now consider a situation where a modification of the part of the value chain did not have an immediate impact on the end-customer but allowed the internal customers to meet their desired outcomes.

Substitute a Manageable Risk to Reduce Another

The basic principle here is to identify a critical activity in the value chain and develop options to increase the efficiency and effectiveness of this activity. Let us start by considering the pharmaceutical industry.

A successful major drug can contribute years of profits to pharmaceutical companies as patent protection can significantly reduce competitive risks. However, the process of developing drugs is risk laden. It takes approximately $800 million and 12 to 15 years to develop and market a major drug. Further, of the many projects that

pharmaceutical companies are constantly engaged in, only a fraction
lead to a breakthrough, and then there is the FDA hurdle. For this
reason, most pharmaceutical companies invest in multiple projects,
much like venture capitalists invest in multiple businesses hoping for
that one big hit. To protect their intellectual property, most drug
research is done in secret; researchers rely on the small, personal networks within their companies, which means that the in-house
research scientists don't have many places to go for help. In the
1970s, Merck broke from the pack by having a focused set of research
projects with more resources and managed the risks of fewer projects
using sophisticated risk management techniques that it developed in-
house (we will analyze the Merck situation in detail in Chapter 9,
Strategies to Shape Markets: Products, Process, and Platform).
However, the major breakthroughs in chemistry and biochemistry at
present are increasingly coming from collaborative efforts in arenas
where secrecy is not that paramount. Even the Merck model that was
so successful in the 1970s and 1980s cannot capitalize on this trend.
In Chapter 3, you saw how Eli Lilly set out to solve this trade-off by
investing in a capability to harness the power of collaboration while
minimizing the risks to their intellectual property.

You may recognize several examples from previous chapters that
describe successful strategies based around this principle. Consider
the strategies of Cisco Systems, FedEx Custom Critical, Sony
PlayStation, and Eli Lilly. All of these companies identified the activity that was critical for their respective core objectives. In particular,
for Cisco, this was manufacturing; for FedEx Custom Critical, this
was delivery; for Sony, developing new games; and for Eli Lilly,
developing new drugs. All of these companies decided to outsource
part of this activity and developed a capability for managing the
adverse consequences of the outsourcing.

High Risk: Creating an Entirely New Value Chain

Anytime you are developing a completely new product or service, you are taking on the risk of investing in new capabilities, which may have little or no salvage value if you are wrong about the demand.[7] Focus groups are not very useful in reducing demand risk when the product or service does not yet exist. To understand demand risks, you need to have a deep understanding of higher level needs and aspirations that can be tapped.[8] Also, even if you succeed, your first-move advantage can be temporary. If a business model is based on capabilities that are easy to imitate, you must try to analyze your options against competitive risks before you make the investment. We now consider some techniques to reduce such demand and competitive risks. The basic objective is to identify and exploit a white space or a sweet spot (both are explained in the following) in an existing market.

A *white space* is a need that exists but currently no one has the capability to serve profitably. A *sweet spot* in a market is a customer segment that is being ignored by incumbents for whatever reasons. Unlike a white space, incumbents can deliver a product or service to a sweet spot, but they simply choose not to. One way to distinguish between white spaces and sweet spots is to think in terms of capabilities. No one can deliver value in a white space using current capabilities. On the other hand, the incumbents *can* deliver value in a sweet spot using their current capabilities, but they most likely *will* not. For example, airlines can carry packages in their luggage hold, but they choose not to. This is an important distinction with regard to future competitive risks. If someone exploits a sweet spot, the competitive risks are likely to be low because the incumbents are not likely to become interested in a segment that they have knowingly ignored. On the other hand, if a firm commercializes a white space opportunity, there is a higher possibility of competition from new entrants who would like to imitate the business model that they could not visualize previously.

White spaces and sweet spots can almost always be identified at three stages where customers interact with the firm. Using the outcome-objective approach, firms can:

- Identify outcomes that can solve articulated (but not delivered) or unarticulated needs

- Identify outcomes that can simplify the delivery of value

- Identify outcomes that can provide peace of mind[9]

These three stages apply to *all businesses*. With a deeper understanding of the outcomes desired by customers at each stage, managers can identify white spaces, a sweet spot, or both. To illustrate a white space in stage one, consider the hearing-impaired customer segment. The success of text messaging is a result of the communication outcome that was not being met by existing products. Likewise, the hearing-aid battery package discussed in Chapter 2 was a product for the same white space. Microsoft's success in the 1980s and 1990s were based on the need for desktop applications for small businesses. Cisco's success was based on its ability to become the soup-to-nuts network solution provider. BancOne shaped the community banking experience by elevating what the community banks could offer after they joined the BancOne family.[10] The stage two white space is usually a service that is added on to the value delivery chain, making it easier for the customer. This service can be something as simple as streamlining the purchase process. The shelf-display strategy used by Home Depot is an example of helping customers get what they want quickly. The advent of e-commerce in its various forms is a service designed to simplify the purchase process. Amazon, eBay, and Expedia have succeeded in simplifying the buying process in their respective industries. Blockbuster exploited a white space in the video-rental business by providing a broader selection. Alternately, it can be a feature that is added on to the product to increase the efficacy of the value delivery. An example of this is a medical patch that can be used to take medications without having to be reminded to take pills. The grafting of digital technology to the piano by Yamaha is also an example of a stage two white space.

The insurance industry was built on the premise of peace of mind—a three-stage outcome. The new products that are being offered to pay for future college tuition for our children are an extension of products for filling this white space. The software industry has identified a white space known as upgrade inertia and is now offering software on lease rather than purchase. IBM, HP, and EDS are trying to provide peace of mind for computer network administrators. GM's OnStar is trying to provide similar peace of mind to motorists. Of course, just because there is a white space does not mean all firms should attempt to exploit it. Both EDS and General Motors are struggling in their respective white spaces, as we shall elaborate on later. Basically, to exploit these white-space opportunities with lower risks, you have to take on the risks of developing capabilities that may be too costly, may not deliver the objectives, or both.[11]

Capabilities for Exploiting White Spaces

The capabilities for exploiting white spaces have to go beyond the means to deliver the core objectives. These capabilities also have to be difficult to imitate if the development risk is worth undertaking. Consider Starbucks. If it simply tried to compete as one more coffee shop, it is unlikely that it could have been very successful. The white space in this market was the lack of establishments for people who want to socialize but do not want to drink alcohol. This is the white space that Starbucks has captured.[12] At a higher level, America Online used people's desire to socialize, by way of chat rooms, as a cornerstone of its initial strategy.

However, this is a high risk strategy because Starbucks had to create the entire value chain from scratch. A little less risky strategy is to develop niche white spaces, such as Sam Adams beer. However, there is almost no way around avoiding the investment risks in these situations if the firm is incorrect about the desired outcome it is planning to satisfy.

Leverage Complementary Capabilities to Develop White Spaces

When faced with the invention of the automobile, Disney realized the impact it would have not only on travel, but also on how families received their entertainment. In response, Disney created theme parks that served as destinations for families. By rephrasing the outcome, Disney was able to anticipate a new demand.[13] Sony was able to capitalize on the love of music with its ability to produce miniaturized electronics to develop the Walkman. Of course, neither Sony nor Disney was able to avoid competitive risks in the long run, but they did reduce the demand risk by considering different slices of the outcomes that consumers desire from entertainment. It may also be worthwhile to note that Disney made significantly more investment than Sony and possibly took on much more capability risk. However, Disney also managed to keep competitors at bay much longer than Sony.

Restructure a Market to Create White Spaces

This approach involves identifying the dynamics in a marketplace in a way that allows a firm to achieve a position in a market that gives it the ability to do something that has not been possible before. This is the Enron story—reducing uncertainty through aggregating fragmented gas supply sources. This does not rely on a unique skill—anyone with the correct sources of supply could pull it off—but they got there first. Basically, Enron restructured the gas business into a financial services business.

Restructuring a market can go beyond financial or analytical strengths. One company that has been able to effectively restructure a market is Kao, a Japanese toiletry company. It developed Babu, a bath additive that duplicates the improvement in circulation that

Japanese hot springs provide. Babu was the first product to offer these benefits, and its introduction completely restructured the traditional bath gel market. In fact, "it completely wiped out the old Japanese bath gel and additives industry" and, "it's now the only product of its kind that sells in Japan." By restructuring the market from bath gels to products that offered health benefits, Kao was able to reduce its competition and risk.[14]

Find the Sweet Spot of a Market

White spaces may give you a temporary advantage because of being the first mover, but there is always the risk of competition moving in after others develop the market. A sweet spot in a market is a particular service or product that has been ignored by the major players and is likely to continue to be ignored by the major players. The sweet spot thus immediately avoids competitive risks, but managers do take on both capability risks and demand risk if their assumption proves to be incorrect. Roberts Express (now FedEx Custom Critical) started off by solving the following trade-off. How can you provide ground shipping that is more reliable, cheaper, and faster than airfreight? Their sweet spot is 500 pounds, 800 miles or less. At that weight and that distance, FedEx costs a third as much as airfreight and can deliver the goods one day sooner.[15] Unlike trucks, airplanes have to wait until the package is brought to the plane using ground freight, and then there is the loading and unloading time. This concept is very similar to the business traveler driving 200 miles faster than it takes for him or her to fly.

Redefining the desired outcome of automobile insurance from reducing risk to reducing inconvenience enabled AutoGlass to develop a business model around repairing small windshield chips at the car owner's home. Both the insurance companies and the car owners came out winners in this business model. The sweet spot for AutoGlass is that the regular car-repair garages are unwilling to repair windshields at the car owner's home. The risk that AutoGlass took was to develop a capability to do the repair on-site. If the basic assumption held up, AutoGlass had no competitive risks. Competitors were simply not interested.

Develop Capabilities to Exploit Sweet Spots

There are some instances where the sweet spot or white space appear to be risky to your competitors, but really are not. In other words, they may deal with finding and accessing a market segment that already exists but has been misjudged by other players. Sometimes, such segments can be identified from personal experiences. For example, personal experiences of ex-military officers led to the formation of the member-owned United Service Automobile Association (USAA). The ex-military officers knew that military personnel were very good credit risks despite their low income, yet traditional insurance agencies only looked at the income to determine credit risk. However, over the last two decades, identification of such sweet spots typically involve developing analytical skills and an ability to obtain and analyze segment data (data mining). For example, Motorcycle riders are high risk, but Malcolm Forbes, who was a motorcycle enthusiast, should have been able to get a better insurance rate than the Hell's Angels. Progressive Corp found sweet spots in many supposed high-risk insurance categories and developed business models to profit from them. Capital One conducts multiple experiments in coming up with a much detailed credit scoring model to serve and profit from the sub-prime (high credit risk) market. One such sub-prime market is bankruptcies. It is very difficult to get credit after a bankruptcy. Yet Capital One identified the sweet spot among bankruptcies by looking at the cause of the bankruptcy. Capital One found that bankruptcies caused by medical emergencies are much lower credit risk than that caused by business failure or other reasons. Capital One calls its simulations and experiments to identify these sweet spots Information Based Strategies (IBS). You need to note, however, that even though the risks are theoretically calculable, the very complexity of the calculations makes it immeasurable for most. This type of a sweet spot, or a white space, is almost all about managing the risks of developing the capability. Because the capabilities are so difficult to imitate, and demand risk is relatively low, these bets are likely to pay off if a firm can develop the capability. However, these are complex capabilities and firms should take their time with them. Key Corp is developing a credit-scoring model similar to the IBS used by Capital One for the past 10 years. We revisit these capabilities when we consider strategies for shaping a market in Chapter 9.

Sometimes, the quantitative analysis is not necessarily complex but different. For example, a smoker and a skydiver can get life insurance. Yet, Allstate Corporation will not insure you if you plan to visit Israel. Why? Because Israel is on the State Department's travel-warning list. However, the death rate in Israel is about 11 per 100,000 people; that is considerably lower than the accidental death rate in the United States.[16] This unwillingness of some insurance companies to look at data dispassionately has allowed others to exploit sweet spots. For example, the insurance company Centre Group insures a luxury ocean-liner condominium project, a power plant in the Colombian rain forest, and a steel-galvanizing plant in Estonia. Through the use of models—the average risk is subjected to 10,000 simulations—Centre is able to identify the most profitable risks to insure.[17]

The final risk that you must be aware of comes not from the initial capability development but expecting more than it is capable of delivering.

Capabilities Dictate the Limits of Your Business Model

Even if you have identified the appropriate capabilities that can deliver your core objectives, you still have to understand the basic risks in developing your capabilities. Further, you also have to understand the limits of what your capabilities can deliver. Understanding these two sources of risks at the design stage is critically important to avoid problems during execution. You must understand the core objectives that the capabilities of the business can deliver consistently. Trying to push beyond these objectives has been the cause of many business failures. EDS employees are learning this the hard way as they are trying to implement a contract with the Navy for installing the Navy's computer networks. Their capabilities are simply stretched too thin. Reportedly, they had assembled personal computers over a year ago that are sitting in a warehouse waiting to be installed. This delay has resulted in EDS's inability to collect more than $1 billion in sales.[18] Moreover, as you know, personal computers sitting in a warehouse can quickly become obsolete.

Capabilities Dictate the Natural Size of Your Business

When Southwest started operating in the transcontinental market, its quick turn capability in the short-haul market was not very useful because the very length of the transcontinental flight constrained the total number of possible flights to two. Thus, for Southwest to try and expand to the transcontinental market using its quick turns capability invites competitive risks. However, Southwest's capability of getting the most out of its workers could be transplanted to the transcontinental market with very little modification. This led analysts to note that Southwest would still have a cost advantage in the long-haul market because of its labor productivity. Note that Southwest's capabilities are also not suitable for the short-haul markets (150–200 miles) because of the efficient range of the Boeing 737. For this reason, Southwest is now considering acquiring the Brazilian ER 190 to enter the short-haul market.

The American business landscape is littered with successful firms that flamed out by trying to expand beyond their capabilities. Time and again, we have witnessed the acquisition of a successful niche firm by a larger national/international firm that failed to use its scale to grow the sales of the acquired company. Sometimes, such a strategy may succeed serendipitously, as it did with Quaker Oat's acquisition of Gatorade. However, Quaker Oats was unable to replicate the same national rollout strategy with Snapple—Quaker simply did not have the correct capabilities to promote Snapple in the same manner as Gatorade.

Case 1: Little Tikes's Distribution Strategy

Recall the sidebar on Little Tikes from Chapter 3. It was a successful small company, catering to the specialty toy stores. In 1984, Little Tikes was purchased by Rubbermaid Incorporated for $56 million. This purchase price was a significant premium based on an estimated 1983 sales of $30 million (estimate based on 1989 sales). Thomas Murdough continued on as president of the new subsidiary. Between 1984 and 1989, sales grew by better than 25% annual average rate and was approaching about 37% in 1989. In September 1989, with sales at $250 million, Murdough resigned. *Crain's Cleveland Business*[19] magazine stated that:

> "Murdough's reasons for leaving the company were based on what he characterized as a loss of Little Tikes autonomy at the hands of Rubbermaid. Mr. Murdough particularly objected to Rubbermaid's involvement with Little Tikes' marketing program. Shortly after Mr. Murdough's departure, John Nolan, Little Tikes' Director of Sales and Marketing, also resigned."

And from *Business Week*[20]:

> "Nolan and Murdough had followed the strategy of rationing the amount of product sold through the mass discounters, choosing instead to accommodate toy supermarkets and independent toy stores. Although Rubbermaid claims that

continues

Case 1: Continued

Little Tikes is not being forced to follow Rubbermaid's strategy of flooding the discounters with merchandise, it is reported that Little Tikes is already boosting production and increasing shipments. Full-line retailers, such as Coronet Juvenile, are concerned about the apparent change in philosophy. Coronet, for example, allocates 5% of its space to Little Tikes in return for a listing in Little Tikes' national catalogue that is sent to over one million customers two times/year."

The article also stated that Murdough felt that accommodating discounters meant dealing a direct blow to the full-price retailers (specialty toy stores). He said that discounters would not take Tikes' full-line of toys, but instead would select only the most popular and mark them way down, destroying the margin opportunities for other retailers.[21] While it is true that discounters would indeed cherry pick the line, the new management at Little Tikes was able to keep retail prices at acceptable levels by implementing a suggested retail price that retailers were under significant pressure to maintain. This was accomplished by withholding co-op advertising funds (which offset the cost of producing ads) for ads that offered any Little Tikes product for a price less than Little Tikes' suggested list price. Little Tikes' toys were typically priced at the high end for toys of its class.

Little Tikes succeeded because it avoided competitive risks from major players, such as Fisher-Price, and by staying away from the mass-merchandising channel. Little Tikes needed the specialty stores sales forces to communicate the value of the developmental toys to affluent suburban parents. The combination of this communication capability coupled with the unique features of the toys allowed Little Tikes to dominate this niche segment. However, Rubbermaid had to try and recover the acquisition premium and the only channels for the growth strategy were the mass merchandisers. Unfortunately, as soon as Little Tikes started offering only selected items from its full line of products through the mass merchandisers, it became vulnerable to competitive attacks from Fisher-Price as well as Step 2, started by Tom Murdough after he quit Rubbermaid. Rubbermaid was unable to profitably scale Little Tikes because it did not understand the risks of extending Little Tikes' niche strategy through the mass merchandiser channel.

Enron (see Appendix for the full article) was extremely successful when it was trading in only one commodity—natural gas. By the end of the 1990s, Enron was involved in over 1,200 commodity markets. The sheer numbers of commodities markets that Enron was trading overwhelmed Enron's capabilities[22] by its own admissions. Long Term Capital also found out the perils of expanding too fast the hard way. Long Term Capital attracted a number of wealthy clients using sophisticated hedging strategies to make large bets on small market moves. For a while, its model seemed to be working until the late 1990s when it went beyond the parameters set by the model. This led to one of the most spectacular financial collapses that required a bailout by the Fed. These days, smart money managers will close a mutual fund if the amount of capital goes beyond their capabilities to successfully invest. On the other hand, if a firm truly understands the logic of its growth strategy, it is not constrained by a certain size. Through most of the 1990s, Cisco's ability to manage the risks of outsourcing its manufacturing allowed it to acquire and scale up small, privately owned (mainly network switching) companies. This was something that other acquirers simply could not match. However, even Cisco succumbed to the sheer volume of its acquisitions as it began to make tactical mistakes in 1999 and 2000.

Summary Thoughts

In this chapter, you explored many options of how to consider the reduction of capability risks. Firms can identify options that allow them to utilize existing capabilities or off-the-shelf capabilities that represent the lowest risk. These options are easier to identify by using the outcome-to-objective framework than by focusing on the customers' perceived needs. If a firm has to invest in new capabilities, it is very important to avoid competitive risks, even if temporarily by identifying a white space or a sweet spot. Firms may also be able to reduce these capability risks by substituting one capability risk for another or acquiring a capability that allows it to outsource the risky capability. Further, managers will have to consider the risks inherent in both developing and using a capability. Complex capabilities can provide protection against competitive risks, but they have to be developed slowly and rigorously. There is also the danger of pushing a capability beyond its limits, which can derail a business model.

We feel that you will be able to significantly reduce capability risks by considering one or more of these options when designing your strategy. However, these options are primarily at a strategic level. In Chapter 5, *Lowering Capability Risks with Visible and Invisible Outputs*, you will consider some techniques for reducing capability risks at the operational level.

Endnotes

1 In the Appendix, we will demonstrate just how Enron was so successful. This is quite contrary to current perceptions.

2 To be fair, Toyota does this too in an annual idea contest from workers. However, Saturn made this a part of the organization's fabric.

3 This needs to be put in context. Obviously, Saturn had to invest in capital equipments, and it will probably never recover the capital costs, even though it has operating profits. However, in comparison to the automation push by GM in the 1980s (unsuccessfully) or Lexus (successfully), Saturn's capital investments were decidedly modest.

4 We will revisit this issue later under diversification strategy in Section 2. In this case, if the space pen were built on a leveragable capability, and it could lead to profitable opportunities elsewhere, then the risk of the investment may not be as high.

5 Kenichi Ohmae, i. "Getting Back to Strategy." *Harvard Business Review*, Nov.–Dec. 1988: 149–156.

6 Christine Tierney. "Chrysler's Crossfire: German Skill, U.S. Pizzazz." *BusinessWeek* July 7 , 2003.

7 This is also a market-shaping strategy that we will discuss in Chapters 8, *When and How to Use a Low-Price Entry Strategy* and Chapter 9, *Strategies to Shape Markets: Products, Process, and Platform*.

8 We will develop a framework to identify these opportunities in Chapter 5, *Lowering Capability Risks with Visible and Invisible Outputs*.

9 Much of these ideas are based on Chatterjee, S. 1998. "Delivering Desired Outcomes Efficiently: The Creative Key To Competitive Strategy. *California Management Review* 40(2). (Reprinted with permission.)

10 We look at these examples in detail in Chapter 9 when we develop frameworks for market shaping that exploit white spaces.

11 In Chapters 8 and 9, we will develop some detailed techniques for managing these capability risks.

12 Seth Godin. "Walt Disney, Steve Jobs, My Mom—and Now You—Have Shared the Secret of Rifting." *Fast Company March* 2000: 258.

13 Ibid.

14 Kenichi Ohmae. "Getting Back to Strategy." *Harvard Business Review* Nov.-Dec. 1988: 149–156.

15 Conversations with Kevin McClellan and John Palma.

16 Peter Coy. "Where Insurance Doesn't Travel." *Business Week* December 1, 2003.

17 Keith H. Hammonds. "No Risk, No Reward." *Fast Company* April 2002: 82.

18 Gary McWilliams. "After Landing Huge Navy Pact, EDS Finds It's In Over Its Head." *Wall Street Journal* April 6, 2004.

19 Mooney, Barbara. "Murdough Back To Kid Stuff." *Crain's Cleveland Business* September 23, 1991: 1

20 Mallory, Maria. "Why Little Tikes' Managers Picked Up Their Toys and Left." *Business Week* (Industrial/Technology Edition), 1989, Nov 27: 83.

21 Ibid.

22 Enron admitted this much when one compares Enron's confidence in its risk management capability published in its 1992 annual statements (when it was trading only in one commodity—gas) and its equivocation in its 1999 annual statements.

> EGS will continue to offer reliable gas delivery at predictable prices, all of which will be accomplished with limited commodity risk to Enron. Enron Annual Report, 1992.

> The use of financial instruments by Enron's businesses may expose Enron to market and credit risks resulting from adverse changes in commodity and equity prices, interest rates, and foreign exchange rates. Enron Annual Report, 1999.

5

LOWERING CAPABILITY RISKS WITH VISIBLE AND INVISIBLE OUTPUTS[1]

In Chapter 4, *Designing Strategies with Low Capability Risks*, you saw many examples of how reducing capability risk when investment in new capabilities is needed to modify part of or the entire value chain. These investments are likely to succeed if these capabilities are a critical component of your business model and enable you to reduce demand or competitive risks. To continuously sustain your competitive advantage, you have to keep track of which capabilities are critical and which are not (table stakes, as defined in the next section). In this chapter, you consider some techniques not only to identify the critical capabilities, but also how to make these capabilities more efficient without succumbing to demand risk. This process gives a firm buffer against competitive risks even if competitors try to imitate its business model.

Critical Capabilities and Table Stakes

Firms invest in developing a lot of capabilities, but some are more critical than others in their impact on the core objectives. These are the *critical capabilities*. The other capabilities are "table stakes" and have to be performed at a basic level by all competitors. Thus, to play blackjack in Las Vegas, a gambler needs a minimum amount of capital to sit at the table; these are the table stakes. However, table stakes are no guarantee of winning. The core objective for the gambler is to know what cards are in the deck with a high degree of precision. Therefore, the technique that the gambler uses to remember cards is a critical capability. If the gambler is continually miscounting cards, he knows his technique is flawed, and his risk of losing is high because now he is totally dependent on luck.

Note that a particular capability may be critical to one firm and table stakes for another. For example, Southwest Airlines does its own maintenance, which is critical for its business model, while other airlines outsource most of their maintenance, including JetBlue, making it a table stakes for them. It goes without saying that a firm has to give special attention to its critical capabilities. But how does a firm know which capabilities should be critical? Choosing to emphasize the incorrect capability or ignoring a critical capability invites failure. The next section provides guidance in this matter.

Not All Outputs Are Equally Valued by the Customer

Perhaps the surest way of avoiding competitive risk is to constantly increase the value frontier—give customers more of their desired outcomes at increasingly lower prices. While most consultants and business practitioners would readily agree to this premise, there is very little available to guide you on how to do this in a routine and repeatable fashion. As we saw in the dotcom bubble, many firms went bankrupt by providing increasing value to the customer without any regard to the cost of delivering that value. They clearly did not suffer from demand risk but rather suffered from capability risks. In this section, you consider how fine-tuning your capabilities can simultaneously increase the value frontier and reduce your costs.

As we have seen in previous chapters, the capabilities of a firm are composed of many activities and resources. Typically, an activity (supported by resources) results in an output that is used by either an internal or external customer. However, not all of these outputs are equally important in a firm's ability to command a price premium. Customers are more concerned about outputs that are visible to them. This insight should be the basis of fine-tuning capabilities.

Reengineer Activities That Deliver Invisible Outputs

Consider the activities whose outputs are normally invisible to the customer. Without a doubt, such activities do contribute to the overall value of the product by directly or indirectly influencing product or service attributes that customers care about. However, the customer does not really care about the exact manner in which a firm carries out the activity, unless the output from the activity is directly visible. To take advantage of this distinction, a firm must always try to minimize costs in activities that result in invisible outputs, so long as there are *no adverse effects on the visible outputs*. Further, a firm must do this irrespective of the price point for its product or service. This internal cost minimization does two things. First, if the firm is not facing serious competition, it can increase its margins by virtue of achieving efficiencies in the activities leading to invisible outputs. Second, the firm is in a much better position to tackle competitive risk if it has a total cost structure that is already low enough to allow it to compete on the basis of price. In other words, just because a firm is currently selling a premium-priced product does not mean it should be complacent about increasing efficiencies by reengineering invisible outputs.

In the early 1980s, Mercedes was the car to beat in the luxury performance segment. However, Mercedes was very expensive because it was literally handcrafted, using a manufacturing process that became a benchmark in this segment. Without doubt, this handcrafted manufacturing process added attributes of finish and quality that were valued by customers. However, this process was not increasing the value frontier because the added value was coming at increasingly higher prices. Further, the manufacturing activity was normally invisible to the customer. Lexus reengineered the manufacturing of a luxury car and built a car equivalent to a Mercedes, but one that cost significantly less to manufacture. Lexus could then offer the car at a price point that was an order of magnitude below that of a Mercedes and increased the value frontier. The basic opportunity that Lexus exploited was that most customers did not care how a car was manufactured because this activity is invisible to them. Now consider some examples of how firms are already putting this principle to practice.

Toyota has taken to painting only the bottom half of a compact car's wheel well because the top half is invisible from most angles. This saves Toyota a penny per car.[2] Both Toyota and Honda (see Table 5.1) have decided to cut content from their cars where the output is not visible to customers while boosting features that are visible to customers. Ford had taken the same strategy in not painting its ashtrays, which saved it 25 cents per car. Ford used to have 14 types of cigarette lighters that they have presently reduced to a single type—for a total savings of four million dollars per year. A luxury hotel chain in Dallas installed motion detectors in guest rooms that shut off the power when guests are not in the rooms. Even Lexus has taken to saving money where it feels that customers will not notice. Most luxury cars have chrome-tipped exhausts. The earlier models of Lexus also had this feature. However, in the past two or three years, Lexus has redesigned the exhaust, so the end of the exhaust does not stick out behind the car and, therefore, is not as visible.

After this redesign, Lexus stopped using the chrome tips even for the flagship LS 430.

Table 5.1 Honda Saved Enough Money in the New Civic Where Customers Wouldn't Notice...

Replaced rear disk brakes with cheaper drums; switched to a simpler, less expensive antilock system.

Integrated dashboard clock into radio display.

Replaced trunk hinge with a simpler design that cut costs in half.

Used 30% fewer threads in rear seat materials and replaced vinyl and interior trim with cheaper fabrics.

Bumpers, dashboard, and other parts are now made with fewer pieces, cutting manufacturing costs.

Air conditioning that is factory-installed, rather than dealer-installed, trims price from $1,200 or more to $850.

...To Add Features and Refinements Where Customers Would Notice

A more powerful 1.6-liter engine that meets California's tough new emissions standards.

Hydraulic engine mounts and electronic controls for automatic transmission make for a quieter, smoother ride.

Radio standard on all models; doubled number of speakers to four.

Rear seat folds in two sections instead of one, adding versatility.

A higher roof and improved design create a more spacious car with extra rear legroom.

From *Business Week*, September 18, 1995

Reengineering has recently fallen out of favor. For one thing, reengineering was not used in the manner recommended by Hammer and Champy and became synonymous for layoffs. For another, it was not clear how to quantify the benefits from reengineering. We suggest that reengineering has its place because it can give a firm the much-needed buffer from competitive risks by lowering costs. The only caveat is *reengineering should be targeted primarily to outputs that are invisible to the customer* and in a manner that the visible outputs are not adversely affected. Consider the example of IBM Credit, which Hammer and Champy (1993) used in

their book. IBM Credit, like the credit arms of many other companies, is a very profitable business that finances the purchases of IBM's
customers. Hammer and Champy point out how IBM Credit used to
take up to 14 days to process a loan application, a lag that led to a loss
of computer sales to other vendors. Using the outcome-based framework, it is easy to see how the initial long-winded process came to be
established and eventually abolished. IBM Credit, like most credit
institutions, was internally focused on risk management: It wanted to
be profitable by reducing defaults as much as possible. However, the
internal output of risk management (low default), which is invisible to
the computer customer, led to a visible delay that detracted from the
desired outcome of the customer—quick resolution of their loan
application. The resulting reengineering meant that IBM Credit
could process a credit application in under a day. It is not clear if, in
the process, IBM's default rate has gone up, but IBM clearly made a
trade-off by giving more importance to the visible output that leads
to quick turnaround, perhaps at the expense of internal risk management. To summarize, single-minded focus on invisible outputs without considering the impact on what is visible to the customer is a risky
strategy.

It Is Risky to Be Too Thrifty in Visible Outputs

Caterpillar is extremely conscious about what is visible to the customer. Caterpillar continuously tracks the quality of its products using
a process called Continuous Quality Improvement (CQI) programs.
The process was delivered to track defect rate—the core metric for
product quality of its machines.[3]

Caterpillar found that even for products like a tractor, poor paint
quality is quickly noticed by the customer, which can affect his perception of the overall quality of the machine. The TTT division paint
line team adopted CQI to improve the paint finish drastically. By taking apart the entire painting process, the team changed task pattern,

processes, and tools resulting in almost total elimination of paint defects. Customer complaints about paint quality declined from 113 in 1990 to 0 by 1996.

During its glory days of the late 1980s, Rubbermaid charged a premium price for its basic housewares products. However, instead of trying to capture the margin from its premium price, Rubbermaid provided value to its most important constituents—the retailers. It used the extra profits realized from manufacturing efficiency not only to offer better margins to the retailers, but also to provide them with what Rubbermaid called "invincible customer service"—an output very visible to the retailers that erects a very high hurdle for Rubbermaid's competitors.[4] Now consider Rubbermaid's reaction to the rise in plastic prices in 1993. Rubbermaid had already negotiated the prices for its products with Wal-Mart for the year prior to the increase in plastic prices. Yet, Rubbermaid decided to increase prices without clearing it with Wal-Mart first. Clearly, price is possibly the most visible aspect of a product to the likes of Wal-Mart. The result was not much of a surprise to anyone who has followed Wal-Mart's interaction with its suppliers. Rubbermaid was dropped as a vendor.

Going back to the Lexus example, it is interesting to note that it managed activities such as sales and service, marketing, and advertising quite differently from the manufacturing situation described previously. In dealing with these areas that impinge on the customer's experience (a visible output), Lexus did not spare any expense to ensure that the purchase experience was as pleasant as it could be. Lexus dealers were literally sent to boot camps where they received extensive, and expensive, training on how to ensure that the customer's visit to the dealership was a memorable one. This investment paid quick dividends when an early recall of the first Lexus model actually worked to Lexus's advantage because it allowed customers to experience firsthand how good the dealer's handling of a problem really was. Lexus also advertised that it could instantly retrieve the maintenance history of any Lexus car anywhere in the country through a satellite linkup.[5] All this may sound like overkill, and it certainly did cost money, but it touched upon factors that are very visible to the customer.

Investing in visible outputs can pay a huge dividend if there is an emotional component to the outcomes that customers desire. This becomes even more important in service industries where the product can not be returned, such as child care, and even more important for services that are used very occasionally, such as wedding planners. However, even for physical products, emotional components can lead to reduction of competitive risks. Increasingly, product design takes this emotional component into account and investment in capabilities that can deliver a visible emotional outcome is well worth the investment. Consider the following quotes.[6]

> **"Good technology is not an end in itself. People must have an emotional attachment to products."**
>
> **—Stefano Marzano, Head of Philips Design,**
>   **in *Echikson*, 1999.**

> **"They were talking about the iMac in a language usually reserved for small, fluffy animals and close family members."**
>
> **—Jonathan Ive, Head of Apple Design,**
>   **in *Redhead*, 1998.**

The iMac is a classic example of using visible outputs to cover up shortcomings in other areas. The iMac offered precious little in terms of functionalities over comparable computers. For this reason, industrial design is increasingly taking the emotional and visible impact into consideration beyond strict functionality.

Invisible Outputs May Be Visible to Some Customers: What to Do About It

Now consider the danger of trying to save money from invisible outputs without considering what is truly invisible to the customer. Dell Computer used a 2GHz chip in its smart step laptop computers. However, business users who were more computer-savvy than home users found out that this 2GHz chip would run at the fast clock speed only when connected to AC power. Dell was trying to save $350 by not using the mobile version of the microprocessor. Dell thought that the microprocessor was invisible to the customer but, in this case, it backfired.

There is a similar lesson to be learned from Ford's strategy to build the Jaguar on the same platform as the Mercury. Sophisticated Jaguar customers could quickly tell the similarities even though the platform is normally hidden from view. This led to an adverse reaction from potential Jaguar buyers. Now consider what Lexus does. Lexus builds the entry-level ES 300 on the same platform as the Toyota Camry, but uses a completely separate platform for the flagship LS 430. Recall the commercial high-rise building that installed mirrors in the lobby that we discussed in Chapter 4? We suggested that the same tactic would not work in a residential high-rise building. The reason behind this is that what is invisible to an occasional visitor will become visible to the resident who frequents the lobby every day. The lesson? What is normally invisible to some customers is visible to others who are more sophisticated about the performance attributes of their products. This goes back to the importance of granularity in defining a firm's customer.

Bob Nardelli, a rising star at GE, took over the reins of Home Depot and decided to make it more efficient. As part of his cost-cutting venture, Nardelli started to replace the retired trades people that used to help do-it-yourself customers with temporary staff—sometimes college students during summer. This efficiency enhancement move is actually more risky and resulted in lost sales. Why?

Home Depot succeeded in taking over the do-it-yourself big-box industry by providing handholding to the weekend project warriors. The trades people served a very visible role. The temporary staff were totally ill-equipped to do this, and Lowe's was the beneficiary of this strategy. Home Depot has now reversed this trend by focusing on what led to its original success.

Exploit Hidden Value in Invisible Outputs

Very often, a firm can generate value from customers with very little cost by simply communicating some of its internal outcomes to them. To counter the threat from Japanese cars, BMW's advertisement copy changed from "the ultimate driving machine" to "even people of means are asking...What makes this car worth the money?" The advertisement then goes on to explain how the car is manufactured to precise tolerances—outcomes that are normally invisible to the customer. The BMW advertisement illustrates a growing trend, exploitation of values from outputs that are normally invisible to customers. This is a very cost-effective way of creating value.[7]

In 1993, James Dyson had the breakthrough idea that customers would like to know how effectively their vacuum cleaner was performing. Dyson started to sell his cyclonic vacuum with a transparent housing. Customer feedback suggested that making the inner working of the vacuum cleaner visible added to their trust of the product. Similar rationale has been used by many businesses in service industries.

A Honda dealer in Cleveland makes a point of showing prospective customers its ultra-clean and modern repair facilities (normally invisible to customers) as well as emphasizing the door-to-door limousine service it offers should the car ever need repairs (an output that is invisible until the customer needs to have the car serviced). Factory tours are becoming common business practice to impress industrial customers. This is especially true for businesses where reliability is absolutely critical, such as in service industries like FedEx Custom Critical (see the case study in Chapter 3, *Identifying Multiple Capability Configurations*). Lexus advertises its satellite hookup for retrieving individual cars' service histories. Japanese retailers have taken to publicizing "made in Japan" to reap the value of patriotism in fighting Wal-Mart. Many restaurants try to create value by opening their kitchens to their customers. Examples include table-side, acrobatic, food preparation at Benihana and glass-enclosed clay ovens in many prominent Indian restaurants. Coors has always tried to create value by citing the source of the water that goes into its beer, as has Perrier, for its mineral water. Intel has tried to increase brand loyalty by persuading PC manufacturers to publicize the brand of microprocessor used in the PC advertisements "Intel Inside."

A variation on the aforementioned technique would be to deploy inexpensive (or low fixed-asset investment) resources that can improve visible outputs that are highly valued by the market. The proliferation of talk shows is one such example. Talk shows are very cheap to produce compared to regular programs and are easy (less costly) to discontinue if they prove to be unpopular. Basically, just like Sony, talk show companies were trying to maximize variety with a little upfront investment. They could quickly scale up if the talk show caught on (just like Sony's ability to quickly manufacture a popular game), but had few fixed investments at stake if it failed.

Remove Visible Outputs with Negative or No Value

Finally, some visible outputs may actually detract from a firm's value. For example, the 2003 BMW 7 series has a control panel that is extremely simple. Instead of trying to find many small buttons that operate the air-conditioner or the CD player, the driver can drill down a series of voice-activated menus to get to the item that he or she would like to turn on. Unfortunately, this good idea backfired because drivers were more used to seeking out buttons. In the mid-1990s, Delta Airlines initiated a cost-cutting move with a targeted reduction of $1.5 billion per year. One change was to omit lettuce from its in-flight food service. It seems customers did not care, and the change saved Delta $1.5 million per year. Breyers Ice Cream removed the pledge of purity from its ice cream packages for the same reason, at a savings of $100,000 per year in printing and labor costs. Chock Full O'Nuts stopped including a plastic scoop in each coffee can when it realized that customers did not care.

There is, however, a danger in the strategy. For a while in the mid-1980s, airlines started charging for on-board food in a drive to "unbundle" services. Customers did not appreciate this change, and ultimately, most companies reversed the trend and tried to absorb the cost of service.[8] Surprisingly, the airlines are doing this all over again. The message you have to remember is only remove visible outputs that consumers would not notice. Recall the IBM Credit example earlier in this chapter. The negative value that IBM computer buyers saw in the time it took to have their credit approved had to be removed.

In the context of our framework, competitive objective is the concept that captures the logic of how the business model can simultaneously deliver value to the customer and capture part of the value for its shareholders. What we suggest is that you focus on developing tactical-level core objectives that support the competitive objectives such that the visible outputs generate a price premium, while creating efficiency from invisible outputs. Thus, with a proper configuration of capabilities of visible and invisible outputs (see Table 5.2), a firm can develop core objectives that reduce the risk of customer dissatisfaction (demand risk) as well as profit-erosion (reduce competitive risks). Table 5.2 illustrates the kind of emphasis the different capabilities should receive depending on their type.

Table 5.2   Are the Outputs of the Capabilities Visible To the Customer?

	Yes	No
The outputs increase value for the dollar.	Develop capabilities to differentiate even if it means more expenses.	Make the outputs of the capability visible.
The outputs do not increase value for the dollar.	Hide the capability.	Reengineer capabilities for efficiency.

Check Your Assumptions and Logic When Investing in Capabilities

Ultimately, firms invest in capabilities to exploit an opportunity. We have suggested many ways that firms can reduce the risk of these investments. However, at its core, the risk arises because there is an inherent uncertainty that cannot be quantified. Whenever a firm is making a capability investment decision, it is making certain assumptions about the demand, competition, and capability. Inherent risk in these assumptions will always exist that later will be proven wrong in some or many instances. A second source of risk exists as well. This risk is developing a business model that does not logically follow from the assumptions you made. We now suggest ways to manage both of these risks.

Assumption Risk

Incorrect assumptions manifest as one of our three sources of risks when a strategy is put to action. What we would like to stress in this section is how to reduce the adverse impact of assumptions that prove to be inappropriate. Faulty assumptions regarding market demand will plague just about every company, and this is not necessarily bad. Quite often, the risk is one of timing—the market may not be ready for the product or the product configuration. Segway scooter,

Newton PDA, and Interactive TV are all examples where the demand assumption may have been incorrect. Interactive TV has sputtered, for instance, because viewers weren't as keen to play with their programs and commercials as marketers hoped. We do not know if satellite radio will take off. The important thing is to have an understanding of the types of organization that can take assumption risks and others that are ill-suited to do so.

As we saw in Chapter 4, assumption risk is most serious when a firm is trying to develop a completely new value chain (market shaping), whether it is Starbucks, Yamaha, or Disney. When you are shaping a market, you are basically making assumptions not only about demand, but whether the underlying capability can deliver the product in all its expected attributes, including costs.

Develop Resiliency

Assumption risks about demand change over time, and you need to have the resiliency to not give up after the first failure, provided you are consistently using our framework, or a similar one, to understand the sources of risk. Apple was early with the PDA and gave up, while Microsoft never gives up. Most of its products failed miserably the first time out, but they kept coming back with the ones that they really believed in. As stated earlier, Lilly has consistently made new drugs from compounds that failed in their previous attempts. The best companies are not too hard on themselves regarding assumptions for a completely new product. If you penalize employees for being less than 100% on delivering a new demand, it will choke out all risk taking. On the other hand, you should be extremely critical regarding assumptions about capabilities needed to deliver the core objectives. This is an assumption where the variability can be predicted with a lot more precision because this is internal to the firm. Yet many firms grossly overestimate their capabilities for delivering a completely new product or service, as you have seen from examples described in previous chapters, such as Continental CALite.

Take Baby Steps Before a Big Plunge

If you are taking capability risks where the assumption is suspect, you are more vulnerable if you are taking on risks on an ad hoc basis, as opposed to a company that is used to continuously taking risks using a risk-management framework. Consider Sony and Motorola. Sony probably has many failures that we never hear about and some, such as Betamax, that we do. Yet Sony is in a much better position to keep taking these risky bets because it has developed a process that has many elements of our framework by which to reduce these risks. In particular, Sony is constantly looking at customer outcomes and marries Sony's existing capabilities to deliver products and features that can visibly deliver these outcomes. The use of Betamax to develop compact Hi-8 cameras that are easier to hold and the CD capability to provide a variety of new games on the PlayStation platform are all illustrations of this process of seeking out new outcomes that can be delivered using existing capabilities. While Sony does develop some of its own technology, like the Betamax, it has been equally successful with off-the-shelf technology, such as the CD-ROM.

On the other hand, Motorola has been quite successful in two basic technologies: wireless and microprocessors. Motorola has been in the wireless business since World War II when it developed the walkie-talkie. The cell phone business is a natural extension of the walkie-talkie. In the late 1980s, Motorola was equal to Intel in the chip (microprocessor) business. Yet, Motorola lost its lead to Nokia by being late with digital technology in the cell-phone business, and Motorola is about to spin off its chip business. In our opinion, Motorola is primarily an efficiency-driven company[9] that has historically made incremental progress on its wireless technology by staying ahead of competitors on the technology dimension. However, with the advent of innovative companies, such as Microsoft, Dell, and Nokia, which used off-the-shelf technology to deliver customer outcomes, a pure inside-out focus was destined to lose.[10] Companies such as Microsoft and Nokia are masters at understanding and

managing demand risks. This was not the case with Motorola historically. For such a company, a multibillion-dollar bet on the one dollar-
per-minute satellite phone system called Iridium proved to be too
risky. That failed venture also coincided with Motorola's fall from
grace in the mid-1990s.[11] As a postscript, in 2004, Motorola is doing
a turnaround by shrewdly adopting and developing alliances around
the off-the-shelf CDMA technology to counter Nokia's bet on GSM.

You are much better off taking baby steps with smaller risks and
not betting the company on any one venture. The cumulative experience will put you in a better situation to manage the capability risks
if you do decide to place a large bet. The same argument holds true
for companies that make acquisitions. Acquisitions are a quick way of
acquiring or deploying capabilities. Acquisitions are a risky business,
but if you make that a practice, you are much better off than firms
that do a one-off acquisition.

Logic Risk

The second source of risk, faulty logic, usually stems from overconfidence and superficial analysis that can be avoided by focusing on the
core objectives. For example, in the mid-1990s, many airlines that
tried to imitate Southwest assumed that the key to Southwest's success was to have a point-to-point route structure and frequent flights.
Thus, Continental CALite started its Southwest imitation by starting
frequent point-to-point service between Dayton, Ohio, and
Greenville, SC—a route that hardly filled up the planes. It is critical
for the low-risk strategy design to minimize such logical errors.
JetBlue, on the other hand, only flies profitable routes—it is sacrificing risky growth for profit. This makes complete logical sense.
JetBlue is under very little competitive risk both because of its cost
structure and the entry barriers it has created (see Chapter 7, *When
and How to Use Differentiation Entry Strategy*, for more details).
Under the circumstance, trying to grow very fast would increase
demand risk. This would be a logical error. Some say that JetBlue is

taking a risk by acquiring a second type of aircraft (Southwest and all its imitators have only one type). However, JetBlue is avoiding the major risks by keeping the smaller jets in a totally different organization, essentially cloning the Southwest strategy on profitable routes where smaller jets would be more efficient. JetBlue analyzed the risk of mixing the two organizations at the design stage of its strategy of acquiring smaller jets. JetBlue concluded that any synergies from combining the two organizations would be offset by undermining the core objective of quick turnaround. In this situation, trying to generate synergies by combining the two organizations would actually be a logical error. This clarity comes from developing a well-defined set of core objectives that is critical to avoid logical errors.

Of all the types of risks, logical mistakes usually happen because of not thinking through the business model carefully. If you have to take people to task, the logical mistakes are a good candidate because here, you or your team are in reasonable control. Unfortunately, even the best companies make logical mistakes—sometimes repeatedly. Dell Computer has revolutionized manufacturing and logistics and used that competency to dominate the direct sales channel. Yet in the early 1990s, Dell did not have faith in its own ability and tried to sell its computers through the retail channel where it had no distinctive advantage over the likes of IBM and Compaq. To its credit, Dell pulled out of the retail channel. It seems to us that Dell is repeating the same mistake right now. Dell has recently decided to sell Lexmark printers under the Dell brand name to its direct customers. To us, this seems like a logical inconsistency. The money being made in printers is not from the printers themselves, but from the cartridges, and most cartridges are sold through retail channels where Dell has no presence.[12] Coincidentally or not, Lexmark has been recently disappointing Wall Street.

Logical errors add a degree of risk to a company's strategy that should be rooted out as much as possible. Once again, this can be avoided by focusing on outcomes and the internal objectives needed to deliver those outcomes. The customer using a Dell printer values uptime that is most easily solved by a quick trip to Office Depot rather than waiting for Dell to ship a printer cartridge in a few days. Dell is trying to address this problem by incorporating a feature in its printers that will alert the customer to order cartridges before they run out.

Finally, when is the risk of making a logical mistake high? It usually happens when time gets compressed. Unfortunately, some of these time compressions are self-inflicted, especially around acquisitions.

Unfocused Objectives and Hubris

Assumptions and logic risks, which should be tackled at the design stage, can be exacerbated by two common failings that usually manifest themselves at the execution stage. These are unclear/shifting objectives and hubris.

Understanding the risks in assumptions and logic is only good to the extent that there is clarity on the competitive objectives. For example, Enron had a schizophrenic approach to its strategy. It started with a vertically integrated strategy, shifted to an asset-light strategy (roughly analogous to outsourcing), but never really abandoned its vertical integration strategy. As described in the Appendix, the two strategies had completely different core objectives. This confusion prevented Enron from developing the appropriate capabilities needed for success in either strategy. On the other hand, JetBlue had total clarity on its competitive objectives when it decided to acquire the smaller planes. The objective was simply to clone the business model in a different route and not to generate efficiency across the entire organization.

Lack of clarity on the competitive objectives can become a serious obstacle in making mergers and acquisitions work. In 1999, Prudential acquired the boutique Silicon Valley Investment Bank, Volpe Brown, to get into the booming Internet firms underwriting business. During its negotiations with Volpe Brown, Prudential's dealmakers drew up a list of 12 bankers and analysts considered critical to the firm's value. Yet many of these critical personnel left when Prudential closed Volpe's trading desk and integrated the trading operations with Prudential's own. Prudential paid a premium to buy the underwriting business, and trying to recover the premium by consolidating the trading desk was the wrong synergy to go after.

On the other hand, FedEx acquired Caliber systems in 1997 to develop a ground network. FedEx soon found out that the two companies had vastly different cultures and infrastructure. Despite increasing pressures from Wall Street to integrate the two companies to realize synergies, FedEx waited until 2000 before combining the ground networks, and even now they are not completely integrated. Basically, there was a danger to the FedEx brand if its service-level deteriorated. The lesson here is to never lose sight of what the core objective is in a merger or in any strategic decision. This means that if you find out after the merger that the anticipated synergies are harder to come by, the worst thing you can do is to try to force it and make a bad situation worse.

Finally, even the best companies are susceptible to hubris. We are not talking about the garden variety arrogance displayed by the likes of Enron. But for many companies, a string of successes, sometimes caused by a favorable economy, can lead to what we call "complacency creep." A healthy dose of paranoia and a framework such as outcome-to-objective, which encourages continuous self-examination, will go a long way to prevent the risk of hubris. This self-examination should be a part of designing any new strategy.

Summary Thoughts

In this chapter, we have provided you with a framework to identify tactical options to reduce capability risks. The basic principle driving this framework is that investment in capabilities should be contingent on whether or not outputs from the capability are visible to the customer. Applying this principle will allow you to get more bang for your investment dollars, both in terms of delivering the outcomes that customers desire as well as becoming efficient in your internal processes. Clearly, the former reduces demand risk and the latter reduces competitive risk. Finally, all the frameworks and concepts developed in this book are vulnerable to risks from incorrect assumptions and logic. Clarity on understanding the business model using a framework such as what's developed in this book will go a long way in helping you avoid errors in assumptions and logic.

In Chapter 6, *Organizations That Can Benefit from the Outcome-to-Objectives Framework*, we describe the characteristics of organizations that are the best suited to benefit from the types of frameworks described in this book.

Endnotes

1 This chapter draws on Chatterjee, S. 1998. "Delivering Desired Outcomes Effectively: The Creative Key to Competitive Strategy." *Calafornia Management Review* 40(2). (Reprinted with permission.)

2 Porter in (Michael Porter. "What is Strategy." *Harvard Business Review*. Nov-Dec 1996) suggests that this is an example of the Japanese car manufacturers' running into the productivity frontier, and that the only way they can keep prices down is to skimp on quality (:69). This is patently incorrect. Both Honda and Toyota have added value in visible outputs in an effort to expand the value frontier and not simply shrink from the productivity frontier. Although Porter is correct that Honda did introduce cheaper fabric in its cars to save money, Honda guessed correctly that customers would not see the difference but instead would perceive more value in the other features added, at extra cost, thus pushing out the value frontier and providing a higher hurdle for competitors.

3 It tracks these defects by the age of the machine in three brackets: VEHR (very early hour failure), registered within the first 21 hours of operation; DRF1 (Dealer Repair Frequency One), registered during 22 to 200 hours of operation; and DRF2, registered during 201-1000 hours of operation.

4 For example, Rubbermaid helped the inventory management for Wal-Mart by installing an Electronic Data Interchange (EDI) system. Of course, Rubbermaid had to spend a lot of money to make this system operational and to some extent maintain it, but it has paid off in tremendous customer loyalty and access to shelf

space. However, in 1993, Rubbermaid tried to pass on some resin cost increases to retailers, including Wal-Mart. This decision led to Wal-Mart severing its relationship with Rubbermaid.

5 Actually, other luxury car makers also provide this service. However, Lexus capitalizes on it by making the customer aware of its availability. See the later section on how to create value hidden in internal outcomes.

6 European Business Forum. http://www.ebfonline.com/main_feat/in_depth/in_depth.asp?id=380.

Emotional components are visible and add value to product design.

7 Since then, a number of car manufacturers have used variations on this theme in their advertisements, such as the ball-bearing test for Lexus to demonstrate the fit of different panels, and the wine glass pyramid for Lexus and Altima, to demonstrate the vibration tolerances.

8 J. Berger. "In the Service Sector, Nothing Is 'Free' Anymore: Selling Service Separate From the Product Irks Consumers." *Business Week*. June 1987:144.

9 Six Sigma was invented there.

10 Consider the following quotation by Tom Lynch, who runs Motorola's cell-phone business: "There are endless examples of instances where this company has blazed a trail and someone else has reaped the benefits." Adam Lashinsky. "Can MOTO find its MOJO." *Fortune*. April 5, 2004.

11 To give an update, Motorola is much more focused on its core business and efficiency, resulting in a dramatic turnaround in early 2004.

12 This is developed in more detail in Chapter 8, "When and How to Use a Low-Price Entry Strategy."

6

ORGANIZATIONS THAT CAN BENEFIT FROM THE OUTCOME- TO-OBJECTIVES FRAMEWORK

Organizing for Taking Risk

Polaroid, AOL, Palm—these companies developed a market-changing product but could not follow through with an encore because they did not take the next risk in developing a new business model. Most of these companies basically tried to focus on their past successes and strengthen existing competencies rather than develop the next set of capabilities. In contrast, the successful strategies of some of the world's best companies can be explained by the outcome-to-objective framework. Very simply, these companies take risks that others do not because of their ability to anticipate and avoid the risks while reaping the rewards. Moreover, they do this because they can harness the true potential of the organization using cross-functional activities that many can not even visualize. However, to adopt this framework, you need to understand its organizational imperatives;

these processes are risky because they are much more complex than traditional business practices. Unless the organization develops the capabilities to manage this complexity, it is probably better off with the status quo.

What are the organizational imperatives for success with the outcome-to-objective framework? For starters, this is not a framework that simply resides in the leadership suite—it has to be adopted, and understood clearly, by the rank-and-file members without which any hope of cross-functional benefits is impossible. Further, the organization needs to have a process by which it can generate and refine the core competitive objectives on a continuing basis. Basically, the high-level objectives need to cascade down to functional-level objectives that should be developed lower down in the organization but that reinforce the higher-level objectives as much as possible. It should be obvious that before attempting to do any of this it is imperative that the rank-and-file of the organization is on the same page about the business-level objectives. The first step to create an organization capable of adopting this framework is to use core objectives (or a similar framework) to help create a common doctrine.

Core Objectives Help Create a Common Doctrine

Many companies have seen the wisdom of developing a process that allows the dissemination of a common doctrine. A striking example of adopting this process can be found at Emerson Electric, under the guidance of CEO Charles F. Knight. Every Emerson employee must know the answers to the following questions that relate to his or her position: Do you know your "enemy?" What are the economics (add value and cut costs) of your job? How are you reducing costs at present? Have you and your team discussed your job with your superiors recently? Emerson insists that the rank-and-file use specific words that can be measured with precise metrics. For example, a high-level objective of beating competition (victory) has to be measured by specific and precise metrics such as "best cost producer" that is widely understood. Moreover, just like the Southwest example, the rank-and-file at Emerson knows what needs to be done to deliver the metric. The result of all this is every Emerson employee knows whether they are winning or losing, and why. This clarity with their objectives usually leads to more victory than defeats.

Emerson is a traditional company that is run extremely well, much like GE. It is not necessarily dependant on complex coordination among its functions, compared to Dell or even Southwest. Yet the clarity of objectives allows Emerson to be a stronger competitor. It goes without saying that this clarity of objectives is even more important for more complex models. Percy Barnevik successfully integrated the merger of Asia Brown Boveri (ABB) by clarifying the competitive objectives and addressing the critical risks to the rank-and-file during the first four months after the merger. ABB's competitive advantage depended on a complex matrix structure that was simultaneously sensitive to local customer needs as well as generating global economies of scale. To do this, managers at every level (who were reporting to two bosses) had to have complete clarity about the objectives of both bosses, who were often at cross purposes, and it was often left to the managers to understand the trade-offs. Barnevik was known to explain the strategy from a stack of overheads that he used to carry with him wherever he went in the far flung organization. And he went everywhere. The result of his efforts culminated in spectacular success for the company because it could both customize its products for the local taste as well as be price-competitive due to its global scale. He came to be known as the "Jack Welch of Europe." However, when Barnevik retired, the matrix became too complicated, and the company suffered from lack of clarity. Barnevik's tenure at ABB is an example of how a core competitive objective or similar framework can allow an organization to take on risks that others cannot. ABB is also an example of the danger of complex strategies without implementing a framework that fosters clarity and a common doctrine throughout the organization.[1]

Both the Emerson and ABB examples illustrate how a common doctrine was developed largely through the urging of an individual. However, other organizations are trying to codify this process. For example, Motorola tries to develop the doctrine of Six Sigma quality, and the common language and decision-making system that goes with it throughout its organization through its Motorola University. Koch Industries uses its Koch Management Center to disseminate its common doctrine of beliefs and common vocabulary that it calls "management technology."

Core Competitive Objectives Must Be Pushed Down in the Organization

To get the most out of the core competitive objectives framework, it has to be replicated at all levels of the organization. Consider Dell Corporation and its retail counterpart Wal-Mart. Over the years, both companies have seized market share from their competitors and their top line has benefited accordingly. Most companies track their sales figures, but this is not central to Dell's or Wal-Mart's business model—if anything, these companies can offer a wider and customized selection of products and services at lower prices as a *result* of their business model. Of course, by now, most business school students know about the revolutionary supply-chain management capabilities that allowed Wal-Mart and Dell to develop their competitive advantage. However, the real reason behind Wal-Mart's and Dell's success is not that they invested in a supply-chain management system, but their deep understanding of the critical risks in implementing such a complex system and how to avoid such risks.

The framework you have seen in this section suggests that to mitigate the risks, you need to identify the correct core objectives. Both Dell and Wal-Mart base their success on having minimal inventory without sacrificing speed and variety for the customer. Thus, one high-level core objective for Dell and Wal-Mart can be something like very low day's sales outstanding (a measure of inventory in the channel). Since for Dell, and to an extent for Wal-Mart, the suppliers ship what the customers buy (pull through), the inventory management numbers are much more important than raw sales in terms of knowing whether the business model is functioning properly. Sales can fluctuate because of macroeconomic conditions, but the day's sales outstanding should not vary; if it does, the cause is usually identified and a fix attempted before it shows up in the quarterly statements.

> **"All of the gains we have had have been because we did some deeper level of integration with the core systems of our suppliers and implemented deeper ways of using the data, rather than just a basic online presence. As you get deeper levels of integration, the benefits rise tremendously."**
>
> **—Michael Dell**[2]

However, Dell and Wal-Mart do not simply rest on a high-level core objective, even if it is specific and measurable. The core objectives are usually pushed down further into the organization and the lower level core objectives cascade up to business unit-level objectives. This is important to make sure the processes that allow Dell to deliver the core objectives are functioning properly. For example, Dell monitors the time it takes between receiving an order and having the PC on the loading dock. At present, it is set at four days. This lower-level objective allows Dell to track the capability risks in its business, almost in real-time, using this specific and measurable functional-level objective. Further, this objective reinforces the higher level objective of minimizing inventory in the supply chain as well as delivering the customer outcomes (quick delivery). Dell is constantly trying to improve on the lower level objectives that allow it to be ever more efficient and, thus, reduce both the capability and com-petitive risks. On any given day, observers at Dell assembly plants who are seemingly standing around and doing nothing, in effect, are trying to see how they can constantly improve the assembly.

Dell's core objectives also are pushed out to its partners. For example, Dell gives a guarantee (service-level agreements are around 99 percent) that if one of its installed servers goes down, it will be repaired within 1 hour. This is an extremely visible outcome for the server customers, and meeting this outcome 100 percent of the time significantly reduces competitive risks in an industry where major players are eager to take business away from Dell. While the actual repair is done by Dell or Dell-contracted repair persons (increasingly more of the latter), it is up to UPS to have the correct parts ready for pickup by the repair person from one of their field-stocking locations that includes the acquired Mailboxes, Etc. retail outlets. Moreover, after the repair is done, the Dell repair person drops off the excess parts to the UPS field-service locations for restocking. The invisible part of this process is it is up to UPS to not only have the correct parts ready for pickup, but also to reduce the total inventory of parts.

The same principle is in play with other facets of Dell's business. For example, its sales force is not simply taking orders, but also mak-ing sure they are pushing for the most profitable custom configura-tion to their customers. Basically, Dell is ready for not only capturing the demand for their product, but also maximizing sales opportunis-tically. Of course, this reduces demand risk by giving Dell an addi-tional buffer. How do they do this? When customers call in to order a computer, most sales representatives use a custom-built application called Symphony to configure the system. Symphony is linked to Dell's vendor inventory and enables the salesperson to precisely predict how long it will take to ship a system out (this is the four days mentioned earlier) as well as how changing a component can affect assembly time. Symphony does more. It can also track "every change to a configuration—say, upgrading a laptop carrying case from standard issue to the $219.95 Kenneth Cole leather edition. The system shows how the profit margin changes."[3] This example leads us to the next topic: how the outcome-to-objectives framework can be used to reduce demand risks in a wide variety of businesses.

How Frontline Employees Can Reduce Demand Risk

The Dell Symphony approach can be adopted by a wide range of industries to reduce demand risk as well as increase sales. According to Hackett benchmarking research,[4] 76 percent of data that companies collect to predict demand is historical, and just 24 percent is leading or predictive. The reason is very simple. In most companies, the demand prediction is done by someone at the back office extrapolating past trends. This makes most firms vulnerable to demand risks, except for the very stable industries, such as food or pharmaceuticals (and even in these industries, there is room for improvement, as we will illustrate). On the other hand, everyone agrees the best knowledge regarding actual demand resides with frontline employees. Even if a company does not implement a complicated customer pull through supply chain, like Dell or Wal-Mart (and there are risks in this also, as we will illustrate with Cisco later), it can still tap into the knowledge that resides with its frontline employees to reduce demand risk and increase sales opportunistically. So, why don't more companies involve their frontline employees? The reason is it is extremely complex to predict demand by incorporating the multitude of input from many frontline employees. In other words, there is a capability risk. However, those firms that developed the requisite capabilities have witnessed lowered demand risks that have significantly and positively impacted their bottom line.

The first thing a firm must do to benefit from frontline employee input is to make sure there is a common template; otherwise, the input cannot be interpreted. Second, the firm needs to make an investment in the appropriate information technology that can facilitate the process.[5] Let us consider some examples.

Most pharmaceutical companies would give their eyeteeth to know why some drugs sell better than others, or why some retail channels (pharmacies) are more profitable than others. Their sales force is usually too busy making their rounds with a quota of up to 12 customers a day to analyze the impact their visits are having on the bottom line. Even the sales managers have no metric to determine what contributes to the reduction of sales and profits in a particular region. Even if there were some core objectives, the measures are rarely available contemporaneously to take corrective actions. As a result, most sales managers continuously make adjustments after the fact (from the back office using historical data), and sometimes the causality they are using to understand sales changes may have changed during the interim. Often, the exact source of the problem, whether it was the sales person, the pharmacy, or the drug remains unresolved.

Novopharm, a division of Teva Pharmaceuticals, has built customized applications (computer models) around the core objective of improving sales-force effectiveness. These applications process data and provide real-time results that are accessible to sales representatives on their laptops. The result: Novopharm is gaining market share. This application is very similar to Dell's Symphony portal and similar to the weather updates and flight plan changes that are automatically updated to JetBlue pilots' laptops, allowing them to take actions on-the-fly.[6]

The key here is to develop a common template around a set of core objectives that is part of the common doctrine of the organization. This basically allows firms to do their planning in real-time, giving them a tremendous advantage over others. Some of this software is available off-the-shelf. However, you should only use the software if it can be customized to your specific processes and not change your processes to accommodate the software. We like to call it "being business smart in technology."[7]

The preceding examples illustrate how an organization can reduce demand risks by tapping into the knowledge of the frontline employees. Now let us consider the case of Cisco Systems to illustrate the risk of utilizing frontline employees when the organizational imperatives break down. Cisco not only uses customers and their salespeople to input orders (not forecasts), but it also uses a sophisticated supply chain to minimize channel inventory. In fact, Cisco has even less fixed assets than Dell because Cisco does very little of its own assembly. Cisco had so much confidence in its data that it boasted the ability to close its books in 24 hours if needed. Despite this in 2001, Cisco had to write-off $2.2 billion of inventory. In terms of our framework, Cisco salespeople failed to adhere to the common doctrine that made its business model so successful. Basically, the advantage of customers and corporate salespeople entering orders implies there is virtually no demand risk. This is a complete pull-through process where the only risk is Cisco's capability to minimize channel inventory. The problem was that at the height of the dot com bubble, both customers and the sales force started inputting orders in the system that were not actual orders but *forecasts*. Because of the shortage of networking equipment, some customers took to double ordering (from multiple vendors) to be assured of delivery.[8] Likewise, salespeople did not want to miss out on a sale and aggressively input orders that they hoped to land but did not have in hand.

How to Develop Core Objectives Deeper in an Organization

The ability to develop core objectives at functional or department levels that cascade down from organizational-level core objectives is what sets world-class companies apart. There are two hurdles in implementing this process. First, senior management is rarely in a position to set functional-level core objectives. However, it is imperative for senior managers to be able to evaluate whether the functional-level objectives are collectively working together with the business-level core objectives. The second problem is that, in many organizations, different product or functional groups have evolved autonomously over time. Trying to force each unit to conform to an organizational core objective too quickly can lead to major disruption. Let us consider a few examples to illustrate these challenges.

The primary broad competitive objective of healthcare provider companies is to generate efficiencies. Memorial Healthcare System of South Broward County, Florida has identified 250 specific and measurable core objectives (using our terminology) for managers across all its departments. While this figure is much higher than the Hackett study, the large numbers are caused by multiple legacy systems, which provide an integrated picture only to the leadership team. Memorial's solution: Provide its 200 managers access to all of the objectives using a knowledge management system, and allow them to customize the core objectives that are relevant to their departments. According to published reports, this has led to a reduction of 25,000 hours in management time.[9]

Of course, a system like this is not easy to assemble. Many of the companies identified in this chapter have taken advantage of information technology to fine-tune their core objectives. However, the answer is not to get a knowledge management vendor to sell you the latest software. You must first identify the core objectives and supporting capabilities, and only then can you seek out the help of technology to automate the process. If the basic capability mapping is flawed, then this will only lead to flawed real-time metrics. It is almost a certainty that if core objectives are imposed from the top, especially at the functional level, they will be flawed. Developing deeper core objectives is a dynamic process that typically involves the collaboration of people most familiar with the process. One process that many world-class companies, such as Memorial Healthcare System, have adopted is to let managers customize what they need because managers are in the best position to put the data in context. An even better approach is for managers to share their knowledge to develop core objectives and best practices (capabilities) that cut across organizational boundaries. This approach will often unearth creative solutions that are virtually impossible to visualize using a top-down approach.

Context and Collaboration Are Critical to Create and Implement Core Objectives

Let us now revisit the case of Sony PlayStation. According to our terminology, Sony's core objective is to come up with a variety of new games that have some chance of being accepted in the market. Now consider the organization that Sony PlayStation adopted to deliver this objective.

Case 1: The Sony PlayStation Organization (A)

Game developers are mostly rebellious young people with a sense of independence, and the last thing they care for is micromanagement. Sony's management implemented a system that set upfront clear project progress milestones, completion time, and backup plans to manage the unexpected. Developers can do what they want to do, but they are held responsible to the agreed upon deadlines. Internal roles within a team are also clearly defined by the level of sophistication involved and the specialty (programmers, modelers, animators, and so forth). The management at Sony also creates an arena for competition between development teams; the winners are not just those who develop the coolest games, but those who did on time.

How does Sony decide which traits are most important when selecting PlayStation's creative staff? For starters, Sony looks at young people. Phil Harrison, SCEA's Vice President for Third-Party Relations and R&D explains the acronym, "Young people don't have preconceived notions about how things should be done; they just come up with solutions…" Most of the management team at SCEA is in their 30s.[10]

Sony PlayStation has to come up with creative games *fast*. The creativity is partly delivered by the traits that Sony looks for in its game developer staff. The creativity is complemented by a unique approach to develop teams as explained in the following case study. However, to deliver the other core objective of quickly developing new games, these somewhat rebellious developers are also aware of strict deadlines. How does Sony manage the risk of trying to discipline these rebellious developers? They are quick to pull the plug if a team does not deliver, as also described in the following case study.

Case 2: The Sony PlayStation Organization (B)

With the demanding gamers in mind, Sony has also developed a unique approach to team management to deal with the external demands of the market. With the large number of projects being developed at one time and considerable experimentation with content, some projects never see the light. About 15 percent of the projects are aborted, which is an expected outcome from management's perspective, but for the team working on the project, it is a tough call. According to Ken Flock, the President of SCEA, "When you terminate a project, you have to break up the team. Failure usually means that the team dynamics weren't working. Chances are that the dysfunction will continue into the next project." Surprisingly, Sony reshuffles teams that are successful too. "After a killer project," Flock says, "the number two person is ready to become number one on a new project."[11]

Sony's approach to its organization development in some ways mimics its high-level core objectives of "maximize variety." Basically, Sony is maximizing the variety of the team composition in a manner that gives them the highest probability of developing new games quickly. If a team cannot deliver, it is quickly disbanded. This does not imply that the individual members are not creative or capable. It simply means that the team chemistry cannot deliver the company-wide core objective of speedy development of new games. Sony simply tries a different combination of team members to see what works. Finally, teams are not allowed to get jaded, which would negate the objective of "variety." Thus, the teams are broken up even if they are successful.

There are some important takeaways from the Sony story to any firm that is planning to use its people to develop creative solutions such as that are possible with the outcome-to-objective framework. In any organization, there are loners and gregarious people. There are methodical learners and quick studies. There are agitators and the consummate team players. The Sony story suggests that if the firm has intrinsic faith in a person, then it is possible to complement the methodical learners with quick studies and the agitators with the diplomats to get creative, yet rigorous business models. To illustrate, creativity is critical in rephrasing customer needs as outcomes and in identifying multiple objectives. Rigor is important in working through various capability configurations that can deliver the outcome with the least risk to the firm. Of course, none of this is possible unless the team has clarity about the core objectives. The movie A Beautiful Mind is a good example of how the most iconoclastic person, such as John Nash, can flourish with the right support system. Another example is the late Nobel Laureate in Physics, Richard Feynman. His anthology of autobiographical essays was titled, What Do You Care What Other People Think? Further Adventures of a Curious Character. He was strictly a loner who was nevertheless valued by his colleagues who took care of many of his responsibilities, freeing him to make his contributions to science.

Codifying Knowledge Through Core Objectives

We are firm believers in knowledge management systems provided they are properly used to develop core objectives. Massive company-wide information gathering is not the way to develop core objectives. Such all-encompassing initiatives are usually too complex to succeed.

Yet, part of the fascination with complex knowledge management systems may be driven by academic research on social network theories that strive to demonstrate the complexities of the decision-making process. We will go out on a limb and say that it is virtually impossible to codify these processes using knowledge management systems because most of the knowledge in complex networks is tacit. For example, in the early 1990s, there was a great deal of investment made by pharmaceutical companies to codify the process of identifying intermediate chemicals that form the building blocks of new drugs. An article in the February 25th 2004, *Wall Street Journal* suggested that this has basically failed because the process of identifying these chemicals is largely tacit. On the other hand, Lilly managed to tap worldwide networks of scientists to get the same result. Thus, companies that invest in data warehouses to capture any and everything find they rarely get any value out of it without the context to make the information useful.[12] One solution is to let individual managers customize the knowledge and provide the context. For example, most Dell managers use an intuitive interface with their data warehouse called Dell-Data-Direct (D3) to customize 10 or 15 reports, much like Memorial Healthcare. A second, and complementary, solution is to identify the objectives that dictate how the knowledge is going to be used for the benefit of the entire organization. This calls for a different, collaborative process.

Case 3: Raytheon's "Communities of Practice"

Raytheon is trying to develop a portal called "communities of practice" where managers and technical staff (such as supply-chain and Six Sigma staffs) can collaborate to develop best practices to deliver their core objectives. However, this portal can also be accessed by the leadership level to ensure the practices being developed are consistent with the broad competitive objectives of the company.

For Dell managers, D3 also allows them to create what-if scenarios and share the findings with other managers to collectively develop the best practices. This example illustrates the two issues identified earlier. Allowing functional managers to draw from the same knowledge base is the first step to bringing the different objectives in line with overall organizational objectives. Functional managers are in the best position to have the context to use the data appropriately and customize their own core objectives. Collaborating with others at the same level and higher (Dell managers can only collaborate with colleagues that have the same or better security clearance) not only forces managers to refine the objectives, but filters them upwards to enhance organizational conformity. You should recognize the similarity between this process and the iterative process that we suggested previously, of selecting one objective from the multiple objectives identified through the outcome-to-objective framework, testing the capabilities that necessitate knowledge from lower in the organization, and finally, selecting the objective that can be delivered with the least capability risks.

Core Objectives and Control Systems

The key to avoiding risks is to know whether you are winning or losing before you have lost a great deal. Unfortunately, most companies' control systems actually hinder instead of help. To exploit risky opportunities, corporate control systems that can manage to both control operations and increase risk-taking must be built. The formula employed by the best companies is to control what you must, not what you can. How do world-class companies manage to track so few items? Their core objectives guide them to the few metrics that provide immediate feedback on how the company is doing. Other steps: shorten the time, and the number of intermediaries, between measurement and action and increase the speed with which managers at all levels receive feedback. Southwest is immediately aware when a plane is on the ground longer than accepted norms. Dell is immediately aware when a computer has taken more than four days to be ready for shipping. Thus, control systems should be set up to establish and monitor core objectives at all levels in the organization. It does not mean that other data should not be gathered, but this data should be structured in a way that is available to managers who want to drill down to resolve an observed variance in a core objective. There is one caveat: Do not set up such a control system quickly; it must be tested for robustness many times. However, after you achieve it, you are much less likely to be surprised if you are tracking fewer items and taking quick action on these.

Closing Thoughts on Section 1

In this section, we showed you how to design a strategy where you can anticipate most of the risks of failure before you actually implement the strategy. The key take-away from this is that this design process is not a one-off event, but rather a replicable process that you should be able to repeat over and over again. In fact, the whole idea of anticipating risks means that you can abandon a strategy if it looks too risky at the design stage and use the same replicable process to try a new variant of the strategy. If you can clearly define the logic of your business model by succinctly articulating your core competitive objectives so it is understandable by the organization's rank-and-file, then you are in very good shape for anticipating what is possible and what is too risky. In the next section, you consider frameworks that extend the same process to understand and avoid the risks in growth and diversification strategies.

Endnotes

1 In the Appendix, we demonstrate how Enron's culture evolved from being thorough and rigorous to a "cowboy" mentality that was allowed to run rampant without any checks and balances. We argue that part of Enron's failure is in its inability to codify its business model and disseminate a common doctrine (and we do not mean greed) throughout the organization.

2 Source: *Ariba* magazine, Winter 2001: 22-28.

3 Chris Murphy. Dell is proud and protective of the business processes it uses to take advantage of technology. *InformationWeek* Sept. 8, 2003. http://www. informationweek.com/story/showArticle.jhtml?articleID=14500036.

4 *European Business Forum*: http://www.ebfonline.com/main_feat/in_depth/ in_depth.asp?id=380.

Emotional components are visible and adds value to product design.

5 As an aside, we are not a great fan of technology for technology's sake, but this is an example of being what we like to call "business-smart in technology." First clarify the objective, and then seek out the correct technology that can deliver the objective.

6 The JetBlue example is more geared to customer satisfaction and internal efficiency than pure demand maximization. However, the common theme is that the frontline personnel were empowered and allowed to make the decisions because they had a common doctrine.

7 An example of off-the-shelf software is Minneapolis-based Adaytum's ePlanning software, which has been used successfully by many financial services companies to increase inputs from employees by a factor of five. Cadence, a Tempe, Arizona-based network services company uses dynamic planning software from Stamford, Connecticut-based OutlookSoft Corp. to narrow its ex-post forecast accuracy from 25 percent to between five and 10 percent. What led to this improvement? According to company sources, the forecasts used to be made by the VP of Sales from intuition and conversations with a few senior executives at customer firms. After the software was introduced, every salesperson and outside consultant input a forecast.

8 Scott Berinato. "What Went Wrong at Cisco." *CIO Magazine*. Aug 1, 2001.

9 Jeremy Epstein. "Who Knows What When and How?" *Darwin Magazine*, April 2003.

10 Paul Roberts. "Sony Changes the Game." *Fast Company*, Issue 10, August 1997.

11 Ibid.

12 Kent Greenes, Senior VP and Chief Knowledge Officer at consulting firm Scientific Applications International makes a similar point as Tony Kontzer. "The Need To Know." *InformationWeek* Aug. 18, 2003. http://www.informationweek. com/story/showArticle.jhtml?articleID=13100330.

SECTION 2

THE RISKS IN GROWTH AND DIVERSIFICATION STRATEGY

One of the most vexing problems for a successful firm is to figure out how to grow out of the niche that brought it its success. Your firm might enter a new business either by creating (shaping) a new market or entering an existing market (adapting).[1] You will, of course, recognize this constitutes a choice between demand risk and competitive risk. Other than creating a new industry (which we discuss in Chapter 9, *Strategies to Shape Markets: Products, Process, and Platform*, which has its own set of risks), most firms that try to grow out of their original niches have to consider entry into an established market. Unfortunately, a lot of firms do not apply the same principles in the new market that were the cornerstones of their success in the original niche.

Very simply, the basis for low-risk growth and diversification has to be rooted in the same principles we have developed so far. With two exceptions, a diversification strategy succeeds only if you are also a strong competitor in the market that you choose to enter. The first exception is when you deliberately choose to lose money in one business in order to profit from others. Some feel that this is a strategy Hewlett-Packard has embarked upon in the PC business by cutting prices to a breakeven point to counter Dell Computer. Hewlett-Packard expects to make up the money from other services that it offers with its PC sales. We will not explicitly consider this strategy in this book,[2] but it should be clear that success in this type of a "loss-leader" strategy is still dependent on being competitive in the other businesses.

The second exception brings us to the concept of leveragable capabilities. When you are trying to compete in a single market, you are concentrating on developing what we call business-specific capabilities. To increase the odds of success in diversification strategy, you need to develop a capabilities set that can be used in multiple businesses. This is an important concept that we use throughout this section.

Leveragable Capabilities: The Key To Reducing Diversification Risk

As we saw in Chapter 4, *Designing Strategies with Low Capability Risks*, the highest risk involves investment in a brand new value chain where a firm has to acquire all the capabilities from scratch. Sometimes this is impossible to avoid. However, as we will illustrate, even firms such as Microsoft, which have shaped or created brand new markets, have consistently relied on their own or their partners' capabilities to reduce the risk of these strategies. The basic difference between capabilities that are specific to a business and capabilities that can be used to reduce the risks in diversification strategy is the latter is much more leveragable—these capabilities can be used in multiple businesses. Leveragable capabilities can be used to overcome entry barriers (reduce capability risks) when entering existing markets, or erect entry barriers around a new market (reduce competitive risks) that a firm creates. At various points in the next four chapters, we expand on this difference and how this leveragability manifests in different types of corporate strategy. However, it may be useful to lay out what exactly is a leveragable resource.

Most firms first invest in a capability that is targeted for a single business. If you are successful using the framework developed in the previous chapters or a variation thereof, you inevitably will run into a point where growth in the core business slows down. The least risky option is to carefully consider the parts of your current capabilities that can be leveraged into a new business. This process is illustrated in Figure 1. The first point of interest is, therefore, to identify exactly what it is you can leverage to other businesses.

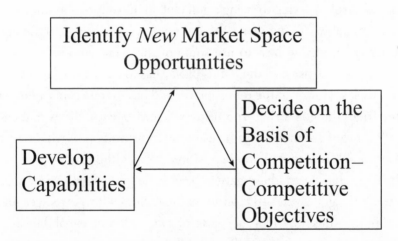

FIGURE 1   Using existing capabilities for diversification: Virtuous cycle.

What Is a Leveragable Capability?

Everyone talks about leveraging capabilities. But in practice, it is not so easy to identify what is leveragable and what is not. Let us consider an example from the world of sports. Here is a fact that many people may not be aware of. Most right-handed professional tennis players play golf left-handed, whereas most right-handed basketball players play golf right-handed. In the words of one of these ex-tennis players, the reason for playing golf with the weaker hand is because there is a strong similarity between the tennis backhand and the golf swing. For this reason, it is much easier for a "good" tennis player to learn the golf swing as if he or she is hitting a backhand. There is no such similarity between any of the moves involved in the basketball game and the golf swing. For this reason, most professional basketball players would pick up golf the way the rest of us do—play it with our dominant hand. Basically, tennis players can leverage some of their activities into playing golf and that gives them an advantage in the sport, which is not available to basketball players.

Now let us think about what exactly the tennis player is leveraging to golf. Even though there is a fair amount of similarity between the two strokes, trying to swing a golf club identically to a tennis backhand probably will not work. What a tennis player brings to the golf swing is knowledge how to use some of the same muscles that are used in both strokes, so the tennis player has to train a smaller subset of muscles. However, the tennis player still has to train other muscles to perfect the golf swing. In business, likewise, capabilities that can be leveraged are unlikely to be a simple transposition of what a firm does in one business to another. Moreover, like the muscles used in the tennis backhand, these have to be complemented with other muscles for the golf swing—the business capabilities a firm leverages into a different business may be parts of two different capabilities. In other words, business-specific capabilities reside at the intersection of activities and resources, while leveragable capabilities reside at the intersection of capabilities. A growth strategy, and the success of it, depends to a large extent on how you can identify parts of your existing capabilities that, in combination, can be leveraged into a new business.

Case 1: Cendant Corp: Leveragable Capabilities

Cendant Corp. has been able to leverage its information capability across multiple businesses with little need to acquire new capabilities. Since the early 1990s, Cendant has acquired troubled businesses with strong brands and, more importantly, information assets. Through the acquisitions of Avis Rent-A-Car, Coldwell Banker, and Howard Johnson hotels, for example, Cendant has gained reservation systems, listing services, and customer databases. Rather than acquire new capabilities in these industries, Cendant has spun off most of the physical assets (hotels, offices, rental agencies, and so forth) and has franchised the information assets to the new owners. By leveraging its information capability to acquire informational assets, Cendant has increased its ability to spot and respond to market trends and shifts.[3]

Some Characteristics of Leveragable Capabilities

Business-specific capabilities are more visible to customers (thus, affecting the price premium), while leveragable capabilities are usually more involved in the delivery mechanisms (thus, affecting the cost structure). Typically, leveragable capabilities result in outputs that are invisible to the customer. Going back to the golf example, it is difficult to charge a premium price for an exercise regimen to strengthen the golf muscles, whereas golf clubs command a premium price. Leveragable capabilities get you in the playing field, but you will still need business-specific capabilities to deliver it. For a final illustration, let us revisit an example (Case 5) you saw in Chapter 1, *How to See Gold Where Others See Risk: Identify More Choices to Get the Gold.* about how Company X outmaneuvered a new competitor for shelf space at Home Depot.

Leveraging Category Management Capability

Once Company X had successfully taken over the category management of its specific niche product, it decided to leverage this newfound capability to manage the entire paint and sundries section of Home Depot, saving Home Depot time and effort, and it actually did a much better job than Home Depot might have done itself. Further, with this newfound arrangement, Company X managed to expand its product line covering several categories based around the original product. It did this with the full acquiescence of Home Depot by demonstrating that it was easier for the consumer to have a similar category in one place. In other words, the category management capability that Company X had developed and executed to fight off competitive risk became a leveragable capability that allowed the company to diversify into more product lines.

To underscore the importance of having the right leveragable capability as the foundation for a diversification strategy, note that prior to its acquisition by the holding company, Company X had attempted to broaden the brand name of this product (say, "protector") to other products in the same market space. In the process, the original brand name sank perilously close to being a commodity and was in danger of losing its high franchise value. The strategy was abandoned.

However, after Company X took over the category management of the paints and sundries department at Home Depot, it successfully extended the "protector" product line by making sure to distinguish between the various product lines related to the original brand. None of this would have been possible without the category management capability it had developed. This took very specific market/shelf presentation, distinction between related brands, and a well-presented, customer-focused display. All these risks were considered, given weight, and the project moved forward—very successfully. According to company leadership, this was a great example of leveraging a strong brand name through potential pitfalls by virtue of acquiring a second set of capabilities.

With this background on leveragable capabilities, we can develop frameworks to help you reduce risks in diversification strategies. In Chapter 7, *When and How to Use Differentiation Entry Strategy*, and Chapter 8, *When and How to Use a Low-Price Entry Strategy*, we look at two generic strategies for adapting to a market. In Chapter 9, *Strategies to Shape Markets: Products, Process, and Platform*, we look at market-shaping strategies.

Endnotes

1 These two terms, adapting and shaping, have been widely used in the practitioner literature.

2 See Chapter 10, *Develop Multiple Migration Paths*, for Microsoft's diversification strategy, many of which are loss leaders.

3 Keith Hammonds, H. "Size is Not a Strategy." *Fast Company* Sept. 2002: 78.

7

WHEN AND HOW TO USE DIFFERENTIATION ENTRY STRATEGY

Adapting to an existing market usually avoids demand risk because the market demand is fairly well understood compared to shaping a new market, which we discuss in Chapter 9. However, adapting to an existing market forces you to contend with the market incumbents and, therefore, subjects you to competitive risks. Finally, adapting to a new market usually implies that you have to overcome entry barriers. Thus, you are also susceptible to capability risks.

In Early Product Lifecycle—Differentiate

Two basic adaptive entry strategies exist: differentiation or low-price. In most entries, there are elements of both strategies present to a greater or lesser extent (recall the Lexus example). However, one may be less risky than the other depending on the product lifecycle of the market that the firm is getting into.

If the market is early in the lifecycle and not all of the desired outcomes are being effectively addressed by existing players, you may wish to pursue a differentiation strategy, even if it is purely through marketing. There are situations where a new entrant may come in with a low-cost strategy early in the product lifecycle, but this has to be more of an exception than the rule. If a particular value proposition is still evolving, you are more likely dealing with customers who are early adopters and are much less price-sensitive than customers in a mature market. Moreover, in an evolving market, you are likely to find opportunities for differentiation because all the value propositions have not yet been fully developed. For example, the SUV automobile market is still being fought primarily on the basis of differentiation, such as the new Nissan Murano. SUVs fetch high margins for automakers.

When There Is a Strong Incumbent—Differentiate

Several risks exist in trying to wage a price war directly against strong incumbents, particularly if the market is evolving. This is because the incumbent can reciprocate in kind by cutting out some of the profits and, unless the entrant truly has a lower cost structure, it will most likely end up the loser in this battle. It is also unlikely that the entrant has lower cost structure in an evolving market because the production technology is most likely evolving and not as easy to standardize as a mature market. By identifying a sweet spot, the new entrant can enjoy profits without bringing attention to itself from the strong incumbent.

When FedEx created the overnight delivery market in 1973, this was a white space that went unchallenged until the late 1970s when some of the freight forwarders, such as Purolator and Emory Freight, entered the space. However, these new entrants were quite content to play in their own niche that did not bring them into head-to-head confrontation with FedEx. The result was a period of sustained growth and profits for the entire industry. Now for the exception: If a firm can leverage its existing capabilities, it *may* be able to offer the same outcomes as the market innovator at a lower price. However, even if a firm succeeds with a low-price strategy, it runs the danger of decimating the profit structure of the industry, sometimes forever. When UPS entered the Air Express industry in 1982 and aggressively focused on price against the market leader FedEx, the entire industry went into a tailspin leading to a massive consolidation in 1987. UPS could do this because of its deep pockets and its extremely efficient ground network. However, even UPS could not match FedEx in all its overnight offerings until it had completed its own air network, which took UPS 15 years. UPS may have learned from its initial entry strategy because such rampant price cutting has not taken place in this industry since 1987.

If you do decide to resort to a low-price strategy in an early stage market, you have to be very confident that you have or can attain the lowest cost structure. Failing this, you will simply hand the market over to the lowest cost player. In 1992, Compaq ushered in the PC revolution by slashing prices. However, the ultimate winner was Dell, the low-cost producer who, until that point, was a struggling PC direct marketer.[1] Now consider Sony. Sony has been both an innovator (Walkman) and a fast follower with a differentiation strategy (VAIO laptops and PlayStation). It rarely resorts to price competition unless forced by the likes of Microsoft and Xbox.

How To Execute a Differentiation Entry Strategy

To illustrate a differentiated entry strategy, let us now go back to JetBlue airlines, which we examined in Chapter 3, *Identifying Multiple Capability Configurations*. JetBlue is taking on the most successful airline in America—Southwest. While Southwest has been around for a fairly long time, its impact on the airline industry began to be observed only in the early 1990s. The point-to-point airline industry is finally beginning to attract strong competitors. A number of major airlines are once again trying to compete with Southwest after having failed with earlier attempts. A number of startups, such as AmericaWest and AirTran, have successfully implemented the Southwest business model.

Among the startups, JetBlue has garnered the most attention. You may wonder whether JetBlue is a good example of a differentiated entry strategy given that it competes on low-price. Not only has JetBlue developed a different set of capabilities to deliver some of the same core objectives that Southwest adheres to (see Chapter 2), but it has also managed to differentiate itself significantly from Southwest.

How JetBlue Has Differentiated Itself in the Point-to-Point Space

Routes & Schedules

JetBlue has a geographically diverse flight schedule of long and short hauls, making it less vulnerable to competition from any single competitor. This strategy also allows it to select the best possible markets and adjust its schedule to accommodate seasonal fluctuations in demand in certain markets. For example, it offers increased service on its New York to Florida routes in winter, when demand is higher. Currently, it serves 22 cities in 9 states and Puerto Rico. It operates 180 flights daily with 80 daily flights between JFK and Florida, 22 daily flights between JFK and upstate New York, and 32 daily flights between JFK and the western United States.

Airports

JetBlue established New York's JFK airport as its operating base on the East Coast. Even though JFK has better facilities compared to La Guardia and Newark (more runways permitting more flights per day), it was least preferred among major U.S. airlines. JFK experiences congestion only during the period between 3:00 p.m. and 8:00 p.m. (due to peak domestic and international air traffic), as opposed to La Guardia and Newark, which remain congested throughout the day. Because JFK is one of the airports that comes under the FAA's High Density Rule, during the congestion period, there is a limit on the number of scheduled flights between 3:00 p.m. and 8:00 p.m., and only slot holders are allowed to operate during this interval. However, according to a 1994 ruling, slot exemptions could be given to qualified air carriers to fill voids in underserved markets and generate needed price competition in specific markets. JetBlue qualified to get 75 slot exemptions and gained access to otherwise slot-restricted JFK airport with the help of Sen. Chuck Schumer, (D-N.Y.). The gates are in newly renovated Terminal 6, which was a deserted garbage heap when JetBlue took it over a year ago. JetBlue is able to operate throughout the day, including during the slot-controlled period on account of these slot exemptions. However, JetBlue schedules almost two-thirds of its flights outside the slot-controlled period. Further, the only increase in domestic departures that can occur during the slot period at JFK would be in the form of regional jet service to small and medium, non-hub airports by airlines currently using less than 20 slots. These airlines are eligible to slot exemptions and JetBlue, it seems, stands out as one of them.

Passenger Comfort

The A320 has a wider cabin than the Boeing 757 and 737, and each aircraft is designed to carry 162 passengers in a single-class coach equipped with wide leather seats and satellite TV at every seat (the first and only airline to offer this service). These aircrafts are also the quietest and most fuel efficient jets in air. Some of the other ways that JetBlue differentiates itself from Southwest and even the major carriers are as follows:

- More leg room with a 32-inch pitch between rows.
- Pre-assigned seating, ticketless travel, and no Saturday stay.
- No overbooking of flights.
- Change fees are only $25 per passenger, compared to $100 charged by major carriers.
- In-flight passengers are treated to soft drinks and blue-tinted potato chips.

continues

How JetBlue Has Differentiated Itself in the Point-to-Point Space: Continued

- Onboard "Crunch-fitness" yoga program to relieve stress.
- Delayed customers are provided free snacks and drinks.
- Customer self-service kiosks, currently installed at JFK, Oakland, and Ft. Lauderdale.
- Live TV in every seat.
- The CEO works as a flight attendant once a month.

Identify a Sweet Spot

JetBlue's choice of JFK as its primary airport is a classic case of identifying a sweet spot and developing capabilities to exploit the sweet spot. JetBlue has stayed away from direct confrontation with Southwest, though it may be only a matter of time. Southwest favors secondary airports and would never consider JFK because it could not afford to get bogged down during takeoff and landing. Southwest likes to space its flights fairly uniformly throughout the day. This would be a major issue with Southwest, given JFK's slot restriction periods. JetBlue, by virtue of its combination of short-haul and long-haul flights, can afford to be a little more flexible. However, JetBlue has shrewdly scheduled most of its flights outside the slot exemptions period when the takeoff and landing delays are less likely and the extra runways of JFK allow for the scheduling of more flights. Further, JFK is not only a sweet spot because of Southwest; it is also a sweet spot with regards to the major carriers. The absence of direct competition with the major airlines allows JetBlue much-needed time to get its operations in smooth flow.

Takeaway

When a firm is entering a market with existing players, it is not a good idea to take them head-on, especially if the incumbents are strong and entrenched (unless the entrant is UPS or Microsoft). It is much safer to try a flanking entry or identify a sweet spot—something the incumbents are ignoring for whatever reason. Early in the product lifecycle, you are also more likely to be able to identify sweet spots and possibly outright white spaces. A corollary to this objective is you may have to temper your growth aspirations even if you are successful with your initial sweet spot entry strategy. Unless you have the capabilities to take on the incumbents, drawing attention to the sweet spot may increase your competitive risks significantly.

Develop Capabilities for Differentiation

JetBlue is targeting more of a business passenger than Southwest. Because JetBlue purchased brand-new planes that come equipped with TV monitors on every seat (with live feed), it has managed to differentiate itself in a manner that would be very expensive for Southwest to copy if it wanted to retrofit its older planes.[2] JetBlue is also offering other services and amenities (see the bullet points in the preceding case study) that match the profile of its customers perfectly and is not being offered by most other short-haul airlines or even the major airlines. Basically, by raising the bar on the visible amenities, JetBlue has put Southwest in a position where it has to try to match the same services or fall below the value frontier if and when JetBlue enters Southwest's markets.

Takeaway

Consider the visible-invisible matrix we developed in Chapter 5, *Lowering Capability Risks with Visible and Invisible Outputs*. Part of a differentiation strategy should be to focus on the visible part of the value chain that directly addresses outcomes that customers desire but are not being fulfilled by existing players. This is especially true for consumer markets. JetBlue has focused on visible attributes to be distinct from Southwest. The same principle holds true for industrial markets except you have to communicate how your product or service visibly impacts the revenue or costs of your industrial customers.

Develop Capabilities That Are Difficult to Imitate

JetBlue's access to JFK became even more valuable since, under current law, the slot restrictions were scheduled to be eliminated on January 1, 2007. This allows JetBlue to schedule even more flights out of JFK. Further, JetBlue is actively involved in making the entire metropolitan New York area more accessible to travelers from all the region's airports. The Port Authority of New York and New Jersey is in the process of implementing a $10 billion JFK redevelopment project, which includes new terminals, improved roadways, and construction of AirTrain, a direct light-rail link between JFK and the New York subway system and Long Island Rail Road. These improvements are a part of New York Governor George E. Pataki's visionary "Masterlinks" program (unveiled in May 1996), a comprehensive and integrated plan geared toward improving access to the region's airports. JetBlue is working with the Port Authority of New York and New Jersey to bring about these improvements. It was Governor Pataki's vision and support of the power of JetBlue's low air fares and providing easy access to New Yorkers to the JFK airport that led to the crystallization of this public-private airport redevelopment program, as well as JetBlue's boosting air traffic at JFK. JetBlue recognized this window of opportunity to gain access to JFK through the slot exemptions and set up operations just in time to take full advantage of the influx in passenger traffic brought about by the AirTrain project. The service between Jamaica Station and JFK started in 2003, while the link between Penn Station (New York's busiest transportation facility, which is being redeveloped for this purpose) and Jamaica Station started in 2004. The entire link enables passengers to check-in their baggage at Penn Station and be at JFK in 25 minutes via AirTrain. After everything is up and running, it will be almost impossible to imitate JetBlue in these routes.

Takeaway

If you can negotiate a successful entry early in the product lifecycle, you want to reap the benefits for as long a time as possible. Just because you have identified a white space or even a sweet spot does not mean that you are immune from competition. Even if the incumbents at the time of the entry stay away from your sweet spot, your firm is likely to attract fresh entrants by its very success. Erecting entry barriers is particularly important if you have exploited a white space and brought this to the attention of industry heavyweights instead of entering a sweet spot that the incumbents may continue to ignore.

Consolidate Capabilities Before Expanding the Sweet Spot—Slowly

JetBlue is extremely disciplined about its growth strategy. It only expands routes that are profitable. However, because of its unused capacity of flights during slot-controlled periods, it is embarking on acquiring a new set of capabilities to exploit this capacity in the least risky fashion. JetBlue plans to tap into increased departures that can be scheduled out of JFK during the slot-controlled periods by scheduling flights to non-hub, small- and medium-sized markets. The new capability? One hundred of the latest EMBRAER 190 regional jets from Brazilian aircraft manufacturer, EMBRAER. With a sticker price of $3 billion, this contract of twin engine, 100-seater regional aircrafts will enable JetBlue to bring lower air fares to more small and midsize U.S. markets. Although the new aircrafts will cost them a penny more than the A320s (when compared on the same routes), JetBlue officials say that in the markets it plans to enter, it will still be offering fares that are 50 to 60 percent lower than those currently offered in those markets. JetBlue's contention is that on a route where, prior to its entry, the fares hover at around $200 one-way, it doesn't really matter whether it offers a $60 or $65 one-way fare. Moreover, the flexibility of the 190s in flying short- or long-haul could enable JetBlue to take advantage of the slot exemptions at JFK and the unused nine slots at Long Beach Airport. It also intends to boost off-season business (for example, upstate New York and Florida in winter). Lastly, because JetBlue is the launch customer for the EMB 190, it has been awarded sizable discounts over the list price along with approval of a laundry list of customizations. All the 190s will have the same features and facilities as the A320 and will deliver the same JetBlue experience. The first 7 of these aircrafts were expected to be delivered by 2005, with close to 16 aircrafts to be added each year through 2011. To appreciate the brilliance of JetBlue's strategy, one has to simply look at the response from Southwest. Southwest is being forced to imitate JetBlue's strategy to keep pace, including possible acquisition of the EMB 190 jets.

Takeaway

A major cause of failure of differentiated entrants is they try to expand their sweet spot too quickly without securing the base. They might suddenly find out that what was once a sweet spot is now attracting attention from the industry heavyweights. This scenario has been played out time and again in the high-technology market space, especially where Cisco and Microsoft dominate. If a firm finds itself in that situation, the firm needs to seriously think of an exit strategy before the business gets wiped out (see Chapter 9 for details on exit strategies). However, if you have satisfied the previous three objectives, you are in a better position to expand the sweet spot because the entry barriers may be able to fight off incumbents even if they decide to come into your territory.

In Chapter 8, you will consider entry strategies based on low price. You also will consider the market characteristics that reduce the risks of such a strategy. In particular, you examine one of the foremost proponents of the low-price strategies, Dell Computer, and how it has leveraged its low-cost operations into many markets by under pricing incumbents. Firms contemplating a low-price entry strategy can learn some important lessons from Dell.

Endnotes

1 Compaq, along with Hewlett-Packard, is repeating this price-cutting strategy in 2004. However, the PC business is a mature business right now, and Compaq can leverage its strengths in services and printers to make a battle of it in the PC business, even if it breaks even or loses money.

2 Melanie Trottman. "Southwest Air Considers Shift In Its Approach." *The Wall Street Journal* December 23, 2003.

8

WHEN AND HOW TO USE A LOW-PRICE ENTRY STRATEGY

An entrant should always consider a differentiation entry strategy if it is at all possible. Differentiation gives the entrant some time before competitive risk becomes a problem. However, under some situations, differentiation is not a good option because the basis for differentiation is not sustainable and the competitive battle quickly becomes one of price. Let us consider some examples.

For a Mature Product, the Entry Strategy Should Be Low Price

Opportunities for differentiation are likely to be less if the product or service has been around for a long time. Even if you manage to develop a basis of differentiation, you are likely to attract the attention of the incumbents. Unless this basis of differentiation is impossible for others to imitate, a firm will soon be competing on par with everyone else. For this reason, if the market is mature and the existing products or services meet most of the desired outcomes, then we suggest you think of a low-price entry strategy.[1] In the mature stages of the product lifecycle, customers are likely to be price-sensitive, unlike the early adopters. Of course, this implies it is necessary to develop a cost structure that is lower than the incumbents. You can consider several avenues. The size of the market is likely to be much larger compared to a niche market, which lends itself to scale economies. Also, the production technology should be sufficiently standardized in a mature market such that efficient methods from other industries can be adapted to reduce costs below that of the incumbents.

Risks for Differentiation Entry Strategy in a Mature Market

Case 1: Clorox's Entry into the Detergent Market

Clorox is famous for its bleach products. Clorox is also an aggressive and competent marketing organization. It was once a part of Procter & Gamble. In the late 1980s, Clorox targeted the profitable detergent market dominated by Procter & Gamble's Tide. Clorox decided to add bleach to the detergent product as a way of differentiating itself from normal detergents, including Tide. Unlike private-label detergents sold at the deep discount stores, Clorox's entry was seen by Procter & Gamble as targeting its core customers. The result was an all-out marketing assault by Procter & Gamble and a withdrawal by Clorox.

The Clorox story illustrates two important risks in trying to adapt to a mature market using a differentiation strategy. First, the detergent market was not really suitable for differentiated entry strategy given its mature stage in the product lifecycle. Now, Clorox obviously felt it had added value by reducing the hassle of adding bleach to detergent, something that was probably quite visible to the consumer. However, in a mature market, it is much more difficult to find a sweet spot that is being ignored by the incumbents. The detergent with bleach concept was not exactly a sweet spot but more of a white space. No one, including Procter & Gamble, had considered this possibility until that time. However, this was a white space that, left unchallenged, could threaten Procter & Gamble's core detergent business. In other words, Clorox's entry was seen as a broadside attack against Procter & Gamble's detergent business dominated by Tide, not as filling a niche segment. This may not be necessarily fatal if the incumbent is unable to imitate the basis of the entrant's differentiation, or if the entrant is able to erect entry barriers. Clearly, this was not the case for Procter & Gamble because it introduced Tide with bleach in a hurry. This is the second major risk of trying to enter a mature market with a differentiation strategy. The basis of differentiation gets copied, and the battle quickly becomes one of price. In summary, if your firm is entering a white space, you have to have a strategy to defend the white space. Basically, you have to be honest with yourself as to whether your capabilities can be and will be imitated by the incumbents or other entrants. You need to do this analysis at the design stage of the entry strategy to avoid all the aggravation and losses of pulling out after-the-fact.

Takeaway

If the differentiation is perceived as a threat to a strong incumbent's core business, the risk of failure will go up astronomically. If you have to enter with a differentiation strategy where there are strong incumbents, the low-risk strategy is to identify a sweet spot if you can find one.

Capabilities for a Low-Price Strategy

While JetBlue is a good example of how to differentiate from the market leader, Southwest, which has shaped the point-to-point air transport market, JetBlue's entry into the short-route markets using

the EMBRAER 190 regional jets is a good example of how to leverage a capability from the core business to under price the existing
players in a new, but mature, market. The key is to have clarity in
which parts of your current capabilities can be leveraged into a different mature market to reduce the cost structures of those markets.
Moreover, the capabilities that the entrant leverages have to be
unique, so it cannot be copied by the incumbents the entrant will be
under pricing. In the case of JetBlue, the combination of slots in JFK
and the relationship it developed with the Port Authority of New
York, along with its naturally efficient operations, imply that it can
rapidly dominate small regional markets that can be served from JFK.
Likewise, Southwest's entry into the Philadelphia market should be
cause for serious concern for USAir. The only consolation to USAir is
that Philadelphia International Airport violates one of Southwest's
key principles of using secondary airports. Unfortunately for USAir,
Southwest has so much lower cost elsewhere that it can subsidize its
Philadelphia operations until it settles in.

The remainder of this chapter examines strategies for leveraging
a capability for a low-price entry by focusing on Dell Computer's
diversification strategy. Most people still think of Dell as a PC manufacturer. The following pages detail the fast and furious pace at which
Dell is trying to change its corporate strategy and what we can learn
from it.

Dell Computer: Leveraging Low-Cost Operations to Multiple Markets

Case 2: Dell's Growth and Diversification

Since the company's inception in 1984, its direct marketing
approach is widely believed to be fundamental to Dell's initial and
continuing success. However, in an attempt to gain market share
from market leaders IBM and Compaq, Dell surprisingly abandoned this strategy in early 1989 and tried to sell its products

through traditional retail channels. After a few years of dismal performance with traditional retailers, Dell reverted back to direct marketing exclusively in 1994. Dell truly began to embrace an efficient build-to-order model at this time. In early 1997, Dell added ordering through the Internet to its traditional phone ordering system. In 1998, Dell's Internet sales were about $6 million a day or approximately 15 percent of the firm's revenues.[2]

Operations

The highly successful Dell Direct Customized model is based on a reconfiguration of the supply chain, a tight integration of B2B and B2C capabilities, and new approaches to dealing with customers. Orders go directly into Dell's production schedule after the payment is authorized by Dell's merchant bank. The suppliers receive these orders continuously and ship these products very close to the time that Dell's manufacturing plants are ready to assemble the computer. The logistics of having the parts delivered on time is handled by logistics and transportation providers, such as FedEx. On receipt, parts are kitted immediately before production and built up in cells. The assembling operation involves one person putting the kitted parts together and testing and loading the final product with software before shipment. Accessories such as monitors, printers, or scanners are shipped directly by their manufacturer, and the logistics provider insures their arrival at the customer's site on the same day as the main product. The only PCs that Dell does not assemble are laptops. Laptops are sourced from a vendor in Asia. Dell had major quality problems with its laptops in the mid-1990s.

Dell's supply chain management allows it to operate with only seven hours of inventory[3] compared to 13 days for Compaq and 10 days for IBM. Dell cultivates its suppliers assiduously. Dell doesn't believe in switching suppliers simply to reduce costs. Similarly, Dell has also focused on its cash conversion cycle time, reducing the difference between the time it pays its creditors and the time it takes to get paid to negative eight days in some instances.[4] The suppliers are true strategic partners in their common success, even when the suppliers may also be dealing with Dell's competitors.

continues

Case 2: Dell's Growth and Diversification (Continued)

By most estimates, Dell has a 10 percent cost advantage over its closest competitors, such as Gateway. Dell is constantly tweaking and refining its factories. Dell does not hesitate to decommission what it considers to be less-than-efficient plants and ship the manufacturing into newer plants, as it recently demonstrated in Europe.

Research and Development

Dell's research and development expenses are quite paltry—$440 million a year in 2003 versus $4 billion a year at Hewlett-Packard.[5]

However, Dell holds many patents. Almost all of them are for manufacturing processes, which reveals Dell's priority.

To tackle problems with reliability, Dell not only sought the highest performing components, but also spent its research dollars on ensuring that the components worked as a system to provide customers with a PC that worked straight out of the box. Dell's PCs were not the speediest among its peer group but consistently had the highest reliability ratings.[6]

Dell made most of its market share gains between 1995, when it had a 3.4% market share, to around 16% in 2000 (IDC estimates for desktops, laptops, and PC servers). In contrast, Hewlett-Packard and Compaq combined hold a 16% market share that has remain unchanged since 1995. Analysts wonder how Dell will sustain its growth in future decades.

Dell's core capabilities are suited to deliver its core objectives of direct merchandising and customized PCs while carrying almost no inventory. The objective is simple, but Dell's competitive advantage lies in its ability to manage the complexity of this supply chain process.

According to Dell board member, Alex Mandl, CEO of Gemplus[7]:

"People have tried to duplicate what Dell does, and they can't. It sounds like a simple model, but getting all this going and perfectly executing it is difficult, if not impossible. Many have tried, all have failed."

One new market segment that Dell focused on in the late 1990s was large corporate accounts.

Case 3: Going After Large Corporate Accounts: 1997

Today, customer segmentation is key to Dell's success. Dell categorizes its customers into consumers, medium-sized businesses, large corporations, enterprises, and education. Each segment has its own sales, marketing, and technical support teams.[8] This segment-specific strategy has its genesis in Dell's decision in 1997 to explicitly focus on commercial and government accounts that are generally less price-sensitive than consumers. These markets were dominated by IBM, Hewlett-Packard, and Compaq with well-established corporate sales forces. While Dell has since developed its own corporate sales force, in characteristic fashion, Dell gets the corporate sales over the Internet or telephone. Today, 90% of Dell's sales go to institutions—business or government—with 70% going to very large customers buying over $1 million in PCs every year. By focusing on this segment, Dell has been able to enter the higher-margin workstation and server business. Dell's commitment to servicing this segment and not engaging in the ultra-competitive consumer segment is evident by its announcement in early 2000 that it has no intention of competing in the sub-$1,000 PC market.

Dell was the first to develop a customized web site for its 30,000 plus corporate customers called Premiere Pages. As of 2000, the Premiere Pages account for three-fourths of Dell's daily online

continues

Case 3: Going After Large Corporate Accounts: 1997 (Continued)

revenues, which are nearly $20 million. However, the Premiere Pages concept goes beyond a customized ordering mechanism. The Premiere Pages is a place for sharing information between Dell and its customers and across Dell's customers. The focused information that customers can get from its customized web site can generate new business opportunities, such as serving corporate customers PC needs from soup-to-nuts.

The Premiere Pages also provide Dell's customers advance notice about new product introductions and allow customer inputs to shape developments of new products. The extensive customer involvement not only breeds loyalty, but also reduces errors and speeds fulfillment. In some cases, Dell's manufacturing plants are directly linked to the customers' ERP systems using a service called Direct Commerce Integration, thus automating the procurement processes. This saves money both for Dell and its customers. Dell captures the essence of its success with all customers, particularly corporate, as OBE or "out of the box experience."

The interesting observation to make here is the fact that Dell *waited until the late 1990s* to enter the highly profitable enterprise PC market. Let us consider the capabilities that Dell would have to acquire if it wanted to be a player in this market earlier. Typically, this would involve a dedicated sales force for these accounts. By waiting until the late 1990s, Dell entered the market when the enterprise buyers were comfortable making their transactions over the web and, thus, avoiding much of the need to have a large corporate sales force. Dell could now leverage its operational capabilities by offering a very low price without having the additional costs of enterprise-specific marketing where it was probably no better than IBM or HP. What we like about Dell throughout the 1990s is its discipline in not chasing markets. The only mistake it made was trying to penetrate retail channels. It has patiently waited for a market to develop that lends itself to Dell's capabilities before entering it. This insight leads us to the first key for reducing the risks in adapting to a market with a low-price strategy—you must understand the characteristics of the market where your firm is most likely to succeed by leveraging its existing capabilities.

Develop a Profile for Your Target Markets

Let us now extend this simple framework to understand the other markets that Dell has entered or plans to enter.

Case 4: Dell's Leveragable Capabilities

For the bulk of its existence, Dell stayed tried and true to its direct sales of customized PCs using off-the-shelf standardized components and software (Windows and now Linux). Dell has tried to diversify into the international market with its direct sales strategy. However, Dell has not been very successful in Europe or Latin America. Dell also has a presence in Asia. It is not clear if Dell's Asian markets have met Dell's own internal expectations. Dell gets just 18% of its revenue outside its home market. Sun, by contrast, gets 46% of sales from outside North America.

Noting that many consumers are interested in purchasing "complete systems," which include PCs, monitors, printers, servers, switches, and so forth, Dell has traditionally taken on the role of a reseller. Beginning in 2000, however, Dell began to manufacture its own Dell-branded version of these items, expanding its product line to include many of the items for which it had previously only been a reseller. These new product lines, encompassing switches, network storage machines, handheld computers and, most recently, printers, were the beginnings of a true diversification out of the PC business. Recently, Dell revealed plans to manufacture electronic cash registers for retailers. In August 2000, in an interview published in the *Wall Street Journal*, Mr. Dell laid out his diversification strategy.[9]

continues

Case 4: Dell's Leveragable Capabilities (Continued)

By using the lean production it has developed over the years, Dell hopes to under price rivals and gain market share.

"We're going full-steam ahead, running at Sun and EMC, and we'll take Compaq out along the way," Mr. Dell says confidently.

Dell is targeting small servers for Internet start-ups and corporate websites, with plans to move into bigger, more complex computers. Mr. Dell promises a new Dell data-storage system that will deliver the same amount of storage for a fraction of the price of a product from EMC, a Hopkinton, Mass. storage-equipment maker. "I think EMC stands for Excess Margin Corporation," Mr. Dell says.

An EMC executive says Dell has little to offer in data storage. "The only storage associated with Dell is onesy [simple] disks in PCs," says Ken Steinhardt, EMC's Director of North American Marketing. Data storage is rapidly becoming more software-intensive, an area where Dell has no experience, he says. Moreover, there is no standard software that can be used across all storage systems, like Windows or Linux.

Of these two markets that Dell chooses to enter, which do you think Dell has a better chance of succeeding in? To understand this, let us think through what Dell is all about. Dell is not a technology company—its R&D investment is about one-tenth that of HP. Dell is basically a custom assembler of off-the-shelf components. It can assemble electronic components faster and with lower inventory than any other player in the PC market. Now consider Dell's core PC business and where it has succeeded and where it has not. There is clearly a demand for PCs internationally, as demonstrated by Sun's server sales. Yet why is it that Dell is not as successful in markets outside North America? Perhaps Dell Computer is not as focused internationally as Sun. However, there is possibly a different explanation. To understand this, you need to think about the components of Dell's manufacturing capability. While Dell is very good in its factory layout and constantly tweaking its factories, including periodically scrapping some for new ones, the real money is being saved by the finely-tuned supply chain it has developed with the co-operation of its vendors. This supply chain is simply not replicable without (a) presence of the same or equally sophisticated vendors in the foreign markets, and (b) UPS or FedEx. Yes, FedEx and UPS. Very few people realize how dependent companies like Cisco and Dell are on FedEx in being able to keep their inventory levels low. Take FedEx (or UPS) out of the equation, and it becomes impossible to replicate Dell's model. On the other hand, Sun is fairly self-contained in terms of its ability to manufacture and sell its servers. Therefore, it is far easier for Sun to expand into other markets compared to Dell.[10]

Based on the previous discussion, we can come up with a profile of the markets suitable to leverage Dell's capabilities. Dell provides customization at the assembly stage and not at the component stage. Indeed, Dell uses only standardized components in markets where the underlying technology has matured. In such a market, if Dell can establish relationships with component vendors that can link up to its supply chain system (including drop shipment), it can easily manufacture/assemble the end-product at a much lower cost than incumbents. Of course, all of this is contingent on the availability of outside logistics and transportation providers, such as FedEx or UPS. The profile of an ideal market in which Dell Computer is likely to succeed can be described as follows:

- Components as well as software are standardized.
- Technology is mature.
- Vendor-managed replenishment of inventory is possible.
- Logistics providers, such as FedEx or UPS, are available.
- Customization is at the assembly stage.
- Current incumbents are enjoying high gross margins.

Using this profile, we can better understand the markets in which Dell is likely to have the most success.

Server Business

The server market started its growth phase in the late 1980s and has been a tremendous money maker for incumbents, such as Sun, HP, and IBM. This is a mature market. There are well-established component vendors, and there is standardized server software available at the low-end of the server market. Therefore, it is not a surprise that Dell is slowly beginning to dominate the low-end of the server business.

What about the high-end of the server business? In the high-end, the role of R&D in product development and customized software is much more important. Using our framework, we can predict it will be very difficult for Dell to develop a capability of product innovation through R&D. Accordingly, this is not a market in which Dell is likely to succeed. The only scenario under which Dell would be able to penetrate the high-end server market is if the Intel architecture becomes powerful enough to be used in this segment along with the standardized Windows- or Linux-based software.

Storage Business

We have the same reservation about Dell's ability to succeed in the storage business. Data storage systems are powerful computers (usually linked by a network), which are used to store and manage critical corporate data by means of specialized software. Unlike the desktop and PC markets, a wide range of software are used by storage system vendors. In 1998, Dell entered the storage market with its PowerVault storage. Since then, Dell has dabbled in developing its own storage systems, has acted as the value-added-reseller (VAR) for systems manufactured by others, and has acquired a data storage specialist company, ConvergeNet, in 1999, for $340 million (it has since folded).[11] In 2000, Dell enhanced its storage offerings by partnering with Quantum, a storage manufacturer, to create Dell-branded storage solutions.[12] Also in 2000, Dell announced it had entered into a strategic alliance with Microsoft to develop advanced storage systems. The combination was expected to allow Dell and Microsoft to attack the larger players in the storage market, such as Compaq Computer, EMC, and IBM. According to Dell's Vice President of Storage Systems, Dell's approach of "standardization and lower prices will appeal to customers forced to pay $20,000 or more for network-attached storage. Up until now, implementation of network-attached storage has been on proprietary operating systems or proprietary platforms. We want to reset the bar in terms of price performance using standard products."[13]

However, there is a fundamental difference between the (low-end) server business and storage. A large part of the capability needed to succeed in the storage business is not the hardware but storage management software. Further, unlike the low-end server business where there is standardized software, there are multiple software architectures being used in the storage business. The result? Dell signed a five-year, multibillion dollar co-branding agreement with EMC in 2001 that allows Dell to be the primary reseller of EMC's $200,000 CLARiiON line of enterprise storage systems. Dell also licensed some technology from CLARiiON.[14] The only conclusion we can reach from this arrangement is that Dell could not succeed on its own in the enterprise storage business.

The central takeaway from our analysis of Dell's diversification moves can be captured in Table 8.1. Basically, if a firm can leverage its capabilities into a market that is new (to it), the adapting entry is a relatively low-risk diversification. Thus, Canon's entry in the personal copier market was low risk because it could exploit its miniaturization and optoelectronic leveragable capabilities. However, if the diversification requires extensive capability building, it is a risky proposition.

TABLE 8.1   Markets Suitable for a Low-Risk Entry

| | | Need for New Capabilities | |
		High	Low
Ability to Leverage Existing Capabilities	High	Emergent markets— High risk, high return	Least risky
	Low	High risk	Probably unattractive market

Let us follow through with the Dell story and its printer strategy.

Case 5: Dell's Printer Strategy

While Dell's diversification strategy from 1996 to early 2002 covered a broad array of product line, Dell always avoided head-to-head confrontation with the market heavyweights, at least initially. Dell's entry into the printer business was a departure from the strategy as Dell printers targeted the market leader Hewlett-Packard directly just as Hewlett-Packard was busy integrating its merger with Compaq Computer. Note that Dell was already a major competitor for Hewlett-Packard in the enterprise computing business, though the enterprise computing business was not as important for Hewlett-Packard as it was for IBM and Compaq.

In the area of printers, Dell was, at one point, one of the largest sales outlets for Hewlett-Packard printers. HP is the world's largest printer maker, with sales of approximately $9 billion.[15] Dell's role as a reseller began to change in 2002, when rumors began to circulate that Dell planned to enter the printer market. As the rumors grew, HP took a preemptive move and announced in July 2002 that it would no longer supply printers, cameras, scanners, and handheld devices to Dell. HP spokesperson Diane Roncal, commenting on the end of the HP-Dell agreement, stated, "The basis for the relationship is no longer valid, given the company's intent to sell Dell-branded printers."[16] Analysts estimated that in 2002, HP printers sold through Dell represented approximately 3% of HP's sales.

In September 2002, Dell confirmed the rumors by announcing it had entered into an agreement with Lexmark International Group to sell printers. Under the agreement, Dell made Lexmark its preferred supplier for the remainder of 2002 and began work with the firm to develop a line of Dell-branded inkjet and laser printers as well as a line of Dell-branded printer supplies.[17] According to analysts, the attractiveness of the printer market lies in the supplies, such as ink cartridges; "The margins on printers are extremely low, with many machines sold at near cost, and companies looking to make their money on ink cartridge sales."[18]

In line with its past success, Dell's printer and printer supplies will be sold directly to the consumer. Dell announced in February 2003 that it would begin sales of the first Dell-branded printers in March 2003. As it continues to battle for the number one spot in PC sales, the ability to bundle its own printers with PC purchases opens new doors. As Michael Dell stated, "If we can attach printers to those system sales, it's a nice new business for us."[19]

Overall, the move into printers represents Dell's continued pursuit of becoming a one-stop-shop for PCs and peripherals. According to some, "That's the whole crux of this. Dell wants a piece of delivering a complete Dell-branded solution from their consumer customers up to their corporate customers. They want to sell as many things with the word 'Dell' on it to cement their relationship with their customers."[20]

Risky Profile: Be Careful of Tit-for-Tat Market Entry

If we apply the framework developed in Table 8.1 to Dell's printer strategy, it does not make a lot of sense to us. Why are we not enamored with Dell's printer strategy? For one thing, there is not much assembly to be done with the printer. This takes away opportunities of leveraging Dell's manufacturing capabilities. Second, most of the profits from printers come from the selling of cartridges. The bulk of cartridge sales, as is well-known within Dell, are not through direct mail—another of Dell's core capabilities. Third, the printer can benefit from increased R&D dollars that HP is lavishing on its printers on a continuing basis. Dell has to rely on Lexmark to make its printers equal to HP. It is extremely doubtful that Lexmark can win the game for large corporate network printers with HP. Finally, if it were a matter of being a one-stop shop provider to the customer, HP would probably be very happy to drop-ship its printers along with Dell's PC sales. If Dell is trying to hurt HP in its printer business because of its merger with Compaq, and thus becoming a stronger competitor to Dell in the PC business, it is unclear whether the 3% of sales lost from the Dell partnership is big enough to hurt HP. In summary, the printer strategy simply does not have the clarity in leveraging Dell's capabilities that the server strategy and the low-end switch strategy have. Further, there is always the possibility of getting distracted into managing a business that is not needed as a counter threat to HP's stronger PC business after its merger with Compaq. Even Dell would probably agree that the merged HP and Compaq is still not a threat to Dell's PC business. In these situations, the least risky strategy is to solidify the partnership unless there is a compelling case to be made for trying to hurt the ex-partner, provided you have the capability to do so. See Table 8.2 for an analysis of the various market-entry strategies and their corresponding level of risk.

TABLE 8.2   Risks in a Tit-for-Tat Market Entry Strategy

| | | Can Partner Hurt You in Core Biz? | |
		Yes	No
Do You Have the Capability Against Competitor's Core Biz?	Yes	Preemptive attack— Moderate risk	Do you gain by hurting partner? If not, status quo is probably a better idea—Least risk
	No	Solidify partnership to reduce entry threat—High risk	Status quo—Low risk

Risky Profile: Reduce New Capability Risk Through Outsourcing

Next, we will consider Dell's services strategy.

Case 6: Dell's Services Strategy

In Dell's last full fiscal year, 2001, services accounted for about $2.5 billion, or 7.8%, of the company's $31.9 billion in total revenue. In contrast, Hewlett-Packard raked in $9.5 billion and IBM $25.1 billion in services revenue in 2001.

It seems like Dell is very serious about services, in particular enterprise services, becoming a significant source of revenue and profits. According to Kevin Soelberg, Dell's Vice President of Services Marketing and Development, "We are moving into larger and larger enterprise accounts." Indeed, Dell claims Boeing and the Cornell University Theory Center, a research facility, as exemplars of Dell-built supercomputing customers.

Others are not very sure. Part of the problem is that Dell doesn't break out revenue from leasing hardware. Gartner research analyst Michael Haines said, "We just can't get a straight answer on it. A lot of companies count leasing fees in their services. They [Dell] lease a lot of equipment," he said. Some of Dell's customers that are identified as service customers (on Dell's web site), such as South Carolina's Department of Parks, Tourism, and Recreation also agree. "That's pretty funny, the only services [are that] we lease from Dell," according to IT manager, Elwart.

So what does Dell mean by "services?" According to Dell's income sources, two-thirds of the company's revenue that was claimed as services comes from warranty and post-warranty repairs. Less than a third comes from what the traditional definition of services is in the channel—"solution-building a value-added business that relies more on fostering customer relationships than moving product." Further, Dell does most of its service activity in-house rather than at the customer site, and all the activity is confined to Dell hardware. Dell then began a big push to do more service at the customer's site.[22]

continues

Case 6: Dell's Services Strategy (Continued)

This strategy is the brainchild of Mr. Kevin Rollins, at that time Dell's second in command (and current CEO). Dell's plan: to expand into the maintenance and servicing of Dell-branded enterprise PCs and servers by sub-contracting it out to trained technicians who are either self-employed or employed by service companies desperate for work. These service companies would have access to a knowledge base for common problems and solutions, and a majority of the problems can be resolved by telephone service people in low-cost areas, such as India. For on-site service, Dell negotiated a per-visit rate with its subcontractors. For larger service projects, Dell would open the job to auction.

Rollins based this move on the analysis that the bulk of service income came from installation, maintenance, and repair rather than consulting and business solutions. Further, even this type of service is a high-margin business, estimated to be 30%. It is interesting to note that Dell's prior entry into the service business was just before the Internet crash through an alliance with computer consulting firms. Some of these partners, such as MarchFirst, have become bankrupt. In any case, that move was not successful.

Let us think about the pros and cons of the services strategy. Like many other industries, services that maintain hardware are a high-margin business. Because Dell is selling a lot of computers and low-end servers, it can piggy-back these sales and generate service revenues. The question remains, however, if this strategy can be copied by others. If you think about it, Dell is not bringing anything new to the table except perhaps negotiating a low-cost outsourcing contract. Further, by refusing to service other machines, Dell is making itself vulnerable to IBM or HP sub-contracting with similar service providers, but offering a comprehensive service. Despite Dell's claims to the contrary, Dell is not bringing any of its vaunted assembly capabilities into the services arena. Finally, Dell is simply not equipped to offer anything more than repair and maintenance services. The 25% of the service business that revolves around providing software solutions is both the highest margin and may attract customers that would rather stay with one service provider for all their needs. Dell is unlikely to be able to penetrate this market.

On the other hand, this is not a high-risk strategy for Dell because almost everything is outsourced. This is one more example of the low-risk theme that we have seen throughout this book—reduce investments in fixed assets. Further, if Dell does manage to grab market share from other PC or low-end server manufacturers, it can provide a steady stream of projects to its sub-contractors. This will be a win-win for Dell and the sub-contractors. If this works, it may be difficult for HP or IBM to poach on Dell's contractors.[23]

The takeaway from the preceding discussion is illustrated in Table 8.3.

TABLE 8.3   Using Outsourcing to Reduce Market Entry Risks

		Need for New Capabilities	
		High	Low
Ability to Outsource New Capabilities	High	Low risk	Least risk
	Low	High risk	Low risk

The Risks of Not Developing a Profile of the Target Market

Enron is now the poster child of everything that is bad with corporate America. However, in the early 1990s, everyone was extolling the virtues of Enron's brilliant strategy. If you are interested, please refer to the Appendix for a detailed description of Enron's strategy. However, the following case study provides a few highlights.

Case 7: Enron's Leveragable Capabilities

Enron revolutionized the staid natural gas business by raising capital for depressed producers using a technique called "securitization." Simultaneously, Enron created tremendous efficiency by matching producers of gas with users. Basically, this allowed Enron to be able to increase the value of all the assets in the natural gas business because they could now be used with higher capacity.

Enron used this capability to develop efficiencies in the electricity business by first developing a trading capability to offer electricity at a myriad of customized prices and delivery options. Enron then sold off the assets that it had initially acquired to have a buffer capacity. Because of the efficiency that Enron introduced, these assets could now be sold at much higher prices. This was the basis of Enron's asset-light strategy. Enron decided to apply this strategy to a multitude of other industries, such as paper, water, and broadband, to name a few. All of these efforts ultimately failed.

Unlike Dell, Enron never developed a clear profile of the target market where its capabilities could be leveraged. This profile is reproduced in the following from the Appendix:

- Customers want price and supply stability and are willing to comparison shop.

- The product had to be homogeneous and not come in different shapes, sizes, or grades.

- The product could be seamlessly distributed using a national network where Enron controlled the switches.

- Price and supply information could be readily obtained. Inefficiencies in distribution could be corrected by increased liquidity of the market.

- Enron could initially enter the market by offering risk management products and not acquiring assets. This reduced the exit barriers in case of failure. Assets only would be acquired to guarantee initial supply and divested as soon as liquidity was established.

All of the markets that Enron entered into after the wholesale electricity market simply did not fit this profile.[24] Enron simply did not account for the risks of the new markets it was entering. These risks could have been anticipated by profiling the target markets as previously mentioned.

Note that, even though this framework advocates leveraging of existing resources into multiple businesses, it is not an inside-out model. On the contrary, the far-sighted firm will often invest in capabilities that are not completely specific to one business model. Such capabilities that are leveragable into other opportunities can become immensely useful when industry conditions change or new opportunities arise. What the firm is doing is investing to give it more options. The idea here is that when the opportunity arises, the firm will have the flexibility to exercise the option. This idea is developed in more detail in Chapter 9, under platform strategies.

Case 8: Dell Versus Sony

Gateway was the first computer company to offer $2,999 flat-panel plasma TVs through its channels. Flat-panel TVs are early in the product lifecycle, are very expensive, and the technology is still developing. Dell has decided to jump into this market by adopting a low-cost strategy. Characteristically, Sony is also entering this market with a differentiated strategy. It will be curious to see how this battle plays out as flat-panel TVs become more of a mainstream product.

Dell and Sony have very different strategies to conquer the living room. For Sony, the focus is on the TV to be the controlling appliance for the home network. Its VAIO laptop is part of the network, but not the controlling piece. Not surprisingly, Dell's strategy is to place the PC at the center of the home network. Dell's logic: Trying to use the TV to be the main conduit to the Internet would detract from the simple TV viewing experience for the rest of the family. Instead, Dell wants to promote the kind of distributed TVs based on flat-panel monitors with built-in TV tuners (or digital chips) that are already available on some computers. To promote a PC-centric view of the home network, Dell has started to offer home network installation for around $120.

The Dell versus Sony battle is a good test of the framework that you have considered in this chapter. Dell is counting on its purchasing clout with LCD panel vendors to offer a low-cost TV. Sony has started a joint venture with Samsung to procure the LCD panels. However, there is very little Dell can leverage to the consumer electronic market. Dell is in no position to compete with Sony in terms of features that make a TV more attractive. Further, the early adopters who are buying the flat-panel TVs at this point are extremely conscious of the quality of the image (mainly high definition). It is for this reason that the plasma display panel (PDP) TV has taken off because it can project a much better image for movies and sports than the much more expensive LCDs. Yet, most observers feel that PDPs have a limited appeal because they are not very robust and are susceptible to burn in. This situation is a classic example of evolving technology where the customer preferences and technology standards are simply not set. This is not an ideal market for Dell to exploit with a low-cost strategy. Because of the entry by Dell and Gateway, Sony is also not doing very well at this moment.[25] To Sony's credit though, it is still trying to extract a premium from its brand in most of the consumer-electronics products.

So where can Dell make a mark in the consumer electronics marketplace? There is an outcome desired by customers that plays into Dell's strengths. Customers want all their electronic gadgets to seamlessly interoperate with each other irrespective of the vendor. Dell has substantial expertise in understanding device conflicts because that is the central focus of its research and development efforts (see the first case study on Dell in this chapter). They are now in the process of extending this expertise to eradicate conflicts between Dell PCs and devices made by other vendors, including that of its competitors, such as Hewlett-Packard printers and Sony video cameras. If Dell PCs become the hub where you hook up all your consumer electronic gadgets for seamless interoperability, Dell may be able to infiltrate into this marketplace. However, the strategy is more akin to exploiting a sweet spot than a low-price strategy in a mature market. Stay tuned. In the meantime, look at Figure 8.1 and Tables 8.4 and 8.5, which look at Dell's capability matrix in new markets.

In Chapter 9, you will look at the risk factors in shaping a market from scratch. These strategies take a long time to come to fruition, involve much bigger bets, and are inherently more risky. The strategies are usually also the most profitable and most long-lasting.

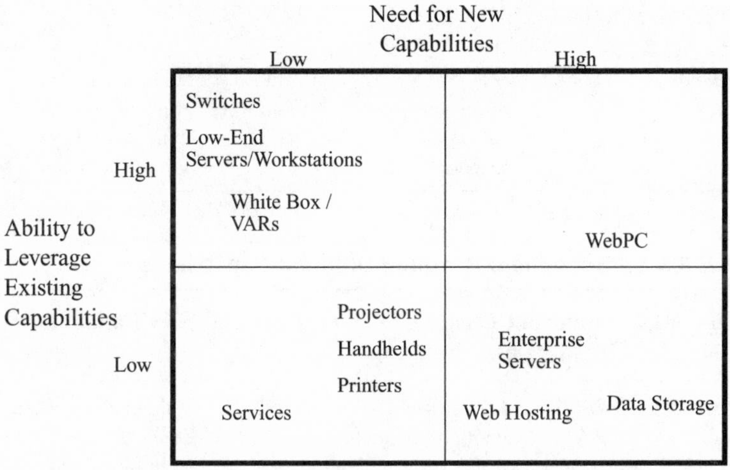

FIGURE 8.1   Dell's new markets span the capability matrix.

TABLE 8.4   Most New Markets Capitalized Upon Dell's Strengths...

Market	Relevant Existing Capabilities		Required New Capabilities	
Servers and Workstations	High	Low prices, transferable product perception from PCs.	Low	Improved chip supply improves existing performance capability to required levels.
Switches	High	Commodity product; low-end segment available for entry niche.	Low	

continues

TABLE 8.4   Continued

Market	Relevant Existing Capabilities		Required New Capabilities	
Projectors	High	Commodity product, leverages supply excellence.	Medium	R&D needed for product improvement. Dell relies on vendors.
Printers	High	Commodity consumer product, leverages supply chain excellence; complimentary to sales of PCs.	Medium	As with computers, R&D required to maintain upper-end niche only.
White-Box/ VARs	High	Focus on manufacturing.	Low	
Handhelds	High	Standards ; emerging becoming price-driven.	Low/ Medium	Dell does not have expertise outside Windows CE operating system.

TABLE 8.5   ...But Others Required Different Capabilities

Market	Relevant Existing Capabilities		Required New Capabilities	
Enterprise Servers	Med	Low prices, competent quality.	Med	Unknown whether Dell's Wintel technology will satisfy performance needs.
Enterprise Data Storage	Low	Dell has to rely on vendors for the hardware.	High	Support for proprietary software.
WebPC	High	Effective manufacturing to ensure quality at low prices.	High	Usability design; market creation.
Web Hosting	Low	Manufactured server products for use.	High	Staffing and training; site location; partners; service reputation.
Services	Low	Product maintenance/repair appears to make up the majority of this business.	High	Staffing and training; reputation and client relationships.

Endnotes

1 At least as a fall back even if you have entered with a differentiation strategy.

2 Michael A Verespej. *Industry Week* Cleveland. Nov. 16, 1998.

3 Kevin Maney. "Dell Business Model Turns To Muscle as Rivals Struggle." USA TODAY. Jan. 20, 2003.

4 Andy Serwer. *Fortune* New York. May 11, 1998.

5 Maney. Op. Cit.

6 Michael Dell. *Executive Excellence* Provo. Jan 1999.

7 Steve Lohr. "On a Roll, Dell Enters Uncharted Territory." *The New York Times*. August 25, 2002, Sunday, Late Edition.

8 Jennifer Mateyaschuk. *Information Week*. Manhasset; Sept. 21, 1998.

9 Gary McWilliams. "Dell Looks for Ways to Rekindle The Fire It Had as an Upstart." *The Wall Street Journal*. August 31, 2000.

10 We are not suggesting Sun has a better strategy. In fact, we feel that Sun is in grave danger of being marginalized because of its rigidity. This example simply feeds into the framework that we develop in Table 8.1.

11 Lohr. Op. Cit.

12 Shankland, Stephen. "Dell Taps Partners for New Storage Offerings." CNET *News.com* 08/31/00. http://news.com.com/2100-1001-245226.html?legacy=cnet.

13 Wilcox, Joe. "Dell, Microsoft Join Forces in Storage Gambit." CNET *News.com* 10/23/00. http://news.com.com/2100-1001-247423.html?legacy=cnet.

14 Boulton, Clint. "Store It Up! Dell, EMC Ink Major Storage Deal." *ASPNews.com* 10/22/01. http://www.aspnews.com/news/article/0,,4191_907821,00.html.

15 Fried, Ian. "HP Quits Supplying Printers to Dell." CNET *News.com* 07/24/02. http://news.zdnet.co.uk/story/0,,t271-s2119667,00.html.

16 Ibid.

17 Spooner, John G. "Dell Dives Into Printer Market." CNET *News.com* 09/24/02. http://news.zdnet.co.uk/story/0,,t271-s2122787,00.html.

18 Krazit, Tom. "Dell Move to PDAs, Printers Called a Plus." IDG *News Service* 08/16/02. http://www.pcworld.com/news/article/0,aid,104055,00.asp.

19 "Dell Printers to Ship Next Month." *Reuters* 02/26/03. http://news.zdnet.co.uk/story/0,,t271-s2131100,00.html.

20 Krazit, Tom. "Dell Will Resell Lexmark Printers." *IDG News Service* 08/16/02. Viewed online at http://www.pcworld.com/news.

21 This is excerpted from Lohr. Op. Cit.

22 Gary McWilliams. "Dell Pins Hopes on Services To Boost Its Profit Margin." *The Wall Street Journal* Updated November 11, 2003.

23 This may be one reason why HP is determined to attack Dell's PC business even at the risk of losses to its own business. HP makes a lot of money from its service business and especially in high-end computer consulting where Dell does not have a presence. The more PCs HP can sell, the more service revenues it can generate.

24 As you will see in our analysis of Enron in the Appendix, it was first a strategy failure, then a governance failure.

25 Sony's troubles may be primarily caused by the beating its PlayStation game console sales have taken courtesy of Xbox's aggressive pricing strategy. Sony does not break out its profits, so it is really difficult to know how well the flatscreen TV businesses is doing.

9

STRATEGIES TO SHAPE MARKETS: PRODUCTS, PROCESS, AND PLATFORM

Who Is a Market Shaper?

In Chapter 8, *When and How to Use Low-Price Entry Strategy*, we made the case for diversification based on leveraging a firm's existing capabilities. Market shaping, on the other hand, usually implies investment in new capabilities. As illustrated in Table 9.1, the new capabilities can be used for shaping a market either through development of a new product (such as Polaroid or the Walkman or the CT scanner), a repeatable process (such as an information technology system or acquisition process), or a platform (such as the DOS or Windows operating system).

TABLE 9.1   New Capabilities for Shaping Markets

	Product	Process	Platform
Adapt	Change price-value relationship. Example: Dell personal computers	Leverage existing capability to change price-value relationship. Example: Dell servers and switches	Make end product on existing platforms. Example: Sony VAIO, Dell Intel servers
Shape	Create primary demand for product. Example: Palm Pilot	Invest in a new process to take repeated bets. Example: BancOne, Cisco, and Merck Pharmaceuticals	Encourage new products for a new platform. Example: Microsoft DOS, Windows, .Net

The basic difference between adapting and shaping is that the market shaper is usually ahead of the curve in terms of introducing new products, services, or dramatically new value propositions. Typically, this position allows the market shaper some immunity from competitive risks by either creating a large installed base around a product or platform or by their ability to stay ahead of the competition in terms of continuous introduction of new value propositions by leveraging a process.

A market-shaping strategy involves the creation of a new or significantly different price-value proposition. Basically, market shaping allows a firm to execute a business model that is immune from competitive risks for a fairly long time. Often, this involves identifying or even creating a white space. Microsoft's success in the 1980s and 90s was based on filling the white space for desktop applications for small, and finally all, businesses. Cisco's success was based on its ability to become the first soup-to-nuts network solution provider—a white space that no other networking company was willing to risk. BancOne shaped the community banking experience by elevating what the community banks could offer after they joined the BancOne family. This was a white space that the Moneycenter banks were not interested in exploiting. Amazon, eBay, and Expedia have succeeded in putting their stamps on simplifying the buying process in their respective e-commerce industries. Blockbuster shaped the video rental business by rolling up the fragmented mom-and-pop video stores. IBM, HP, and EDS are trying to provide peace of mind for computer network administrators. GM's OnStar is trying to provide similar peace of mind to motorists.

A successful market shaper has a chance to acquire a long-standing profit stream. However, the market shaper also faces more uncertainties than a market adapter. The market shaper typically has to place some hefty bets about the nature of the opportunity it is trying to shape. It also has to make significant investments to develop capabilities that will be the foundation for the shaping strategy. Often, the investments have to be made without a clear idea of where the demand is going to come from or the exact characteristics of the demand or the final product. Market shaping is, thus, a classic high-risk, high-reward situation. Consequently, it is imperative for the market shaper to understand where the risks are coming from and how to minimize the risks while maximizing the profit potential. Note that the risk for the market shaper is more than the failure of demand to materialize. Many market shapers have failed not because demand failed to materialize, but because they were not ready to capitalize on the demand that proved to be much larger than expected. Market shapers must tackle both demand and capability risks. Further, some types of market shaping also attract competitive risks *if* the entry strategy is successful in creating a new value proposition. In the following pages, you explore some concepts that can be applied in most market-shaping situations to mitigate the inherent risks without sacrificing the upside.

Core Objectives for Market Shaping: Create Entry Barriers

The basic objectives for any market entry decision, whether it is shaping or adapting product, process, or platform are essentially the same. If and when a market entry is successful, it is imperative to quickly erect entry barriers to prevent others from sharing in the spoils of your success. Very often, a market shaper relies upon a large and loyal installed base of customers as the ultimate entry barrier. If a market shaper, at the very outset, focuses on how exactly it is going to develop this installed base, it will have much clearer insights into the success requirement of the market shaping strategy. This clarity is extremely important to understand the capability risks that it is taking on. Moreover, as we shall demonstrate, the process of creating a large installed base also gives the market shaper early warning signals if its strategy is not creating the demand it had expected. In such a situation, it is imperative to implement an exit strategy (which we will discuss later). This clarity also helps the market shaper to get an early warning signal if it has *underestimated* the true demand and to take the necessary steps, so new entrants cannot capitalize on the underserved demand. These early warning signals allow the market shaper to avoid both the downside risk (and exit) and leaving money on the table for new entrants to capitalize on.

Core Objectives for Market Shaping: Exit Strategies

One thing should be apparent from the aforementioned discussion. Investing in product, process, or platform capabilities with the intention of shaping a market is not for everyone. A firm needs to have fairly deep pockets to withstand the loss of substantial investments mainly because of the demand risks. This brings us to the second risk management objective for market shaping: Knowing when to execute an exit strategy.

Not all market-shaping strategies will be successful, which underlines the inherent risks in market shaping. On the other hand, planning that attempts to anticipate every contingency will lead to extreme risk-aversion. You can significantly reduce the risk of investing in product, process, or platform-specific capabilities if you know when to pull the plug. It is the inability to see the limits of the strategy that contributes to shareholder value destruction. Thus, when the strategic opportunity runs its course, your business needs to look for an exit strategy, or it will actually destroy shareholder value. This takes us back to the original theme of this book. The key is to anticipate the relevant risks ahead of time and to have a clear idea and action plan for when the risk parameters are violated. If you have done this exercise, you will not have to think in terms of risk management, but risk avoidance. In simple terms, the exit strategy should kick in any time the assumptions of the initial entry strategy are violated. In terms of our three risk categories, the demand may have matured or competitors have been attracted to the white space and imitated the firm's capabilities (thus increasing competitive risk). In these circumstances, a well-thought out exit strategy will allow you to maximize your profits and avoid future losses.

Most companies do not pay enough attention to developing a formalized plan of when to execute an exit strategy. However, if the entrant firm takes the time to correctly identify the metrics for its core objectives, such metrics will automatically alert the firm if an exit, or at least a change in strategy, should be considered. Let us revisit the example of Company X and its somewhat risky strategy of adopting category management for Home Depot to fight off the new product from Company Y. Company X tracked its sales and Company Y's sales religiously after it instituted the category management strategy. If the strategy had not worked, this tracking would have alerted Company X to seriously consider an advertising battle before Company Y's product became firmly established with the public.

Managers in U.S. firms are naturally optimistic, and this is good. However, this optimism should always be tempered with knowing when to pull the plug. Some companies have institutionalized this practice. The pharmaceutical company Novartis pays an individual on its drug-development teams a nominal sum if she or he halts a development project. This is to check and prevent the "losing gambler" syndrome, where a lost cause becomes a sink for escalating commitment to recover from past mistakes. Most people know that all Toyota assembly-line workers have the right to stop the assembly-line. However, this kind of practice only can be implemented if a common doctrine is understood by the rank-and-file (see Chapter 6, *Organizations That Can Benefit from the Outcome-to-Objectives Framework*).

In the following sections, you examine the core objectives for market shapers in the context of three basic strategies (product, process, and platform).

Strategies for Market Shaping: How to Acquire a Long-Standing Profit Stream

Product

Market shaping based on a single product will have many character-istics similar to that of adapting. Basically, a single (although new) product (or service) has well-defined parameters that allow you to have a clearer idea of not only the demand but also the capabilities needed to deliver the value. This clarity, as we have stressed through-out the book, is the first step to reduce demand and capability risks. However, even products that set out to significantly improve existing value propositions have some demand risks. The PDA is now ubiqui-tous, and both Palm and Blackberry have become the product of choice for their respective specialized applications. Yet Apple could not exploit any benefits from its investment in the development of Newton—the first PDA that was commercially available. Basically, when the end-market is a white space, as the PDA market was in the early 1990s, demand risks are particularly great, and there is always a risk that the demand does not materialize. In the case of Newton, the product may have been simply too early in the market with features that were not appreciated at the time of the initial introduction.

One basic strategy exists that can turn demand risk to a firm's competitive advantage is to let the market tell you what the demand is and develop capabilities to quickly respond to it. Trying to guess what the demand is going to look like is very difficult, and that is where companies fall prey to the demand risk. As you have already seen many times, a part and parcel of this strategy is built around flexible manufacturing and the ability to outsource critical parts of the value chain while retaining control over the quality. You have already seen an example of this with the Sony PlayStation, Cisco, FedEx Custom Critical, and Eli Lilly's R&D strategy. The second component of this flexibility is the capability to scale up quickly. This is imperative to lock in all possible customers and create an installed base if the value proposition catches on. This is what Sony Playstation did in spades. The following case study illustrates the exact opposite and how the risks can overcome a firm that is trying to shape a market with a single product, but did not try to take advantage of flexible manufacturing—even when it had the chance.

Case 1: The Shaping of the Medical Imaging Business: The CT-Scanner

Perhaps no single product changed the nature of the X-ray business as much as the CT-Scanner. Most of us do not know the inventor of the ubiquitous CT-Scanner. It was invented by John Hounsfeld when he was the Chief Research Scientist with EMI. Even though EMI had no prior expertise in the medical diagnostic field, EMI was able to market the CT-Scanner on its own partly because all of the major components could be purchased off-the-shelf. This outsourced market-entry strategy reduced the risk in case the scanner did not take off. The second advantage EMI exploited was that none of the major players, like GE or Siemens, had entered the market with competing products.

EMI had grand hopes that its success in the CT-Scanner business would allow it to enter the very attractive medical diagnostics business. However, EMI was too conservative in its entry strategy.

continues

Case 1: The Shaping of the Medical Imaging Business: The CT-Scanner (Continued)

It was more worried about whether demand for its scanners would materialize and did not consider a plan to take advantage of greater than expected demand. As demand for the scanners outstripped EMI's capacity to supply them, competitors rushed in the void despite a patent protection, encouraged by EMI's lack of a legal response. In the end, EMI was taken over and the scanner business spun out.

EMI had the first-mover advantage. It also had patent protection. Further, as the CT-Scanner was the end-product, it was easy to quickly estimate the demand for this product after the major hospitals started to endorse the product. Unlike a platform (such as DOS, which we will look at later in the section, *Platform Strategy*), it was not dependent on complementary products, such as application software for its success. Yet, EMI failed because it did not have a strategy to scale up and capture an installed base that was there for the taking. The reason was that EMI did not have a contingency plan in case the demand for its product was higher than anticipated. In reality, the demand for the CT-Scanner far exceeded its initial predictions. Had EMI developed a plan for scaling capacity up quickly, it would have been able to significantly delay the entry of competitors. The tragedy of the EMI situation is that EMI could have expanded capacity without making fixed asset investments because most of its components were off-the-shelf.[1]

EMI could not move beyond the CT-Scanner and failed in its desire to shape the medical diagnostics business. This highlights a second risk of market shaping that depends on a single end product. These products have the possibility of becoming a one-trick pony without an encore. Another classic illustration of this risk is Polaroid. Polaroid simply could not extend its capabilities beyond the instant photography value proposition. Kodak is still having a difficult time transitioning to digital imaging. Palm is having similar difficulties in extending the Palm platform beyond PDAs. This risk is not necessarily fatal if the firm knows when to execute an exit strategy.

Finally, a market-shaping strategy based around a single product is more vulnerable to competitive risk because it is easier for industry giants to zero in on a product, such as the CT-Scanner or a PDA. It becomes more difficult to fight the competitive risks after the competitors have entered the business. The time to fend off competitive risks is in the beginning by creating a large installed base.

The Risks in Single Product Market-Shaping Strategies

Demand Risks: Every Strategy Has a Natural Size

Many market-shaping opportunities that depend on a single product either have a limited amount of demand, a fairly short-term time horizon, or both. These are likely to be the kind of highly visible "big hits" that gets a lot of industry and investor attention, such as CML's Nordictrack or Salton's George Foreman grill. CML capitalized on the mid-1980s health craze by introducing indoor cross-country ski as an alternative to treadmills and stationary bikes using a shrewd marketing campaign. Likewise, Salton introduced an electric grill for making hamburgers by making a claim that this grill drains the fat out. To a large extent, both products were helped by celebrity endorsements, and in particular by ex-heavyweight boxing champion George Foreman, who became the spokesperson for the Salton hamburger grill that came to be known as the George Foreman grill. For these types of products, the market shaper has to be extremely aware of the demand risks and when to modify the strategy as demand slows down. For example, both CML and Salton had to struggle to decide whether and when to offer their products through retail outlets as the direct mail demand slowed, often due to competitive products. Often, these firms refuse to accept the increased demand and competitive risks or fail to execute an exit strategy. To maximize

shareholder value, these firms should have seriously considered selling out to a larger player when they were dominating the market
instead of suffering from the hubris that they could repeat their one-
trick success over and over. There is a second, and perhaps more
egregious, error. These CEOs frantically started searching for the
next "home run" to keep the momentum going without rigorously
understanding whether the initial formula can be applied to the new
product. Salton is a shadow of its former self. Its stock price is a fraction of its all-time high when the George Foreman grill was rolling off
the shelves. CML has been taken over by Icon fitness at a small fraction of the market value that it commanded at its peak. Sometimes,
the consequences are far more serious. Quaker Oats shaped the
sports drink market with Gatorade and tried to apply the same formula to Snapple. The size of the sports drink market was simply not
comparable to a niche product such as Snapple and, therefore, the
business model that worked so well (with the help of Michael Jordan)
was inappropriate to market Snapple. The Snapple decision led to a
billion dollar loss and the ultimate sale of the company to Pepsi.

Competitive Risks: Every Strategy Has a Natural Time Frame

Consider the case of EMI again. Despite allowing competitors to
come in, EMI was making more money than it ever had in its history. Unfortunately, there were both low-priced scanners threatening it
from below and new technology from GE threatening from above. To
a large extent, this situation was caused by EMI's lack of a strategy to
develop an installed base quickly when it had the opportunity.
However, after it had allowed competitive risk to increase, EMI did
not have much of a chance against the competition, and the prudent
thing would have been to exercise an exit strategy. However, EMI
chose not to exit, even though it had several options. It could sell the
business when it was still profitable. It could service its installed scanners at a very hefty profit margin. Instead, EMI chose to increase
capacity in the face of declining demand and increased competition
that ultimately led to its demise.

Sometimes, the endgame is reached when the business reaches a certain size, as discussed previously. Sometimes, the endgame is reached because the core objectives that drove the initial entry strategy can be delivered by capabilities developed by competitors or new entrants. Even if the demand is not going to deteriorate in the immediate future, the demand for the firm's product may suffer if a stronger competitor is attracted to its white space. Under such a circumstance, the capability requirements go beyond the original entry strategy to matching the capabilities of a deep-pocketed major player. Consider Hotmail. Hotmail developed one of the early email systems. However, when Microsoft came calling, Hotmail was smart enough to see the risks of staying the course on its own. Likewise, numerous startups in the networking space saw Cisco as their exit strategy throughout the 1990s. In fact, because of Cisco's ability to offer comprehensive networking solutions, it became very difficult for individual technology providers to breach Cisco's installed base of customers. In the late 1990s, Granite was developing a faster networking technology (Gigabit Ethernet) that it hoped to market on its own. The idea was to try and dominate this space before Cisco developed the technology. In fact, Granite tried to see if there would be a market for its products if it priced them significantly cheaper (20%–50%, the actual number was not explicit from my sources) than Cisco's price. Granite found out that customers were not interested despite the lower price and would rather buy from Cisco at a higher price along with the service that Cisco provides. Granite had no hopes to survive on its own and was acquired by Cisco.

Imatron Inc. developed the electron beam computed tomography (EBCT) in the 1990s that is used to screen for occult coronary artery disease in asymptomatic middle-aged men and women. EBCT was used in the Ultrafast CT-Scanner, which is more powerful than the best available non-invasive test in predicting heart attacks and other coronary disease in apparently healthy people. However, Imatron could not market the technology on its own and, after 5 years, sold out to GE. Basically, you have to make a judgment as to whether you have the capabilities to compete with the big players when they get attracted to your successful entry.

The same story has been repeated many times, especially for smaller companies that have entered industries dominated by giants using a product rather than a platform. In the early 1990s, U.S. Surgical's laparoscopy procedure was an instant hit with surgeons. Yet when Johnson & Johnson entered the market with a competing product, U.S. Surgical dug in its heels. Like EMI, U.S. Surgical also ended up being taken over but not by choice. The key to a successful exit strategy is to exit on your terms. To do this, you need to understand how you are planning to avoid the risks of the initial entry strategies and to track the risks post-entry. You should execute your exit strategy when the risks exceed your *predetermined* risk avoidance parameters.

Now consider a company that has become a verb. We are talking about Google; the search engine that has become the fourth most visited web site in 2004. Investors are salivating at the prospect of a Google IPO. However, Google insiders are much more circumspect. And they have every reason to be. Google is, after all, a single product company and has even less switching costs than the CT-Scanner or laparoscopy. Google's problem is that, from one side, people are beginning to criticize Google for leveraging its near monopoly by directing surfers to web sites who provide Google with ad revenues. On the other side, Microsoft is making a serious effort to develop its own search engine. Of course, Microsoft will certainly integrate its search engine with Windows, but there is a real possibility that Microsoft's search logic may be better than Google's given the resources that Microsoft is bringing to bear on this project.

Exit strategies are not simply restricted to small startups. IBM shaped the computer industry between 1960 and 1970, but paid dearly in not recognizing the competitive risks from mini-computer makers, such as DEC, early enough. Likewise, DEC succeeded in the early 1980s to derail IBM's big iron with its mini-computer but failed

for not having an exit strategy when faced with client/server computing. Novell did not transform its NetWare software when faced with
competing products from Microsoft in the 1990s. The only way you
can take a hard look at the utility of your firm's core competencies is
to continually check the validity of your business logic using an outside-in framework, such as our outcome-to-objectives framework.
Microsoft had an exit strategy from DOS that is now well-known.
However, it also has an exit strategy from Windows that is less widely publicized (see Chapter 10, *Develop Multiple Migration Paths*).
Unfortunately, when confronted with information that challenges the
competitive advantage of the firm, most firms fall prey to an inside-
out perspective and concentrate on improving their existing, and possibly irrelevant, core competencies that do little to avoid competitive
risks. This does not mean that a firm should roll over anytime a new
entrant comes into its space. However, it does mean that a firm must
develop a dispassionate way of looking at options to counter competitive risks; options that should include exit strategies.

Take the Emotion Out of Exit Strategies

Until the mid-1980s, Intel had a virtual monopoly in the DRAM
business. However, in the face of low-cost Japanese entrants, Intel
realized that its competitive risks had gone up dramatically and it
decided to quit the DRAM market in the mid-1980s. Throughout the
world, companies have recently instituted exit strategies as part of
doing business. Nowhere is the strategy being executed as systemati-
cally as by the Japanese electronics firms. In 2001, Sega exited from
the videogame business and Minolta exited from the APS camera
business. In 2002, Toshiba exited from the DRAM business, Hitachi
from the monitor business, Aiwa from the audio system business, and
Sanyo from its VCR business. However, most of these businesses are
mature businesses and one can argue that these exit decisions perhaps were made under duress rather than proactively. A disciplined
exit strategy is much more important for firms that are continually
exploiting white spaces.

Capital One is a classic example of a firm that has managed to succeed by repeatedly exploiting white spaces. Capital One's disciplined exit strategy can be captured from this statement in its 1996 annual report: "Many of our business opportunities are short-lived. We have to move fast to exploit them and move on when they fade." Capital One started its odyssey with its innovation of getting people to transfer credit-card balances with low initial rates. Capital One's core objective was to use analytical techniques to identify people with high debt balances, but who would eventually pay them off, and then lure them to be Capital One customers. However, these techniques soon became table stakes, and cash-rich competitors started to copy Capital One's business model. Capital One's response? By 1998, the company had taken the lead in the business of direct marketing of mobile phone services in the domestic U.S. market.

Several reasons exist for why companies fail to plan for and execute an exit strategy. Some get emotionally attached to their business models. In other instances, success leads to complacency. However, even with the best of intentions, without a framework that allows you to understand the parameters that should drive your exit strategies, you will be reacting to circumstances rather than anticipating them. You will see in Chapter 10 that even Microsoft has a contingency plan to exit from Windows if the situation calls for it.

A market-shaping strategy that is based on a single product is always vulnerable to demand and competitive risks. A well-planned exit strategy allows the market shaper to retain as much of the profits as possible. However, there is a second option that many market shapers do not consider. This option is to extend a single product into a process or a platform. In contrast to a product-based strategy, some firms have embarked on shaping markets by investing in a repeatable process that allows them to continually stay a step or two ahead of the competition.

Process

There is a common theme across all firms such as Cisco, Merck, BancOne, or Capital One that has shaped their respective markets based on a repeatable process over a long time period. The common theme is that these firms identified a set of customer outcomes that the existing players, including themselves, were simply not capable of delivering with their existing capabilities. These firms had the foresight to realize that this is a white space that can lead to long-term profits if they were the first to develop the capabilities needed to capture these white spaces. Basically, most of these strategies do not suffer from demand risks. However, their greatest risk is developing the process to exploit the unmet demand. In other words, their greatest uncertainty is the capability risk. On the other hand, after these firms invested in and successfully developed the underlying process, it became very difficult for future entrants to copy the process by virtue of its complexity. In other words, the process itself becomes the entry barrier, so long as the customer outcomes that the process delivers remain valued by the market. These strategies, therefore, are fairly immune from competitive risk so long as the process remains viable for delivering the business model.

A process-based market shaping strategy *invests in the process first*, often before the company has sold a single product. Note that this is *not* the Dell story. The Dell story is the ability to leverage an existing capability that is basically free because it has already been successfully used in other markets. In other words, the process-based market shapers are taking on a lot more risk up front as the end-result of the investment in the process is unknown.

You have already seen illustrations of this strategy by Progressive Insurance and United Service Automobile Association in the insurance business and Capital One in the credit-card business. Basically, all of these companies developed processes to quantitatively analyze the true risk of a business. These processes allowed them to grow by offering a diverse array of products that other companies in the same industries would not touch. This is also the story of BancOne and its extraordinary track record of successfully integrating new acquisitions throughout the 1980s.

Case 2: BancOne: The Role of Information Technology

BancOne pioneered many technological innovations in the banking industry. For example, it offered the first automated teller machine, credit-card processing system (Triumph), and bank automation system (Strategic Banking System). BancOne basically had two processes it used in all its acquisitions. The first process it developed was focused on the due diligence in advance of purchase. However, BancOne's due diligence was very different from the standard due diligence carried out by most acquirers. BancOne became the acquirer of choice, so it got a much better look at the insides of the prospective target than other acquirers. For example, as part of the due diligence, a prospective target was encouraged to talk to other previously acquired affiliates of BancOne to reduce any anxiety that the target may have in joining the BancOne fold. As part of the same process, BancOne assigned "mentor banks" to help out newly acquired targets. The second process that brought the acquired banks up to BancOne's standards very quickly was a process of sharing best practices and comparing one bank's performance against benchmarks. This process was known as the MICS (Management Information Control System). MICS produced a monthly report that allowed all of BancOne's acquired branches to compare their performances to each other based on the number of financial ratios.

"A case can be made that the information system has itself contributed to BancOne's success. The information structure has allowed the bank to introduce a 'share and compare' review process across its local market entities. Perhaps most important, it has contributed to a climate of continuous improvement that should serve BancOne well over the long term."[2]

Success in an acquisition strategy depends on the ability to allow the acquired entity to hit the ground running and scale up their earnings to justify the acquisition premium. BancOne's goal: Increase the acquired bank's earnings by as much as 40 percent.[3] The MICS reports facilitated a "share and compare" mentality in which individual banks were encouraged to seek out and learn from other members of the BancOne organization that excelled along specific indices. Finally, the MICS financial reporting platform allowed BancOne to do what other purchasers could not after an acquisition—almost guarantee a target's profitability would rise post-acquisition. This created a virtuous cycle that includes a higher PE that would be used as a cheap currency to buy more banks.

Now consider the investments made by another successful acquirer, Cisco Systems. Like BancOne, Cisco also developed a unique acquisition process (described in detail in Chapter 10) that it repeated over all its acquisitions. But a key reason for Cisco's success was that Cisco could acquire small technology startups and scale up very quickly, which allowed it to recoup its acquisition investments faster than other acquirers (see Figure 9.1 on the Cisco integration strategy).[4]

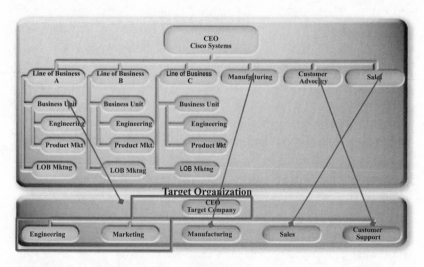

FIGURE 9.1 Cisco Systems: Organizational integration of acquired units. (Source: Cisco Acquisition Strategy & Process Presentation, Cisco Systems 2000.)

Now consider Merck's risk-management process, which allowed it to dominate the pharmaceutical industry for nearly two decades starting from the mid-70s.

Case 3: Merck's R&D Strategy: The Role of the Risk Management Process

In 1975, Roy Vagelos joined Merck as president of its Research Division. Vagelos pursued, what was considered by most, an aggressive and counter-intuitive R&D strategy. He sharply increased the research budget, modernized the labs' facilities, and successfully recruited a large number of talented scientists. Further, instead of spreading the research budget over many projects, as was the norm in the industry, Vagelos felt "success comes from investing more money in a few projects rather than less in many projects."[5] This was in stark contrast to the industry practice of hedging the R&D bets over many projects. Vagelos felt that there were two basic metrics for success in the pharmaceutical business—risk and focus. Vagelos established some basic criteria for R&D projects, which included selecting areas where there were unmet therapeutic needs, where science was advanced far enough for Merck to have a legitimate chance of coming up with a breakthrough, and where Merck had enough knowledge of a particular disease to have some idea of how to arrest it. These moves were designed to build the critical mass necessary to succeed. However, this approach also meant that Merck had to let go of some projects that looked attractive, such as breakthrough drugs for life-threatening diseases. For example, Vagelos realized that drug companies profited more from developing annuity drugs— medicines for chronic diseases such as high blood pressure, diabetes, infections, and arthritis—versus drugs for acute illnesses. Channeling R&D efforts toward the discovery and development of chronic disease medicines that patients would have to take for years, combined with the supplier-dominated structure of the industry, provided prospects for significant, recurring cash flow to fund future R&D activities. This focused (the preceding being just one example), systematic approach to R&D led Merck to adopt what came to be known as the "rational drug discovery process."

This process had been responsible for almost all of Merck's blockbuster drugs since the 1970s. Some of Merck's most successful drugs—Mevacor and Zocor that reduced cholesterol, Pepcid for ulcers, and Vasotek for high blood pressure and congestive heart failure—illustrated the success of the rational drug discovery process.

Merck's finance division greatly contributed to the overall success that the firm had enjoyed. This 500-plus-member team, led by CFO Judy Lewent, utilized a scientific approach to risk management and analysis to contend with the rather unpredictable pharmaceutical industry. In addition to traditional cash flow and net present value concepts, some of Merck's more advanced financial methods included Monte Carlo simulation, option analysis, and game theory. Monte Carlo simulation allowed project modeling and evaluation based on simultaneous changes in numerous variables. A particular emphasis on Monte Carlo simulation and the integration of other financial and scientific techniques resulted in the development of the Merck Research Planning Model in 1983. This model's inputs included scientific and therapeutic variables, capital expenditures, production and selling costs, product prices and quantities, and macroeconomic variables. The risk management process retained knowledge Merck acquired from all of its prior research activities, whether they failed or succeeded. Choosing between competing projects was helped out by Merck's risk-management process by ascertaining probabilities of success based on prior knowledge of success and failure. Risk management also allowed Merck to cut its losses quickly. Even though it was initially developed to assess risk and return across Merck's entire portfolio of research projects, this model was also used to improve Merck's strategic business decisions. Risk management became one of Merck's core capabilities.

Merck's strategy can be summarized as follows. It developed a process that allowed it to take big bets that other pharmaceutical companies simply could not risk. Merck reduced the capability risks by several strategies. First, it focused its resources on fewer projects, thus increasing the chance of a breakthrough. Second, Merck was relying on chemical formulations that were already proven (similar to Dell's off-the-shelf parts) rather than inventing brand new compounds. The big problem with this strategy is the lack of diversification. To reduce the risk from focus, Merck developed the risk management process that allowed Merck to take big bets that not only had a higher probability of success, but also enabled Merck to cut its losses quickly. Finally, Merck was fairly confident of the end demand (for chronic diseases), if it could come up with a drug.[6] Moreover, by choosing existing chemical compounds as the foundation for the new drugs, Merck also reduced the time the FDA takes to approve a drug. This strategy indirectly reduced demand risk as Merck would get the drug to market faster. Thus, if Merck could execute its risk-management process, there was not much demand risk in the end market. This process revolutionized the drug development cycle and came to be known as the "rational drug discovery process."

As an aside, this process is no longer valid and, to an extent, Merck's unwillingness to adopt a more collaborative model of R&D is seen to have contributed to its recent fall from grace. In contrast, Lilly's strategy of opening up its key problems in the web site (see Chapter 3, *Identifying Multiple Capability Configurations*) is a process that is more in tune with drug development in the 21st century. There is an important risk-management lesson here for all firms considering developing a leveragable process as the foundation of a market-shaping strategy. If you do not understand the limits of the process, you may be sowing the seeds of your own failure. Enron developed an energy trading system that allowed it to dominate the gas and electricity business (see the Appendix). Unfortunately, hubris intervened when it tried to extend this system into markets unsuitable for this purpose (such as paper and broadband). The very risk management platform that led to Enron's initial success also led to its demise.

The final market-shaping strategy involves the development of a platform that leads to the development of a number of end products that get widespread use.

Platform

A successful platform generates positive externalities from its derivative products and usually has a longer life compared to a single product. On the other hand, a platform suffers from much more demand and capability risk compared to a single end-product or process-based strategy for obvious reasons. Precision in predicting demand is almost always absent at the initial phases of developing a platform, which is one reason why developing platforms are so risky. That said, most of the spectacular market-shaping success stories have been around platform strategies. In this chapter and the next, you will consider in-depth the three platform investments Microsoft made during the last three decades: DOS in the 1980s, Windows in the 1990s, and .Net in the 2000. These investments were all big bets on being able to leverage these platforms over multiple product lines. What is the core risk of investing in a platform strategy? Basically, you have to recognize how a platform can deliver desired outcomes through a broad line of end products in markets that are likely to be long-lasting. Suffice to say, the platform developer is taking on the demand and capability risks not only of the platform but also the demand and capability risks in the end market. Moreover, the platform developer is often not involved in developing products for the end market, but the success of its platform is intimately tied to the *success of the derivative products*. Thus, an important core objective for the platform developer is to reduce the risks for other firms making derivative products for the platform.

Develop an Installed Base for the Derivative Products

The first objective for any platform should be to try to develop a high installed base for its *derivative* products. This objective has twin benefits. If a firm fails to develop an installed base or its efforts are not proceeding close to plan, it gets an early warning signal and needs to consider an exit strategy. This failure may be symptomatic of the lack of demand for the value propositions the platform is trying to create in the end market. On the other hand, if the demand exists, failure to quickly create an installed base in the derivative product market will invariably attract new entrants with alternate platform configurations and allow them to profit at the pioneering platform's expense. Thus, the objective of a high installed base will have the second benefit of erecting entry barriers and secure a steady source of long-term profits.

Typically, this effort of developing a large installed base in the derivative product market comes at a cost, so it is important to clearly understand the trade-offs. The most well-known platforms over the last two decades belong to Microsoft. However, the trade-offs Microsoft had to accept in creating its large installed base in the derivative product markets (application software) is less known to the business audience. Some important takeaways exist in the trade-offs that Microsoft made to develop a large installed base for the DOS operating platform.

Case 4: Microsoft: DOS Operating Platform

In the 1970s, Microsoft founders Bill Gates and Paul Allen were trying to promote the BASIC programming language that would make it easier to write software for PCs. Microsoft initially rejected IBM's offer to write an operating system for the IBM PC in order to stay focused on developing BASIC. However, Microsoft got a second opportunity to develop the IBM PC operating system in 1982 when Digital Equipment Corporation, which was adept in developing operating systems, walked away from the project due to IBM's aggressive timetable and personality conflicts. As the contract for developing the operating system for IBM was drafted, Gates and Allen had the foresight to maintain ownership of the operating system's licensing. Subsequently, Microsoft opted to exercise its flexibility with the agreement with IBM and began offering Microsoft's operating system to competitors (PC clones) of IBM. Microsoft also realized that computer users would buy a computer for applications and not the operating system platform. To prevent competing PC platforms from taking over the market by offering applications, Microsoft encouraged third-party vendors to write software based on the DOS kernel.[7] Numerous companies took up the challenge, and Lotus 123 pioneered the first spreadsheet that was easy to use and could be used on a PC running the DOS operating system. Microsoft succeeded in creating a large installed base for the DOS operating system platform.

Microsoft is a classic example of capitalizing when lady luck smiles on you. Perhaps one of the most critical decisions that Gates made early on was to keep the rights to license the DOS operating system. Without this move, the PC may have evolved as a clone of IBM's previous strategy of IBM-specific operating system and software. No one in the early 1980s, including Microsoft and IBM, knew how successful the PC was going to be. However, the genius of Gates' decision was not to miss out on the opportunity *if* the PC was successful. Microsoft wanted to create entry barriers that would keep out competing operating systems. Cloning the IBM PC ensured that Microsoft achieved a high installed base and developed close relationships with original (PC) equipment manufacturers. However, Bill Gates' real genius was to make it very easy to write applications for the DOS operating system.[8] After the most popular applications, such as Lotus 123 and WordPerfect, became available only on DOS PCs, Microsoft succeeded in creating entry barriers for other operating systems. Without these applications, the DOS OS was very vulnerable to competing operating systems, such as the GUI-based OS from VisiCorp that came complete with proprietary applications, or even the Apple Macintosh if it could entice independent software vendors to write applications on the Macintosh platform.

However, there was a huge trade-off for Microsoft in this decision that was instrumental in creating its large installed base in the applications market. After the applications for the DOS platform became ubiquitous, they created tremendous positive externality for the IBM PC and its clones. Microsoft also realized the highest margins were enjoyed by the application vendors and not the operating system. Therefore, after the DOS platform became a virtual monopoly, Microsoft desperately wanted to get into the application business in the 1980s. Unfortunately for Microsoft, its critical decision to invite outside vendors to create applications for the DOS platform had given a tremendous first-mover advantage to the likes of WordPerfect and Lotus, which took Microsoft a decade to overcome.[9] A key component of the strategies to dominate the application space involved a second platform that is less well-known by most practitioners and students of business management.

Case 5: Microsoft: Developer Tools Platform

Despite its success with the DOS operating system, Microsoft pursued its development of the BASIC programming language, which culminated in the developer tools division. When Windows 3.0 was launched, the only native Windows applications were the Microsoft business applications. To facilitate the development of applications for the Windows system (where the source code was not available to programmers), Microsoft started the tools division and offered Visual Basic—a graphical interactive way of programming in Basic. However, Visual Basic was fairly limited in terms of its ability to write complex programs. Subsequently, Microsoft introduced Visual C++, which facilitated the development of complex programs (such as the browsers or Microsoft Office) using C++. In 1997, Microsoft bundled all its developer tools into one integrated package called Visual Studio. The tools division quickly became a profitable division for Microsoft with nearly half a billion dollars in revenues in 1997.

According to Industry Standard, the "platform so streamlined the writing of PC applications that Microsoft co-opted as partners literally millions of developers and independent software vendors, and in the 1990s created an entire software industry. The thousands of applications written for its platform squeezed out almost all competition." [10]

Microsoft is now drawing on its developer tools division to create a new platform for writing software for videogames. The plan is to have a common platform that can be used to write games for both the Xbox console system and for the PC.

Visual Studio and C++ were instrumental in shaping the Windows software industry. Unlike the DOS platform where Microsoft was dependent on independent software writers to develop applications to make the DOS platform ubiquitous, Microsoft was unwilling to give up control over the application software for the Windows platform. To retain control over the Windows platform, Microsoft was keeping the Windows source code secret—an action that made it difficult for independent programmers to write applications for the Windows platform. Without applications, it would have been very difficult to develop a large installed base for the Windows operating system. Microsoft's solution? The developer tools platform. By giving the BASIC programming language a graphical interface, Microsoft made it very easy to develop programs for the Windows platform. Microsoft is now trying to repeat the same strategy in the video game industry by investing in a brand new platform for developing software for videogames that works both on the Xbox console and PCs. However, this is more of an adaptive strategy than a shaping strategy. Microsoft is trying to adapt to the competitive environment that has been shaped by the PlayStation game console that outsells Microsoft five to one. This is a much harder process because the independent videogame developers, who are critical for success in the videogame industry, are quite happy with the PlayStation platform and its success. It will be much more difficult to woo these developers away from a successful and existing platform than it was when Microsoft shaped the Windows platform.[11]

Takeaway

Sometimes, you have to invest in a second capability (in the case of Microsoft it is usually a platform) to create the derivative market for the first platform.[12] Recall the example of the category management capability that allowed Company X to finally leverage its brand.

Position the Platform in a Sweet Spot

Microsoft's platform strategy has been successful because Microsoft executed a strategy to make the products that derived from its platforms ubiquitous. Some companies have succeeded with a platform that is much less dependent on derivative products than the Microsoft example. For example, even a single technology that will be needed for a long time is a good candidate for a platform investment. Honda has stayed true to its investment in engine technology that started with motorcycles in the early 1960s to this date. Honda is making the bet that the demand for engines will have a long duration.

Case 6: Honda and Engines[13]

In the 1990s, "bigger is better" seemed to be the mantra in the automobile business. Just about every major U.S. and European car manufacturer went on a merger binge. In this environment, Honda decided to stick it out on its own by leveraging its engine technology. Moreover, there is a danger that new technologies, such as fuel cells, that are being embraced by the likes of GM may make Honda's engines obsolete. Honda's strategy? Become the preferred engine suppliers to other carmakers, such as the deal it struck with GM for advanced V-6 engines. Honda is staying ahead of the curve to meet tough new pollution standards by developing "super-ultralow emission" vehicles, which will be required starting in 2004. Honda expects to develop internal combustion engines that will have pollution standards lower than hybrid or electric power engines. All of this has allowed Honda to become the world's largest manufacturer of internal combustion engines by being able to leverage the technology beyond cars to motorcycles, lawnmowers, snow blowers, and so forth.

How does Honda plan to retain its advantage in engine technology? Like many other carmakers, Honda is involved in the Grand Prix racing circuit building F-1 engines. Most automakers use the knowledge gathered from racing engines to modify the engines for consumer use. The difference? Most car manufacturers involved in building F-1 engines subcontract the design and manufacture of the engines. Honda carries out all of these activities in-house. This in-house capability has allowed Honda to solve seemingly intractable problems. Consider the following:[14]

> "Honda's F-1 engines rotated so fast that the lubricating oil wouldn't adhere to the connecting rods that link the car's pistons to the rest of the system that propels the car. The conventional solution was to polish the rods' surface, so oil would stick to them more evenly, preventing metal-to-metal contact. Instead, Makoto Tsuji, known at Honda as "the metal guy," coated the surface with tiny pyramid-shaped bumps that kept the oil in place, preventing breakdowns. The advance enabled Honda to use lighter and thinner metals in the crankshaft and connecting rods, leading to the compact engines inside its mass-market cars."

> This ability to have quick access to your platform capabilities allowed Honda to capitalize on the demand for high-powered V-6 engines even though it's main expertise was in four-cylinder engines.

Honda is making two bets in investing so heavily in the engine platforms. One, there is a vacuum among the leading automakers in terms of their investment in engine technology. In fact, many of them are content to buy Honda engines, including GM. In other words,

Honda wants to be the supplier of choice of a core product in the automobile value-added chain. Very much like Intel, Honda has focused on a core product where it has a significant technological lead, is investing to maintain that lead, and is helped by others not challenging that lead by making their own investments.[15] Honda's platform satisfies the core objective of creating a high installed base and entry barriers. It is keeping the technology development in-house that allows Honda to make the innovations for setting the standards in engines and makes it difficult for others to catch up. This is another example of building a second capability to fully leverage the core platform.

However, a platform such as Honda's engine that is not depen-dent on derivative products faces some of the same risks faced by a market shaping strategy based on a single product. It is conceivable that environmental concerns can lead to significant modification of automobile engine technology. Honda has a good chance of succeed-ing so long as the internal combustion engine can compete on pollution standards with alternate power plants. Perhaps for this rea-son, Honda is not nearly as committed as Toyota with the hybrid automobile.

You may be hard pressed to think of a firm that came into being using either a process or platform as its initial strategy, except perhaps Microsoft. This is not surprising because this is inherently too risky, especially if the process and platform entails significant investment. Not surprisingly, most of the major process investments were made by already established firms, such as Cisco and BancOne, or major platform initiatives, such as the .Net platform currently being rolled out by Microsoft. There are, however, exceptions.

Case 7: Estrasorb

Novavax has developed a relatively unconventional, but powerful pharmaceutical technology. It is a superior way for introducing drugs into the human body through the skin; a "macular nanoparticle transdermal" system that can potentially be a carrier for 30% of currently known drugs. Novavax, however, does not want to mix its bets, and at the same time wants to put them in the market fast. Thus, it has targeted existing generic drugs as a vehicle for leveraging its technology platform and is both introducing its own proprietary branded version of these generics and allowing other partner corporations to use its proprietary, patented, transdermal delivery mechanism with their drugs, supposedly for a premium.

An example of a generic drug that Novavax has chosen to combine its technology with is Estrogen, a replacement hormone widely used by women for treatment of menopausal problems, among other applications. This drug's market size is around $1.5 billion and growing, mainly driven by the baby boomers reaching the menopause onset age. Recent studies have confirmed the drug's efficacy for acute/short-term application, stabilizing the market demand for it, and proved it to be almost the only effective treatment for the symptoms of the menopausal period. Novavax has branded the combined Estrogen and delivery platform as Estrasorb.

Novavax's strategy is reminiscent of Merck's R&D strategy from the 1970s. At the time when Novavax started investing in developing the platform capability, it identified a white space where it would face minimum demand risk and almost no competitive risk if it can patent the platform. In other words, the only risk that it is taking on is capability risk. The market for Estrogen treatment is large and is expected to get larger because of the demographics. Moreover, by choosing generic drugs like 17-beta estradiol (estrogen), a drug whose attributes and potential side effects are well known to the FDA, to be delivered through its platform, Novavax has taken out many of the uncertainty about FDA approval. Novavax has a strategy that can be paraphrased as "proprietary generics." It plans to develop branded generic medications that can be delivered through its patented platform. Using generics takes out the demand risk. Using the patented delivery platform takes out the competitive risks. Of course, Novavax has to develop the market for these derivative proprietary generics first for this strategy to succeed.

However, the demand for Estrogen has recently been questioned as a result of the Women's Health Initiative study through the National Institute of Health (NIH). The conclusions of this NIH study were that "estrogen replacement therapy should not be used for long-term treatment, but should be limited to the acute treatment of menopausal symptoms." Other studies have suggested that taking the drug through the skin can reduce some of the problems identified by the NIH study. This plays right into Novavax's platform. Moreover, Novavax is not entirely dependent on the success of Estrasorb because there are other drugs that can take advantage of this platform. Finally, unlike a product-based market-shaping strategy, such as the CT-Scanner or laparoscopy, it will take competitors a considerable amount of time to develop a comparable platform that doesn't violate Novavax's patents.

Tactics for Reducing the Risks in Market-Shaping Strategies

Estrasorb notwithstanding, most of the bets made for developing platforms or processes for shaping a market are high-risk ventures and have usually been made by strong firms. However, there is a lower risk option that many firms have missed out on and some have capitalized on. This option is based on starting with an existing product or a process, but then trying to push it beyond its immediate value proposition towards a platform or a standard setting process. This principle is illustrated with a few examples that follow.

The Ability to Visualize a Platform Beyond the Immediate Product

Two companies faced with the same opportunity for developing a platform will often see different risks in making the investment. To reduce the risks of investing in a platform, you need to have a process that can lead to more clarity about the end products or the markets that the platform can exploit. This clarity is almost impossible to obtain by taking an inside-out perspective. Even companies that have actually tried to market a platform missed out on the true scope by focusing on the immediate business and not the desired outcome of possible end markets. The poster child of this mistake is IBM and the PC business. IBM saw the PC as a niche business and maintained its focus on the mainframe business. The PC became one of the biggest platforms ever. The economic landscape is full of companies that missed these opportunities.

Case 8: The GUI Platform

Consider the ubiquitous GUI. It was invented by Xerox's Palo Alto Research Center (PARC) laboratory in the 1970s but never commercialized. In 1984, the Macintosh was indisputably the best GUI-based personal computer around. Steve Jobs had recently hired John Sculley away from Pepsi to run Apple. The Microsoft DOS PC had yet to take firm root in the PC landscape. In this situation, Macintosh had the luxury of being able to charge a premium price for its computers because the Macintosh operating system was only available from Apple. For a while, Sculley managed to promote the advantages of the Macintosh GUI and rake in the profits. However, in the long run, very few applications were written for the Macintosh platform because of the proprietary nature of the operating system. By the late 1980s, Macintosh was losing market share to the decidedly inferior DOS-based PC. This loss turned into a rout when Windows was introduced in 1990.

John Sculley had the opportunity to shape the PC landscape. However, the capability that he needed to develop was a high installed base, like Microsoft. His mistake was taking an inside-out view of the product and how to market it to the customers. This prevented him from seeing the value of the Macintosh as a platform instead of merely a product. If he had instead looked at the outcomes that the customers desired —increase in productivity—he could have positioned the operating system as a platform for many applications. You can perhaps excuse Xerox for not recognizing the platform potential of the GUI because it was focused on the copier business, and the GUI did not fit immediately. However, it is hard to excuse Sculley for the same mistake, especially because Bill Gates had reportedly suggested to Sculley that he consider licensing the Macintosh operating system. Steve Jobs did not make the same mistake with the iPod. He licensed the iPod to HP, and 70% of the sales gains occurred after the iPod could be played on Windows systems. Now consider a company that trades for pennies on the OTC bulletin board. We won't be too surprised if most people do not recognize this company—Ampex. We encourage you to visit the Ampex web site to take a look at all the innovations made by this company over the last 60 years, some of which we append in Table 9.2. Perhaps, the most startling is the fact that it developed the videotape recorder and the videocassette recorder and failed to market them.

TABLE 9.2   Ampex's Innovations

Ampex	
1956	The Ampex VRX-1000 (later renamed the Mark IV) videotape recorder is introduced on March 14, 1956, at the National Association of Radio and Television Broadcasters in Chicago. This is the world's first practical videotape recorder and is hailed as a major technological breakthrough. CBS goes on air with the first videotape delayed broadcast, Douglas Edwards and The News, on November 30, 1956, from Los Angeles, California, using the Ampex Mark IV.
1958	NASA selects Ampex data recorders and magnetic tape, used for virtually all U.S. space missions since.

1961	Helical scanning recording is invented by Ampex, the technology behind the worldwide consumer video revolution, and used in all home VCRs today.
1963	Ampex introduces EDITEC electronic video editing, allowing broadcast television editors frame-by-frame recording control, simplifying tape editing and making animation effects possible. This was the basis for all subsequent editing systems.
1963	Ampex introduces a new computer peripheral digital tape transport, the TM-7. Its design far surpasses previous tape drives, using 80 percent fewer parts and completely eliminating pinch rollers and brake cylinders.
1964	Ampex introduces the VR-2000 high-band videotape recorder, the first ever capable of the color fidelity required for high-quality color broadcasting.
1967	The introduction of the Ampex VR-3000 revolutionizes video recording.
1968	Ampex invents magneto-resistive (MR) heads, now used in advanced computer disk drives.
1969	Ampex introduces the Videofile system, used by Scotland Yard for the electronic storage and retrieval of fingerprints.
1970	Ampex introduces the ACR-25, the first automated robotic library system for the recording and playback of television commercials.
1976	Ampex introduces the VPR-1, helical scan, 1-inch videotape recorder. The VPR-1's successor, the Type C VPR-2 (1978), becomes the industry standard for video recording.
1977	Ampex introduces the AST process, the first automated scan tracking for variable speed effects, making slow motion possible directly from tape for the first time.
1977	Ampex introduces Electronic Still Store (ESS), which allows producers to store digital video images for later editing and broadcast.
1978	The Ampex Video Art (AVA) video graphics system is used by artist Leroy Nieman on air during Super Bowl XII. AVA, the first video paint system, allows the graphic artist, using an electronic pen, to illustrate in a new medium, video. This innovation paved the way for today's high quality electronic graphics, such as those used in video games.
1981	Ampex introduces the ADO system, which creates digital special effects, allowing rotation and perspective of video images. This changed forever the way television material would be manipulated and created.
1983	Ampex introduces the DCRS digital cassette recorder, offering compact cassette storage with the equivalent of 16 digital, 14 inch, 8 DDR instrumentation reels on one cassette.

Source: http://www.ampex.com/03corp/03corp.html

The true potential of the videotape recorder was in the mass-market, and this potential was exploited by JVC and the Japanese electronics firms. The videotape recorder was a platform that led to not just the mass-market in VCRs, but videogames and the video camera to name a few. It may be instructive to contrast the approach taken by Ampex with that of the Japanese. Judging by the other innovations that Ampex developed following the introduction of the videotape recorder, it is reasonable to conclude that the videotape recorder was seen by Ampex to be a product that can only be used by TV studios. For example, Ampex developed other products that complemented the videotape recorder, such as editing systems, but not products that could ease the transition of the videotape recorder for consumer use. However, to see the true potential of the videotape recorder as a platform for a mass-market commodity, Ampex had to rephrase the end-consumer's desired outcome as "taking control of viewing a TV program at a time of their choosing." Audio tape recorders were already around for over 30 years and were increasingly used by consumers to take charge of listening to music in the order they wanted instead of being dictated by radio or even the record companies. In effect, this was the outcome that JVC and the Japanese capitalized on. Ampex is the poster child of the company that relies on product innovation —innovations that were exploited by other companies that relied on business model innovation coupled with an understanding of the outcomes that the end consumer desired. In other words, Ampex saw the product while JVC saw the platform.

Takeaway

The basic takeaway from both the Macintosh and the Ampex story is that to visualize how a product can be extended to a platform, a firm has to avoid an inside-out perspective. This is critical to recognize derivative products. You have to apply the outcome-to-objective framework or a variation to visualize the platform possibilities.

Extending a Product into a Standard Process

Another strategy that firms have successfully deployed is to take an internal product or process and make it available to other companies to be used to as a background process. If such a process garners widespread acceptability and becomes a process of choice, this leads to a sustained competitive advantage that is very difficult to knock off. Perhaps the most widely known example of this strategy is American Airlines' SABRE reservation systems, which became the airline industry standard computerized reservation system (CRS), along with the Apollo reservation system developed by United Airlines. Let us consider some more examples.

Case 9: Ingram Micro

The computer distribution business has consolidated down from hundreds to a handful. Of these, the clearest market leader is Ingram Micro. Throughout its history, it has developed this leadership by creating platforms out of its existing processes. Ingram was instrumental in getting retailers to accept the SSCC-18 bar code platform that reveals the package's contents. Ingram managed to increase the penetration of the standard from 40% to 90% in the early 1990s by insisting on the standard.

In the late 1990s, Ingram developed an Internet electronic-commerce application that was made available to all of its VARs (over 10,000) worldwide. Using this application, a VAR (value-added reseller) could offer its customers real-time and transparent information about inventory, out-of-the-door cost, and any other personalization the customer desired. Moreover, the VAR did not have to acknowledge Ingram Micro as a provider of the application and could brand the website under VAR's own name. More recently, Ingram is pushing for the adoption of another software platform "IM First," which tracks top-selling products, the status of every item, and what's in stock in each of Ingram's 49 warehouses worldwide.[16]

continues

Case 9: Ingram Micro (Continued)

At present, Ingram is capitalizing on yet another trend that is threatening to revolutionize the VAR business. The margins on selling single products for a VAR are no longer profitable. The watchword in the VAR industry is collaboration. The VARs are collectively providing solutions to customers by finding partners and subcontractors in the virtual space. Ingram Micro Service Network (IMSN) functions as "a centralize dispatch system that connects 550 solution providers and more than 10,000 technicians in approximately 800 North American markets into a centralized network managed by Ingram."[17] Ingram has also developed the VentureTech Network (VTN) that allows more than 350 value-added resellers to network with each other in virtual space.

> "Here's an example of how it works: Information Networking in Irvine, Calif. was asked by a customer in Southern California to perform a Token-Ring-to-Ethernet migration of 400 PC workstations and 70 servers. The task involved planning meetings, design, and project management. But there was one major requirement: The job had to be done in one weekend. Through IMSN, Torrance, California-based Micro World supplied 25 certified PC and server technicians to work around the clock during that time period. In conjunction, Information Networking provided three PC and server technicians, four fiber and copper cable technicians, as well as server project management. After some on-site planning meetings and numerous telephone conference calls, the migration project began on a Friday afternoon at 5pm. Roughly 460 man-hours later, the job was done."[18]

Ingram's platform strategy is very similar to American Airlines and its SABRE strategy. Over time, Ingram would derive more value by analyzing the information it gathers over its platform than the revenue from the platform itself. The availability of Ingram gives hope to VARs that would like to sell HP computers despite the domination of Dell and the direct channel. Now consider the decision by Amazon to develop an e-commerce platform that is synonymous with Windows in this market space.

Case 10: Amazon's E-Commerce Platform

Amazon has been placing a major bet that has got nothing to do with its own retailing. Amazon wants to be the platform of choice for all e-commerce retailers. The e-commerce firms are increasingly using web services developed by Amazon to offer bells and whistles they would not be able to develop on their own. Simplest-Shop.com uses a packaged e-commerce platform developed by Amazon. Visitors to this web site have the choice of buying directly from it or from Amazon (depending on the price). In the latter case, Simplest-Shop.com gets up to 15% of the transaction price as a clickthrough commission. In either case, the checkout and shipping are handled by Amazon.[19]

Amazon's e-commerce platform is proprietary software, parts of which (like the one-click ordering) are patented. For Simplest-Shop.com to tap into Amazon's platform, Amazon had to disaggregate its e-commerce platform in the form of web services (see the discussion on Microsoft's .Net in Chapter 10). These web services are now available to nearly one million e-commerce web sites that are featured on Amazon or provide click through to Amazon. This is a much better arrangement than a simple link to other web sites where the quality of experience could not be controlled by Amazon. Amazon is hiring top program talent to facilitate this transition.

In some sense, Amazon is trying to outsource its e-commerce retailing experience to all its associates, so customers who interact with Amazon will have a uniform experience—from what is visible, such as one-click ordering, to what is invisible. Amazon's partners get a much more sophisticated web site with plumbing and wiring maintained by Amazon. Further, this arrangement allows the associates to offer a much wider selection on their web sites. For its part, Amazon gets access through many more retail outlets to sell its products.

The question we would like you to consider is whether your company is ready to extend parts of its internal processes to become a platform of choice. We suggest that the strategy is not for everyone. Basically, all the companies described here (along with Microsoft's strategy, which we will discuss at length in Chapter 10) already have a very high installed base in their core business. Absent that, major investment in creating a platform of choice can be a high-risk venture. Even for Amazon, this strategy is by no means a slam-dunk. If a firm jumps into developing a platform without considering its ability to quickly develop a high installed base, then it may be expecting too much of its platform. This can lead to major risks.

Expecting Too Much from the Platform

Even companies that have been successful in the past at creating industry-standard platforms must guard against overreaching. Consider Federal Express. FedEx, throughout its history, has made a practice of being ahead of the curve in investing in platform capabilities starting with its Memphis hub in 1972. FedEx has invested millions of dollars in an effort to manage the logistics for Cisco, with the hope that it will create the platform of choice for logistics outsourcing (also known as third-party logistics or 3PL). Essentially, this strategy allows firms to avoid investing in warehouses altogether. Unfortunately, two factors are working against FedEx at this point in time. First, it is unclear how the Internet bubble has affected the demand for 3PL services. Second, unlike the 1980s, when FedEx was the undisputed king in time-definite delivery market space, UPS can not only match FedEx service-for-service, but it can also offer integrated ground and air delivery that FedEx has yet to match. Bottom line: Becoming the platform of choice is not a suitable strategy for all firms. Now consider an investment made by GM in the mid-1990s that was expected to bring a new source of growth for the car maker.

Case 11: GM and OnStar

In the late 1990s, General Motors made a heavy commitment in the OnStar telematic platform. OnStar connects drivers to a call center for driver assistance and to the Internet over a wireless network. Essentially, OnStar allows a driver to be in touch with all his communication needs. In the future, OnStar will even allow car owners to download software that can enable the suspension to be soft for city driving during the week and sporty during the weekend. OnStar was expected to be a big cash cow for GM.

OnStar has lived up to some of its promises, such as helping stranded drivers and locating stolen vehicles. However, it is unclear whether OnStar has lived up to all of its promises, and some reports suggest that it is making money solely because of transfer payments from GM. GM is now considering giving away OnStar as standard safety equipment to differentiate the car and not as a separate service.

In contrast to Honda, GM is trying to piggyback its luxury car division to promote OnStar sales. Unfortunately, GM's car division is not strong enough to promote the kind of sales needed for OnStar to set the standard by developing a large installed base, like Microsoft's DOS. Further, there are already substitutes from cell phones to PDAs to Blackberries that are providing many of the functions that OnStar does. Moreover, the OnStar technology is vulnerable to new entrants, such as Microsoft's autoPC. Basically, GM was not in a strong enough position to promote the kind of initial adoption that was required for these investments to succeed.

Make Sure Your Firm Can Push the Platform to the End Market

How do you know you are not expecting too much from your platform? It is not enough to invest in a platform and hope for the best. You have to have a clear idea of whether the full capability of the platform will be appreciated by the end market. Honda's engine technology has allowed them to diversify into many other non-auto markets and dominate the high (and profitable) end of these markets, such as in lawn mowers. The engine platform is thus a very safe bet because the demands for the other end-markets where the platform can be applied are well known.

In contrast, OnStar is expecting that drivers will desperately want to stay in touch with the outside world and is willing to pay a premium. To be sure, GM is not the only auto manufacturer thinking of a car as a mobile communication platform. (Volvo has a similar concept.) Even the strongest car manufacturer may be better served by outsourcing the development of this kind of a platform because none of the key objectives are easily attainable by them. Despite the support that the OnStar initiative has received from a well-known consulting firm, this is an ill-advised investment for GM. In our opinion, GM would be much better to focus on cars and not be distracted with ancillary services.

Ambitious platform developments are usually conceived at a time of affluence, and it is precisely then that firms must have clarity about the end-markets in which the platform must succeed. The space shuttle was designed for multiple uses and was expected to generate revenue from the corporate sector. It never has, and NASA has learned its lessons. In contrast, the Soviets built the more robust Soyuz for one purpose only—to ferry astronauts back and forth from the space station.

Contrast the decisions made by GM and NASA to Sony. Sony, throughout its history, has invested in platforms and not always successfully. Yet Sony has a remarkable success record on the whole. Sony has several things going for it that make it a suitable candidate for investing in platforms or products. Sony is extremely adept at identifying white spaces where it can push its platforms. The Walkman and PlayStation are both examples of this strategy. However, Sony has a second platform it can leverage across all its market entries—its brand name. Sony has carefully developed a brand name that gives it an edge in the end market even when it licenses the platform from others, such as in the CD and laptop markets. Panasonic entered the PC business much earlier than Sony in the early 1980s. Yet it failed to make a dent in the PC market where Sony now has a substantial presence. This brand name allows Sony to have more confidence in investing in platforms because it can protect its profits more easily.[20] Even for market shapers, it helps to have some other capabilities it can leverage.

Modify Unsuccessful Platforms for Other End Markets

If your firm is planning to invest in platforms, it can reduce its risk if the platforms can be modified for other markets. Recall the space pen that NASA commissioned Fisher to develop. It has since become a novelty and can be purchased at Sharper Image. However, unlike Velcro, also developed by NASA, the space pen has no other use.

Sony is a poster child for developing reusable platforms. Even when it failed with a particular product, such as the Betamax, it managed to use the knowledge gleaned from its failure to successfully enter the Hi-8 video camera market. Sony has just done an encore over the last seven years. As described in Chapter 3, *Identify Multiple Capability Configurations*, its PlayStation division went up against Nintendo and Sega by to choosing a technology platform that allowed Sony to try out risky new games, while Nintendo and Sega were stuck in a series of endless sequels. Sony did this by extending its knowledge from video, CD, and PC technology to develop a flexible and low-fixed-costs platform for creating video games that mitigated the risks of trying out many new games. Sony is engaged in a standards battle right now over the DVD read-write platform. In characteristic fashion, Sony has hedged its bets by introducing DVD players that can read and write multiple formats. The Sony DVD players are at the top of the recommended lists in most computer magazines.

Let us revisit Yamaha's strategy to reinvent the piano business. The investment in digitizing the pianos turned out to be much less risky because of its leveragability. Yamaha's opportunities have expanded beyond the digital units and recordings. Because their piano is now being played by a "professional" (using digital media that captures virtuoso performance), many customers want their piano tuned to professional standards. This increases the need for piano tuners and piano hardware. Additionally, interest in playing the piano is increased by the growth of the piano's popularity, which therefore stimulates the piano instruction market and ultimately Yamaha. All these opportunities arose from Yamaha's ability to correctly rephrase customer outcomes. Therefore, Yamaha's first-mover risk in digitizing pianos is much less than standalone attempts to create a new value chain.

Summary Thoughts

In this section, you considered some concepts that will help you anticipate the risks in your diversification strategies by identifying the high-level objectives, such as shaping or adapting, as well as the product, process, or platform you want to pursue as the basis for your corporate development. You have explored risk-management strategies for each of these high-level objectives. However, these strategies are strictly a snapshot in time. In Chapter 10, you look at managing these risks in a more dynamic context. You will see how to identify choices not only when designing a strategy, but how to keep the options open and defer commitments. By keeping options open, you will be able to commit resources when you have the best understanding of the risks.

Endnotes

1 Compare this to the strategy adopted by FedEx Custom Critical and Cisco as discussed in Chapter 2, *Three Steps to Identify a Low-Risk Strategy*.

2 "Realizing a Management Information System's Potential." *Bankers Magazine*. September/October, 1993. This quote is excerpted from *BancOne: The Evolution of Partnership*. University of Virginia, Darden School, UVA BP-0335. I would like to thank Jeanne Liedtka for bringing it to my attention.

3 "The Magnificent McCoys: Running America's Best Bank." *Institutional Investor.* July, 1991.

4 One of the key components of this strategy was the Autotest process described in Chapter 3.

5 Anita McGahan. "Focus on Pharmaceuticals: Industry Structure and Competitive Advantage." *Harvard Business Review*. November-December 1994: 115-124.

6 This approach is becoming quite common now. For example, pharmaceutical companies are not performing research on new antibiotics, even though antibiotic-resistant bacteria are on the rise. Antibiotics are not chronic drugs.

7 The DOS kernel was an open source software where all the codes were visible to the application developers. This is very different from the Windows software where Microsoft did not give software developers access to the proprietary source codes.

8 Refer to Endnote #7.

9 This is our inference. However, recently unearthed memos written by Bill Gates to his management team from the 1980s through the present provide strong support for our inferences. For example, see John R. Wilke and Don Clark. "Microsoft Is Facing More Telling E-Mails In Minnesota Lawsuit." *The Wall Street Journal*. March 17, 2004: Page B1.

10 Dominic Gates. "Bill's Baby." *Industry Standard*. Nov 20, 2000

11 Microsoft persuaded Electronic Arts to develop games for the Xbox platform and the PC platform in May 2004. The details of the deal are not known, but Electronic Arts was very happy about it, as reported on CNBC. I would not be too surprised if this is a loss leader strategy playing out for Microsoft.

12 Also see Chapter 10, Figure 10.3 and Tables 10.1 and 10.2.

13 This case study draws from many sources, in particular from Norihiko Shirouzu. "Honda Bets Its Engines Will Give it the Oomph to Remain Independent." *The Wall Street Journal*. March 15, 2000.

14 Ibid.

15 GM, for example, is focusing on the next generation of engines that may be powered by fuel cells.

16 Tamara Chuang. "Ingram Micro Teams Technology with Distribution." *Knight Ridder Tribune Business News*. Washington: Dec 6, 2003.

17 Sonia R. Lelii. "Teaming With Success—Solution Providers Are Embracing a New Concept-Collaboration." *VARbusiness* Manhasset. Nov 17, 2003: 87.

18 Ibid.

19 Peter Loftus. "Web Services—Smooth Talk: New Software Allows Different Computer Systems To Communicate with Each Other Seamlessly." *The Wall Street Journal* (Eastern edition) New York, N.Y.: Mar 31, 2003: R-9.

20 A brand name is less useful for a platform that is normally invisible compared to a very visible product.

10

DEVELOP MULTIPLE MIGRATION PATHS

Even though you started this book by considering a framework to identify multiple options, the bulk of this book deals with choosing one of the options that promises the least risk adjusted return, and then developing tactics (capabilities) to implement this option with the least risk. This assumes you have to commit to an option before you start implementing the strategy. However, in many situations, you can reduce risks even further by not making this commitment unless you absolutely have to. If this is possible, the actual risks and returns in each of these options can be better assessed as more information is obtained in the future. Other issues exist as well. Your firm may have to decide on taking an immediate profit by pursuing one option as opposed to a larger profit sometime in the future. An example of this is whether to take the profit from a product or push the product to become a platform. Part of this decision depends on the risk tolerance of your firm as well as the resources it brings to the table.

The worst thing to do is to get locked into *one* migration path that ends up in a "Hail Mary" pass that will fail more often than not. This chapter is about assessing the risks in each of the *multiple* migration paths. Fortunately, the outcome-to-objective framework facilitates this assessment by clarifying the capability risks in each path. The next step is to develop a playbook for managing the sources of risk in *each* migration path.

Migration Paths for Adapting

We have already seen examples of identifying multiple migration paths throughout this book. For example, we previously described the other options Company X considered to counter the threat from Company Y before adopting the category management strategy. The migration paths Company X considered are illustrated in Figure 10.1.

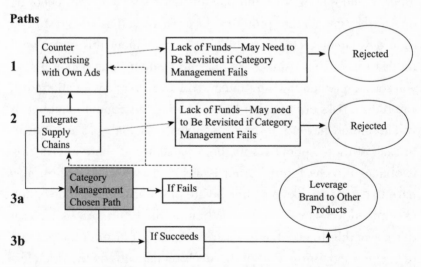

FIGURE 10.1   Company X's migration paths.

Consider the case of Microsoft's ascendancy in the desktop application software market. In the 1980s, even though Microsoft dominated the operating system segment, it was basically locked out of the most attractive segment on the desktop—applications. Today, Microsoft dominates the desktop applications space and most people attribute this to the success of Windows 3.0. However, few realize the multiple avenues Microsoft had embarked on in the early 1980s, each with its unique strategy to dominate the desktop applications space. At least one of these avenues might have meant giving up the DOS operating system monopoly.

The First Path: Become the Kingmaker

In 1984, the best GUI operating system belonged to Microsoft's archrival, Apple computer's Macintosh. Macintosh was plagued with having very little software because it was a proprietary operating system, which made it difficult for other software vendors to write applications for the Macintosh. In 1984, Microsoft made two rather surprising moves. Microsoft offered to write GUI-based applications (Word and Excel) for the Macintosh that soon became the most popular applications for the Macintosh platform. Second, according to published case studies, Bill Gates suggested to Apple's CEO at the time, John Sculley, that he lower the price and license Macintosh for wider adoption—exactly what Microsoft had successfully done with DOS. Sculley, as we know, opted to stay with the premium pricing strategy. Of course, we do not know why Bill Gates ever made this suggestion. However, had John Sculley opened up the Apple operating system to outside licensees, with or without the suggestion from Bill Gates, it is quite conceivable that the far superior Macintosh would have ousted DOS from the desktop (something the iPod is doing in 2004 to other MP3 players). It is almost inconceivable that Bill Gates had not considered this possibility. In this light, Bill Gates' decision to write applications for Macintosh can be appreciated for its genius. If Macintosh became the dominant operating system, Gates would have been number one in the business application space. By writing applications for the Macintosh system, Microsoft hedged against this possibility. Of course, Microsoft also began to learn more about the GUI operating system—knowledge it could incorporate in its own version, Windows. However, in 1984, there was no guarantee that Microsoft would ever be able to dominate the scene with its own GUI system. Just consider what might have happened if Linux was developed in the 1980s. Without a Windows monopoly to fight against, Linux would have a much easier time becoming the dominant platform. Microsoft was a fledgling company in 1984, and for such a company, it may be more prudent to take the immediate profits with the Macintosh applications rather than place a big bet on being able to develop the Windows platform.

The Second Path: Frontal Assault

By 1987, Microsoft had introduced full-featured word-processing (Word for MS-DOS) and spreadsheet (Excel for DOS) applications. However, Microsoft's own decisions in the early 1980s to flood the market with MS-DOS–based applications ceded first-mover advantages for third-party best-of-breed software vendors. The application space in the 1980s was dominated by best-of-breed providers, such as Lotus 123 (spreadsheets), WordPerfect (word processing), and Paradox (database). The common theme underlying the success of all three companies was their ability to deliver a product that was as simple to use as possible given the low memory constraint of the 640KB DOS operating system. Take, for example, WordPerfect. To ease the transition from typewriters to computer-based word-processing systems for office secretaries, WordPerfect developed an opening screen, which is very similar to a blank sheet of paper. Secretaries/ users were encouraged to simply start typing and use the keys that they are used to in order to format the document. This ease of formatting a document by WordPerfect has been unmatched even to this date.[1] This is one reason why, WordPerfect, until very recently, was the most preferred word-processing system for legal documents that require extensive formatting. In contrast, Word for MS-DOS was extremely complicated and required multiple keystrokes to carry out simple formatting, such as a hanging indent. Despite a heavy promotional campaign, Microsoft failed to convert users to its DOS-based applications.

The Third Path: Hide Your Weakness

Microsoft was not ready to give up on the office productivity space. Instead, Microsoft decided to learn about the GUI interface while working with Apple and released Windows 2.0 in 1986. However, the MS-DOS 640KB memory limitation was a hostile environment for a GUI operating system and Windows 2.0 went nowhere. Microsoft also simultaneously hedged its bets by agreeing to develop a GUI operating system for IBM (that ultimately became OS/2). This strategy had two benefits. It effectively eliminated a competitor in the PC-based GUI space. If IBM OS/2 became successful, Microsoft was in a good position to repeat what it had done with the MS-DOS operating system with some caveats that we will discuss shortly. IBM, strangely enough, did not see Microsoft as a serious threat in the desktop GUI operating system business. Clearly, the fact that Microsoft had introduced Windows 2.0 while working on the IBM OS/2 should have been a strong signal to this effect. Some feel that in the mid-1980s, IBM was still on the horns of dilemma between the mainframe business and the viability/potential of the PC business. Basically, IBM did not have an exit strategy for the mainframe business.

Whatever the case may be, by 1990, Microsoft was able to refine Windows with the help of increasingly more powerful microprocessors as well as cheaper memory. Windows had a workable GUI, reasonable multitasking, and most importantly, backward compatibility with the thousands of DOS-based applications available in the market. Simultaneously, Microsoft severed its partnership with IBM.

IBM frantically tried to develop OS/2 on its own, but Windows had too big of a head start, and IBM finally abandoned its quest. By 1991, Microsoft released its Windows-based suite of office applications including Excel, Word, and PowerPoint. The ease-of-use advantage that WordPerfect and Lotus enjoyed in the DOS era was no longer a differentiating factor in the Windows environment because the drop-down menus obviated the need for complicated keystrokes. After Microsoft achieved parity with the best-of-breed vendors, it leaped ahead with integrated applications, fusing together Microsoft Word and Excel (and later PowerPoint), which separated Microsoft applications from the rest of the pack.[2]

The rest of the story is familiar to most of us. Microsoft was able to leverage its monopoly in the Windows operating system market by striking deals with leading PC vendors, such as Dell, whereby Dell would only preinstall Microsoft's suite of office applications on its PCs. Slowly but surely, many new users began to use Microsoft Office Suite as their first applications. Further, WordPerfect and Harvard Graphics refused to embrace the GUI trend quickly enough. This was partly because of arrogance and partly because Microsoft, unlike the open-source DOS, did not give application software vendors access to the Windows source code. There was a mistaken belief amongst many of these best-of-breed application providers that if they refused to come out with the Windows version of their product, Microsoft's applications and Windows would fail. On the other hand, Microsoft kept improving its own applications with inexpensively bundled upgrades. Microsoft achieved its goal of dominating the application space after 10 years of trying.

This story has been repeated in many situations where erstwhile market leaders suffer from a not-invented-here syndrome and refuse to see the validity of a new business model. Most of Yamaha's competitors refused to acknowledge how Yamaha changed the piano business, much like the refusal of WordPerfect and Harvard Graphics to acknowledge Windows. The erstwhile market leaders did not have multiple migration paths of their own to respond to the newcomer's challenge.

Takeaway: You Never Go Broke Taking Profits

There are two important takeaways in the Microsoft story. There is always more than one way to attain your objective. However, the long-term path is inherently more risky because the longer time span will allow unanticipated factors to complicate matters. Traders of financial securities frown on a long-term buy and hold strategy because there are too many uncertainties in doing that. In business, unless you are a market Goliath, short-term profit is usually a low risk strategy—the fledgling Microsoft in the 1980s was not sanguine that it would ever be able to come up with a GUI operating system that the computer-buying public would accept. Basically, Microsoft had an exit strategy option for the chance it took in developing a platform with its antecedent uncertainties. For example, IBM may be reluctant to let Microsoft license OS/2 and instead may opt to write proprietary software as it had done throughout its history. Further, if independent vendors did not, or could not, write applications for IBM's OS/2 (as happened in reality), the platform never may be able to develop a large installed base. Finally, there was always a danger that someone else besides IBM may come up with a GUI system.

Takeaway: Only Risk What You Can Afford to Lose

In 1984, Bill Gates did not want to make the same mistake as EMI in the CT-Scanner market or U.S. Surgical in the laparoscopy market. Everyone was convinced that GUI was the future, but no one was certain which GUI platform would dominate in the mid-1980s. Given Microsoft's limited resources, Gates could have well concluded that helping Apple become the dominant GUI operating system and piggybacking on Apple's success to dominate the application space was a lower risk strategy then being able to develop Windows and leverage Windows to dominate the application space. Of course, had Macintosh become the dominant operating system, Microsoft would have lost all its future profits from Windows. Note that it is very unlikely the Microsoft of today—the market Goliath—will ever consider an option like this that leaves money on the table. Microsoft is losing money in almost all its ventures at present, but this is of very little concern with a 55 billion-dollar cash hoard.

Takeaway: Give Your Competitors a Chance to Make Mistakes

Finally, if you have the option, instead of forcing the issue, let your competitors make mistakes. Even though Microsoft had aggressively pursued Word, Excel, and PowerPoint in the 1980s and failed, it bided its time until it had a way of under cutting the incumbents' competitive advantage. Slowly but surely, Microsoft put itself in a position to win and capitalized on its competitors' mistakes in not embracing GUI and underestimating the threat from an integrated productivity suite. Microsoft's multiple migration paths to dominate the application space are illustrated in Figure 10.2.

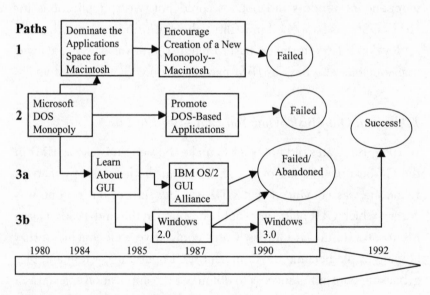

FIGURE 10.2 Microsoft's migration paths.

Migration Paths for Shaping

As discussed in Chapter 9, *Strategies to Shape Markets: Products, Process, and Platform*, these strategies are the most risky because they are vulnerable to demand and capability risks. Cisco did this in the 1990s by means of its acquisition strategy and assembling a portfolio of technologies that allowed it to dominate most segments in the enterprise network market space.

Case 1: Cisco Systems: Setting the Goal to Be the One-Stop Network Solutions Shop[3]

Until 1993, Cisco's fortunes were tied almost exclusively to routers. By the time John Chambers took over as CEO, he noticed customers were placing big orders for ATM switching equipment to beef up their connections between sites. Although Cisco's growth rate was substantial, Chambers felt Cisco had actually stifled its potential growth. With the coming-of-age of the Internet and the growing popularity of corporate in-house intranets, more demands were put on Cisco to provide a complex variety of networking solutions. Chambers thought that if the company was going to grow, it had to make sure it offered all the products demanded by a full range of customers, whether corporation, institution, Internet service provider, or telecommunication carrier. To dominate such a market, executives at Cisco knew it could not hope to develop internally all the needed technologies quickly enough.

In the early 1990s, Cisco knew what its end-objective was—to be the soup-to-nuts solution provider in the networking industry. Being a single provider of routers would have stalled out its growth very soon. Yet with the rapidly changing technology, developing the different pieces of the value-added chain was actually much more risky than bolting on technology that had been developed by others. There were, however, other risks. An acquisition strategy carries with it significant risks because the track records of acquisitions are quite poor.

Very early on, John Chambers had to make a decision about the kind of acquisition(s) it will undertake to become the comprehensive supplier of networking solutions. This was the first migration path Cisco had to navigate.

Case 2: Cisco Systems: Choosing Between Different Acquisition Strategies

With product cycles dropping below 18 months, Chambers set out to buy what Cisco couldn't develop internally quickly enough. Starting with the $89 million acquisition of switch maker, Crescendo, in the fall of 1993, Cisco set a relentless pace for acquisitions.

Cisco's first acquisition candidate was ardently discussed among senior executives. At issue was whether Cisco should merge with another large company—either SynOptics or Cabletron, both of which were about the same size as Cisco. The appeal of a merger of equals was that the combined company would emerge as "Number One" in terms of size. By combining two companies with good management and overlapped customer sets, the result would be a widened customer base and more distribution channels.[4]

However, a merger of equals that created the number-one player would pressure remaining second-tier competitors to rethink their strategies. In Chamber's view, this would force a period of competitor mergers and acquisitions, which might destabilize the industry.[5] There were other risks in a merger of equals. According to Chambers: [6]

"If you merge two companies that are growing at 80 percent rates, you stand a very good chance of stalling both of them out. When you combine companies, for a period of time, no matter how smoothly they operate, you lose momentum. That's a fact. Even today, as good as we are at acquisitions—and I think we really know how to do them today—when you make the acquisition, there is a period when you lose business momentum. Our industry is not like the banking industry, where you are acquiring branch banks and customers. In our industry, you are acquiring people. And if you don't keep those people, you have made a terrible,

terrible investment. We pay between $500,000 and $2 million per person in an acquisition, which is a lot. So you can understand that if you don't keep the people, you've done a tremendous disservice to your shareholders and customers."

There was another option: smaller, targeted acquisitions. Cisco had learned from Hewlett-Packard about breaking up markets into segments, and from General Electric the mentality of being either the first or second player in each segment.

Cisco's decision of not pursuing a mega-merger is analogous to taking a small but certain profit and taking a chance on leaving some profits on the table. Cisco felt that hitting a number of singles is a much safer migration path to becoming the comprehensive provider of networking solutions than trying to hit a home run with a mega-merger. In fact, other major players in the networking industries did merge and failed to make the mergers work.

Takeaway: Understand the Risks in Each Path

The basic takeaway is extremely compelling. To manage the migration paths, you need to know how the sources of risks in each path relate to the end objective you are trying to achieve. In the case of Cisco, the risk in managing the means (acquisitions) was more important than the risk in failing to achieve the end quickly or comprehensively. Contrast this to Microsoft's decision to write applications for Macintosh. We know that it was very important for Microsoft to dominate the lucrative application market space. We also know that Microsoft considered the Macintosh to be a serious competitor in the early 1980s. It seems to us, consciously or not, Microsoft took into account the risks of the different paths it could take to dominate the application space. By hedging its bets by helping out Macintosh, Microsoft was keeping a low-risk path open instead of taking on the best-of-breed vendors in the DOS arena head-on. While Windows turned into a home run, the means to get there and the time it took to get there made it a highly risky means of dominating the application space. Both Cisco and Microsoft, however, were willing to leave some profits on the table to reduce the risks. Let us continue now with Cisco's acquisition strategy as it evolved through the 1990s.

Case 3: Cisco: The Move from Invisible to Invincible

By the late 1990s, Cisco's reputation preceded it into new markets. But in the beginning, Cisco's acquisition strategy was essentially invisible.[7] Although members in the same industry knew about Cisco, the general business community did not. Chambers claimed there was no business advantage to publicity early on, because most of its customer sales were direct; so hearing about the firm in the press was not perceived as an advantage.

That strategy changed around 1995, when it became apparent to senior management that, while product technology was an important part of the business, so was marketing. Management observed Microsoft's behavior and realized it got most of its marketing for free.[8] As a result, a decision was made to become much more visible. Chambers credited the increased company visibility for allowing the firm to move quicker with target acquisitions.[9] The higher profile also helped Cisco keep abreast of competitors' plans to acquire because target companies frequently approached Cisco to see if they were interested.[10]

Cisco's decision to fly under the radar screen in the first part of the 1990s underscored what Cisco perceived the true risk of its corporate strategy to be. For most acquisition programs, deal flow (information about potential targets) is absolutely critical. Cisco could have advertised the fact that it was in the market to buy small companies. Cisco could have also solicited the information from investment bankers. Cisco chose to do neither. What Cisco was doing was avoiding the risks that most acquiring firms fall prey to while making acquisitions. In particular, Cisco avoided getting into an auction situation where the premium for the acquisitions can increase dramatically. By focusing on small friendly deals, Cisco stayed out of the limelight and largely untouched by investment bankers where auctions become almost unavoidable. However, after Cisco's reputation as a successful acquiring firm grew, Cisco became a magnet for small technological startups that wanted to cash out without doing an IPO. By becoming highly visible in the mid-1990s, Cisco managed to increase its deal flow and basically ended up being the acquirer of choice. This subtle shift reduced the risk of overpayment and acquiring the wrong target dramatically. Cisco has successfully managed the migration path not only to become the comprehensive provider of networking solutions, but also mastering a process for successful bolt-on acquisitions.

Migration Paths for Platform Strategy

"Right now, we're all just putting in the foundation for .Net. You've got to get independent software developers enthused and make the strategy clear. But this is a five-year strategy. It was 1983 when we decided to make a graphic interface for the PC operating system. When was Windows a success? Probably 1990."[11]

—Bill Gates on the .Net vision

Microsoft has embarked on a strategy to dominate the web services space by becoming the platform of choice with the .Net platform. Consider now how the businesses that Microsoft has entered into go beyond success in the individual businesses and toward providing the foundation for helping .Net become the platform of choice in web services.

Trying to become the dominant platform is always a risky strate-gy because of the investment risk and the duration risk (this usually takes a longer time to bear fruit). Note that we are not talking about a standards battle, such as one that is currently going on in the DVD recordable market space. One can have a profitable business even after losing a standards battle, as exemplified by Sony adapting to the VCR business after losing the standards battle to VHS. However, as we saw in Chapter 9, winning a platform battle can set the company in a profitable situation for a very long time. For this very reason, many competitors will try to vie for the same platform. The core objective for most competitors is to get the most number of users to buy into the platform as opposed to a competing platform. Microsoft has done it twice with the DOS operating system and Windows oper-ating system. It is now trying to repeat this by developing the plat-form for web services. The stakes are much higher now and this time Microsoft is unwilling to leave any profits on the table (as it may have with DOS) and ensure that Microsoft's .Net platform become the platform of choice for utilizing the Holy Grail of web services. To Microsoft, this would be as big if not bigger than what the application space was with the PC desktop.

Web services let applications share data, and—more powerful-ly—invoke capabilities from other applications (see Figure 10.3) without regard to how those applications were built, what operating system or platform they run on, and what devices are used to access them. Although web services remain independent of each other, they can loosely link themselves into a collaborating group that performs a particular task.

For example, if you connect your inventory system to your accounting system, whenever you buy or sell something, the implica-tions for your inventory and your cash flow can be tracked in one step. If you go further, and connect your warehouse management sys-tem, customer ordering system, supplier ordering systems, and your

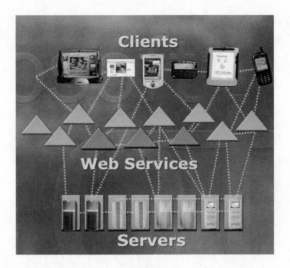

FIGURE 10.3 How web services applications work.

shipping company, suddenly that inventory management system is worth a lot. You can do end-to-end management of your business while dealing with each transaction only once, instead of once for every system it affects. These connections, especially with legacy systems, can be made easily using web services. We have already seen how Amazon plans to use web services to develop its e-commerce platform. An overarching platform, such as .Net—which can enable Amazon's associates to seamlessly access the web services residing on Amazon's servers, irrespective of the operating system of the originating computer—would actually be welcomed by Amazon. The question is what would make Amazon, or any other provider of web services, choose .Net over a competing platform, such as Sun Microsystems's Sun One?

It can be instructive to understand how Microsoft is going about attaining the core objective of a high installed base for its .Net platform. Unlike Windows, the .Net platform cannot leverage the installed base in the DOS operating system as easily. The answer may be found in all other diversification in which Microsoft is engaged.

Case 4: Microsoft's Money-Losing Diversifications

Microsoft is coming under increasing criticism for the various diversifications it has undertaken to compete in online services with AOL (Microsoft Network, MSN), game consoles with Sony PlayStation (Xbox), PDAs against the Palm platform (using the Windows CE operating system), to name a few.

In 1996, the prevailing wisdom was that profit opportunities were in controlling the content and not the channels. To play in this field, Microsoft created the Interactive Media Division that was responsible for the acquisition of WebTV and an earlier alliance with NBC leading to the formation of a 24/7 news channel, MSNBC. Microsoft also modified Windows (Windows CE), so it could run devices such as (TV) set top boxes, automobiles, and even household appliances. Microsoft also invested in e-commerce ventures, such as the travel agency Expedia and an automobile buying site called CarPoint. Microsoft started its online service called Microsoft Network (MSN) to compete with America Online (AOL). To date, MSN has been losing money and has been unable to get significant market share from AOL.

In 2000, Microsoft entered the videogame business with its Xbox game console. Unlike Sony's PlayStation, which is a dedicated game console (and only recently has added networking capabilities for online gaming), Microsoft's Xbox is a full-fledged computer, which has networking capabilities built into it. Xbox customers would be able to play videogames with others over the Internet. However, beyond videogames, Xbox also represented one more device that anyone in a household can use to carry out transactions over the Internet as such connectivity becomes increasingly commonplace and not restricted to the PC, PDA, and cell phones. Xbox has gained some market share with vigorous price cutting, but it has been unable to provide a serious challenge to the Sony PlayStation. To date, Xbox, along with MSN and WebTV, remain a perennial money loser for Microsoft.

Microsoft has rarely entered a business without considering the impact on its other businesses, especially the core business. For example, at the time Microsoft decided to launch MSN, it was a given that the entry would be cost prohibitive given AOL's dominance of that market space. However, Microsoft's priority was to dominate the instant messenger business, and it was willing to take a loss in the online service business. Likewise, the videogame console business has become a huge moneymaker for Sony but a huge money loser for Microsoft. All these losses will be well worth it if these businesses act as a conduit to Microsoft's objective of developing a high installed base for its .Net platform. Very simply, Microsoft has to persuade a critical mass of vendors from PCs to game consoles to PDAs to server manufacturers to incorporate a few lines of the .Net framework code that will enable total interoperability, as illustrated in Figure 10.3. After the .Net framework becomes available in sufficiently large client devices, the tipping point will have been reached, and Microsoft will have succeeded.

The multifaceted migration paths that Microsoft has chosen to reach the goal of dominating web services are, therefore, integral to its corporate strategy. Microsoft needs to develop positive externality in at least one widely used product or service that acts as a gateway to the Internet. For example, if the most popular cell phone, say Nokia, incorporates .Net in all its cell phones, its ubiquity would drive vendors of other device makers to also incorporate .Net. There are yet other avenues. Microsoft's Xbox was the first game console to have hardware built-in that would allow it to interact with the Internet. If Xbox becomes the game console of choice, it will be trivial to add complementary features to transform it into a conduit for online transactions using the .Net platform. The problem for Microsoft is to dislodge Sony PlayStation. Microsoft is willing to lose hundreds of millions of dollars to achieve this end. For Sony, it is only one business. For Microsoft, it is one possible conduit to web service domination. Likewise, if the MSN online service can gain market share from America Online, then it can use its captive audience to promote .Net. It is precisely for this reason you will not see Microsoft abandon any of these businesses in the near term despite the red ink and outcry from investors.

Note this from some internal memos that have been unearthed during the litigation by the state of Minnesota with Microsoft:[12]

> **Mr. Raikes told Mr. Buffett that Microsoft wasn't interested in becoming a media company, as some in the technology industry suspected. The "real goal" of its huge investments in cable-television companies and cable set-top box technology was "to get an 'operating system' royalty per TV," adding that "10s of millions of TV's per year at $10-$20 per TV is a nice little 'operating system' business."**

Of all the money-losing migration paths, Microsoft's savior may be its popular developer tools platform that it initiated in the early 1990s to promote the writing of applications for the Windows platform. The same developer community was clued into the initial components of the .Net platform and has now become a staunch supporter of the developer tools for .Net (Visual Studios .Net). If the majority of software programmers feel more comfortable writing .Net code over other web services frameworks, this may drive widespread acceptance of .Net. If Microsoft (and IBM, who is cooperating with Microsoft) can set the standards by which web services code will be written, Microsoft is home free.

Surprisingly, Microsoft has put a roadblock in its own migration path. .Net has been designed to work best with Windows or its variants, such as Windows CE, which works on client devices. This was a strategic move to ensure that the revenues from Windows would not suddenly drop off. Recall the decision by Microsoft to throw in its lot with Macintosh in 1984 as one option to dominate the application space? Even though the fact that .Net would be less than optimal in terms of interoperating with a non-Windows-based environment, Microsoft is willing to take that chance. The difference between 2003 and 1984 is that Microsoft now has the wherewithal to make a much bigger bet and take on the associated risks. Much of this bet is tied into the many businesses that Microsoft has entered into and is losing serious money in. However, Microsoft is unwilling to give up its cash cow of Windows and Office. Unlike 1984, Microsoft can now take the risks inherent in the "having your cake and eating it too" strategy of tying .Net to Windows.

Microsoft has several challenges before its .Net framework becomes the platform of choice in a distributed computing environment. Microsoft has to weave the new technology into its operating systems and applications, so they're ready to work in the .Net world. However, Microsoft will make no money from this. Another challenge for Microsoft is trying to milk Windows and Office without derailing the transition to .Net. Perhaps the most significant challenge is to get .Net in all the devices and clients that people use, especially portable Internet-connected "smart" devices, like cell phones and Palms. At present, the only smart devices in the market with .Net are the ones using Windows CE. Most of Microsoft's new capabilities are leveragable and have multiple end markets to increase diversification, as illustrated in Figure 10.4.

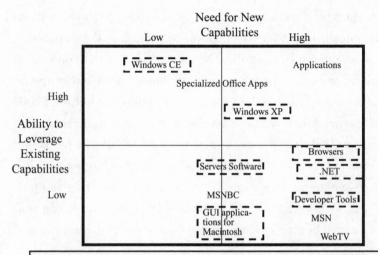

With a less tangible set of leveragable capabilities to rely upon compared to Dell, Microsoft is more willing to develop new leveragable capabilities in its diversification strategy. Most of the new capabilities have multiple end markets.

Legend: ¦ Leveragable New Capability ¦

FIGURE 10.4[13]   **Microsoft is willing to develop new capabilities.**

It may be useful to compare the strategies of Microsoft to that of Dell. Because Dell has basically adapted to existing markets, it has historically concentrated on leveraging its existing capabilities. Microsoft, on the other hand, is more of a market shaper. Consequently, it had to undertake the development of extensive new capabilities (see Tables 10.1 and 10.2), which is a higher risk strategy. In order to mitigate this risk, Microsoft has become much more adept at managing the migration paths than most other companies.

TABLE 10.1   Microsoft Often Leverages Nothing More Than Its Own Position...

Market	Relevant Existing Capabilities		Required New Capabilities	
Application (late 80s)	High	Leveraged evolution of Windows to improve usability and set industry standards.	Med	Reputation and user base (skills); focus on office requirements.
Browsers (mid 90s)	High	Application technology, installed base, distribution channel.	Low	Technology freely distributed.
Developer Tools	High	As provider of the dominant OS, MS could offer the most robust tools for integrating into Windows; later leveraged success of Visual Basic to introduce additional products.	Med	Need to establish expertise and reputation within the server-side environment (Visual J++, InterDev).
Windows XP	High	Released within the Windows line of operating systems.	High	Expanded capabilities with bundled services including email and multimedia.
Windows CE	High	Lower-powered version of Windows.	Low	

TABLE 10.2   ...And Establishes New Capabilities as Needed to Remain Dominant

Market	Relevant Existing Capabilities		Required New Capabilities	
MSNBC	Low	Leveraged brand.	High	Moving into content business.
MSN	Med	Leveraged brand and value of content, thanks to its position within the industry	High	Content capabilities required to compliment technical ability.

continues

TABLE 10.2   ...And Establishes New Capabilities as Needed to Remain Dominant (Continued)

Market		Relevant Existing Capabilities		Required New Capabilities
Specialized office applications	High	Draws upon Office functionality and install.	Med	Expanded and specialized functionality.
Servers (Windows Server, Exchange,SQL)	Med	Leap from the desktop to the server market leveraged MS's reputation and industry position.	Med	Reliability requirements limit MS to the lower end of the market; improved quality required across the market (compared to desktop). Service requirements are critical, which Microsoft was not good at in core software business.
.NET	Low	Developer tools	High	Completely new platform that may make Windows obsolete.

Endnotes

1 Based on *PC World/PC Magazine* reviews from the late 1990s.

2 Microsoft Office was a tightly coupled system—whenever the Microsoft Word program was modified, there have to be corresponding modifications for all the other applications in the suite. Initially, there was a fair amount of resistance from the programmers of the individual applications. However, Microsoft persisted and ultimately succeeded in developing a feature (integrated office suite) that no other vendor could match for a fairly long time.

3 The Cisco examples are based on *Cisco: Early If Not Elegant* (A). University of Virginia Darden Business School UVA. BP-0446.

4 Glen Rifkin. "Growth by Aquisition: The Case of Cisco Systems." Stategy+Business, Second Quarter, 1997. Reprint No. 97209. http://www. strategy-business.com/search/archives/?issue=&textfield=rifkin. Accessed on June 16, 2004.

5 Ibid.

6 Ibid.

7 Ibid.

8 Ibid.

9 Ibid.

10 Ibid.

11 Jay Greene. "Microsoft's Big Bet." *Business Week*. October 30, 2000.

12 John R. Wilke And Don Clark. "Microsoft Is Facing More Telling E-Mails In Minnesota Lawsuit," *The Wall Street Journal*. March 17, 2004: Page B1.

13 The Dell and Microsoft figures were based on a student assignment by Tianqiang Huang, HyunKyung Lee, Emily Lewis-Pinnell, Min Li, Ping and Priscilla Zhong.

EPILOGUE

We hoped to start a conversation about a much neglected and, in our opinion, critical component of business strategy. The reason for the existence of business is to take risks. The question that we posed is not how much money you are going to make from an economic opportunity, but what risks are keeping everyone else away. If you can develop capabilities for taking on these risks and avoid incurring major losses, more often than not, you will be making profits in the long run. Our basic message is that understanding and managing risks should be an integral part of your business processes and not relegated to a backroom staff function.

We have deliberately stayed away from providing templates and laundry lists that you can check off because, in our experience, that is rarely the way good strategies are developed. However, we have tried to put some structure in an inherently unstructured situation involved in designing a strategy for your business. The structure comes around the two dimensions of risk management that we have emphasized throughout the book—clarity and choice. In our experience, filling in a template or checking off the laundry list rarely leads to this clarity or allows you to see more options. We have found that this clarity and choice comes from conversations, sometimes ad hoc conversations, literally at the water cooler. However, the process that facilitates the generation of clarity and choice comes from the presence of the common doctrine that the participants in this conversation can relate to. The frameworks and concepts we have introduced in this book should be the starting point for developing your own individualized doctrine specific to your business. It is by no means the endpoint.

Appendix

ENRON'S INCREMENTAL DESCENT INTO BANKRUPTCY: A STRATEGIC AND ORGANIZATIONAL ANALYSIS[1]

Abstract

Enron's senior management has become the poster boy for all that is bad with corporate America, and justifiably so. Further, it is becoming apparent, even in the popular business press, that the limited partnerships were increasingly used to cover up Enron's strategic mistakes and keep its stock price high. Yet there is hardly any in-depth analysis of what contributed to the strategic mistakes. This Appendix is not about the cover-up but an analysis of the antecedents of these strategic mistakes.

I will demonstrate that the core successes of Enron—and these were unmitigated successes—were rooted in its ability to manage the risks in complex transactions. Yet it was these risks that ultimately brought Enron down. In short, this Appendix is about what we can learn about managing risks in the increasingly complex business environment of the 21st century.

"Make the non-recurring recurring." Jeff Skilling

"We are a cool company." Jeff Skilling

The Secret of Enron's Growth Plans: Recurring Asset Sales

In the latter part of the 1990s, the stock price of Enron closely tracked the profit growth in its wholesale trading business (mainly gas and electricity), which accounted for up to 90% of Enron's revenues and profits. However, it is not well-known that *two thirds* of these profits came from *asset sales*[2] and only one third from trading profits.[3] It was virtually impossible that trading profits alone would sustain the profit growth that was built into Enron's stock price in the late 1990s. However, instead of backing away from unrealistic growth expectations, Enron validated such expectations by claiming the asset sales that had contributed to the growth in earnings would be a *recurring* source of profits. In other words, systematic asset sales would become the de facto underpinning of Enron's growth strategy. Enron was clearly committed to executing this strategy. Even as recently as August 2001, Enron announced plans to sell up to $4 billion in assets over the next 2 years.

There has been no analysis in the business press about the implications of a growth strategy that was based on asset sales as recurring income. I will demonstrate in this Appendix that after Enron mastered the art of managing the risks of being the market maker in the gas and electricity markets, it decided to apply this risk management competency to transform wide-ranging industries. In the process of this industry transformation, they expected to acquire assets and then sell the asset (see the section, *Asset-Light*) at a profit, after the industry had become efficient. This is how Enron expected to use asset sales as the source of the recurring profits. In other words, in the latter part of the 1990s, Enron saw itself in the industry transformation business and not in the energy trading business. I will demonstrate that this shift from energy trading to industry transformation sowed the seeds of its destruction. The off-balance sheet partnerships were simply meant to cover up its strategic errors. In this Appendix, we are less interested in the cover-up and the possible legal consequences that are still unfolding, but more in the strategic processes that led to the enormous mistakes necessitating the cover-ups.

To understand the strategic processes that led to these billion dollar strategic blunders, I demonstrate that there were two visions operating within Enron. Even though Enron has become synonymous with its "asset-light" strategy, Enron was formed based on Ken Lay's vision of a vertically integrated "asset-heavy" energy company. In this Appendix, I demonstrate that the two business models require fundamentally different sets of capabilities and competencies that were never codified. Further, there was a complete lack of clarity about which of these two competing strategic vision's should guide Enron's diversification. This lack of clarity led to an organization that was simply unsuitable to take advantage of the capabilities of a traditional asset-heavy energy company, while it lacked the discipline to take advantage of the complex, risky but potentially rewarding, asset-light strategy. Ultimately, Enron failed on both fronts.

Other firms will still benefit from deconstructing the principles driving the Enron model. However, these are complex principles and the lessons taken from Enron's failure should be knowing how to prevent a complex business model leading to its own collapse. In short, this Appendix discusses what we can learn about managing risks in the increasingly complex business environment of the 21st century.

Enron's Collapse: The Antecedents

The Q3 2001 Earnings Announcement

Enron's meltdown can be traced to a single date: Tuesday Oct 16, 2001. To understand the significance of Oct 16, 2001, it may be worthwhile to break out the different pieces of information that Enron disseminated to the investing community on that fateful day:

1. $1.01 billion in charges, offsetting strong returns from its core wholesale trading and marketing division.

2. The European segment, which includes gas and power operations there and other commodity sales like metals, coal, and crude oil remained flat at $53 million amid lower volatility.

3. Performance details on the relatively new retail services division, which manages energy needs for large corporate clients on an outsourcing basis. The division, considered a high-growth area, reported income of $71 million, more than double the $27 million it earned in the 2000 quarter.

4. The charges included:

   • A $287 million write-down on its troubled water venture and failed spin-off, Azurix.

   • $180 million from the restructuring and scaling back of its broadband telecommunications venture.

   • The biggest chunk, $544 million, was related to various investment losses, mostly from its piece of The New Power Co., a retail electricity joint-venture with AOL/Time Warner.

   • A charge of $35 million connected with "early termination...of certain structured finance arrangements." This was a limited partnership in which Enron had a partial interest.

To summarize, Enron was most successful in the wholesale trading of gas and electricity. It was also very successful in managing the energy needs of industrial corporations.[4] It showed no growth in trading in commodities other than gas and electricity. It failed miserably in its retail electricity venture and in the broadband trading market. Other well-known failures are large power generating and water projects in developing countries, such as the Dabhol power plant in India and Brazil.[5]

Shortly after the Q3 earnings announcement, Enron dropped a bombshell on the financial community. It was forced to acknowledge that it had hid losses in the limited partnerships that should properly be accounted for in the primary financial statements. These losses were mainly in the many new markets that Enron had entered and not in the core energy trading business. Enron restated its prior four years' earnings (see Table A.1).

TABLE A.1   Enron's Four-Year Earnings

Year	Restatement	Original
1997	77	105
1998	570	703
1999	645	893
2000	880	979

Post restatement, Enron's shares slumped to $13.90 at the end of October 2001 and 26 cents at the end of November 2001.[6] I would like the readers to note one thing: Even though there are now allegations of insiders profiting from these limited partnerships at the expense of the employees and shareholders, Enron would have been a very profitable company had it not tried to cover up its mistakes. To understand the sequence of events that led to these mistakes, we need to turn the clock back to 1990. We need to understand how Enron developed its one true core competency—risk management—which was the foundation for all its subsequent growth as well as missteps. The next section details Enron's diversification strategy followed by an analysis of its success and failures.

Enron's Diversification: From Integrated Utility to Broadband Services

EGS

CEO Ken Lay's original vision when Enron was formed was that of a vertically integrated energy company. Soon after the deregulation of natural gas, utilities and local distributing companies were desperate for a supply of gas at a stable price. Conforming to Ken Lay's vertical integration strategy, Enron had the largest pipelines in the USA. However, instead of developing its own sources of supply, Skilling (then a McKinsey partner) convinced Ken Lay to form a gas bank and smooth the supply risk by pooling supplies from a large number of producers. This move was the genesis of asset-light and an alternative to Ken Lay's asset-heavy strategy was born.

Skilling, who joined Enron in 1990 as the chairman and CEO of Enron Finance Corporation (EFC), was well aware that before embracing the concept of a gas bank, Enron needed to develop the capability to offset the risks between sourcing and marketing (selling) of gas in the gas bank business model.[7] In the next *three* years, EGS hired both commodity traders and gas industry experts to develop a rigorous capability similar to that of an investment bank trading desk. Basically, Enron developed the capability of using the price and supply information to hedge the risks of a volatile cash flow. Further, through its own pipelines and contracts with other common carriers (pipelines after deregulation), Enron controlled the "switches" needed to rapidly divert the supply of gas from different producers to different users.

Confident that it could manage the risks of a mismatch in the sourcing and marketing contracts, Enron had one more hurdle to overcome. Only the weakest gas producers, some facing bankruptcy, were willing to sign long-term supply contracts (at the prevailing depressed prices) with Enron. However, the weaker producers were weak because they lacked capital for exploration and production. Without the capacity to produce, it would be meaningless for Enron to enter into a long-term contract with these weak producers, because they would surely renege on their obligations.

The First Special Purpose Entity (SPE) [8]

After a year and a half of hard work, Enron came up with an innovative solution to this Catch-22 through an SPE called Cactus Hydrocarbon III Production Payment (PP) Trust. As depicted in Figure A.1, through a combination of hedging and monetizing the volatile cash flow from gas production, Enron could pay the weaker producers upfront for their exploration and production budgets and, thus, secure a long-term, cheap, and steady source of gas. Thus, by applying its newfound risk management competency, EGS became an unqualified success, and the wholesale gas trading remained profitable until 2001. However, the major impact of Enron's risk management competency manifested in the role Enron played in transforming the North American electricity market.

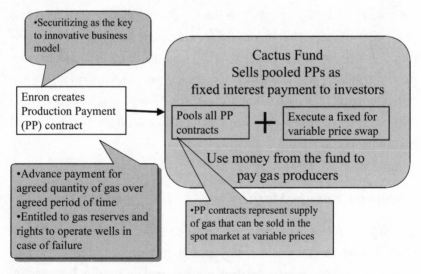

FIGURE A.1   EGS: Securing steady long-term supply.

Electricity

Post deregulation, electric utilities were desperate for stable prices in the wholesale market. Following its gas bank model, Enron entered the electricity market not by producing electricity, but by pooling suppliers and matching them to users—leveraging its ability to hedge price and supply fluctuations (risk management). However, Enron had to acquire two specific types of assets to dominate the electricity business:

1. Peaking (gas turbine) generators as a buffer supply of (peak demand) electricity and also some conventional generating plants solely to gather price and supply information in important markets, such as the Northeast United States.

2. Access to electricity transmission grids "switches" that could be used to distribute electricity from any supplier to any user.

Enron quickly created a countrywide network that could track demand, supply, and price information and distribute electricity from any source to any user.[9] Further, a third of all natural gas traded in the wholesale market was used to generate electricity. Enron was the biggest trader in the wholesale market for gas and could thus use gas for electricity hedges to reduce price risks for electric utilities. The peaking generators that could deliver electricity from stored gas complimented these hedges. This strategy paid off in spades, and Enron's portfolio of long-term contracts increased from $3.8 billion in 1998 to $16 billion in 2000. The wholesale electricity business remained profitable through 2001. Next, Enron sought to transform the European energy markets.

European Energy Markets

In anticipation of European energy deregulation, Enron had concluded more than 250 electricity and energy deals in the EU countries that would help it be the market maker in the burgeoning wholesale electricity market in Western Europe. Like the United States, Enron focused on acquiring the switches for transmitting electricity both across and within country markets with the long-term goal of divesting its power generation assets. As reported in the *Financial Times*[10]:

> **Enron's "tactic is to develop a trading capability in a market, which gives us a better insight into the market and is a precondition for investment in physical assets. This is a rather different tactic to many of the utilities, which have been after the physical assets first and then have sought to develop or inherit a market insight."**
>
> **—Mark Frevert, Enron Europe's Chief Executive Officer**

The European business remained flat but profitable for Enron through 2001. Next, Enron extended it strategy to industrial markets.

Industrial Markets

Enron's initial entry strategy in a new industrial market (such as pulp and paper, textile products, bulk and agricultural chemicals, metals, lumber, and various types of plastics) was to manage the price risks for sellers or producers. Next, Enron started trading the industrial commodity, including physical delivery, which sometimes necessitated acquisition of production capacity to ensure delivery. Enron expected to divest these assets (see the section, *Asset-Light*) when it had secured command of the distribution (switches).

Enron's entry into the industrial markets represented a cultural shift away from the much more deliberate and methodical manner in which Enron entered the gas and electricity business. The company increasingly encouraged its employees to envision new market opportunities and to go after these opportunities aggressively. Jeff Skilling,

Enron's President and, at that time, COO, said, "If you put a circle around Silicon Valley, it would look a lot like Enron. But it's easier to innovate at Enron, because we have a lot less friction."[11] Junior people within the organization with minimal oversight were allowed to rapidly develop new industrial markets. It is not clear how these industrial markets performed. They were probably not losing money but were definitely not on par with the wholesale energy trading businesses.

Third World Strategy: Energy Markets

A significant component of Ken Lay's vision was to be an integrated energy provider to the developing economies. Enron entered the Third World energy market by investing heavily in generation capacity, such as the Dabhol power plant on the western coast of India in 1992. In the late 1990s, Enron may have considered changing its Third World strategy to conform to the U.S. strategy. However, Enron failed to promote privatization and trading in Third World markets and most of its projects in Latin America, and its much-publicized Dabhol power plant ran into severe problems (see some similar examples in the following section on Enron's water ventures).

Third World Strategy: The Azurix Water Venture

On July 24, 1998, Enron acquired Wessex, an UK water company, and announced the formation of a company called Azurix to pursue opportunities in the global water business. Rebecca F. Mark, who had closed the Dabhol deal with the government of India and negotiated many of Enron's Third World initiatives,[12] also championed the Azurix deal. According to Enron, this acquisition would provide the capabilities to compete against the major players in the global water market (such as Vivendi, Thames Water, and Suez Lyonnaise des Eaux) by combining Enron's international financial and project management skills with Wessex's operating and technical expertise in the water business.[13] However, soon after the formation of Azurix, Enron announced its decision to quit this business and suffered a significant loss, as reported in 2001. Azurix's notable failures around the world have been catalogued by Public Citizen.[14]

Azurix lost a 30-year contract due to inferior water quality and paid $1 million in fines (Argentina), pled guilty to 19 environmental charges (Canada), and lost a $100 million pledge in a water pipeline project from The World Bank after allegations of corruption (Ghana). Among its schemes to create a market for trading water resources was an offer to the State of Florida to secure water supply from the Everglades in exchange for funding its restoration. Azurix also tried to develop a water "bank" in a large ranch in California to store water in wet periods and sell it during dry times. Both of these efforts failed.

The Retail Electricity Market

The retail electricity diversification was championed by Ken Lay and Lou Pai (who ran EES, which I will discuss later). In the mid-1990s, Enron decided to aggressively enter the retail electricity markets by under pricing state-run utilities in Pennsylvania, Georgia, and North Carolina.[15] In 1997, Enron acquired Portland General Electric (PGE) for $2.8 billion, primarily to gain new expertise in retail electricity delivery to individual consumers, as well as to avail itself of PGE's transmission grids that served key Western states, such as California.[16] With the purchase of PGE, Enron was looking to become the first vertical provider of electricity to PGE's 7,000 plus retail customers. The bid for PGE was also based on the expected repeal of the Public Utility Holding Company Act (PUHCA).[17] With the repeal of PUHCA, the PGE acquisition would give Enron the ability to engage in gas for electricity arbitrage and swaps, because it would have a strong presence in both markets.[18] However, despite spending $10 million on marketing, Enron managed to sign up only 30,000 of California's 8 million residential customers and quickly exited the California market.

In May 2000, Enron launched The New Power Company
(TNPC)—the first national energy service provider for residential
and small businesses. TNPC's web site was hosted by its alliance partner, IBM, and Enron agreed to pay America Online $49 million a
year for six years for promoting TNPC. This second attempt at
targeting retail customers also failed and resulted in a write-off of half
a billion dollars by Enron.

Broadband

Enron expected to supply broadband capacity to corporate users on
an as-needed basis (as opposed to the long-term expensive contracts
offered by the major backbone providers). Enron put in place 21,000
route miles of fiber-optics network called the Enron Intelligent
Network (EIN), serving 19 cities with expansion plans for 90 cities.
Enron expected to execute agreements to expand connectivity to Asia
and Europe in the near future. The fiber network was intended to
provide back-up capacity and instill confidence in deliverability. The
demand never materialized, and the broadband business was an
unmitigated disaster, as reported in 2001.

EnronOnline

EnronOnline was launched in November 1999 as an electronic transaction platform that offered real-time pricing for commodities. The
commodity trading system marketed more than 1,400 products related to 35 different commodities in 13 currencies and 140 languages,
mostly electricity and natural gas liquids, but also weather derivatives,
emission credits, metal, paper, pulp, and bandwidth. Contrary to its
own past practices, EnronOnline openly displayed its "bid" and "ask"
prices. Further, Enron would actually buy the commodity from a sell-
er and, in turn, directly sell it to a buyer instead of matching buyers
and sellers. This ready market, along with Enron's reputation and

credit rating, ensured market liquidity. The price transparency and liquidity attracted traders, enabling Enron to grow the "notional value" of online energy trades 750 percent in 2000, with EnronOnline accounting for most of them (according to Forrester Research). As of May 2001, the web site conducted $4 billion in trades per day. The October 2001 earnings announcement clearly suggested that EnronOnline was very profitable, and this was one of the few assets that was sold in the open market after Enron's bankruptcy. UBS Warburg was the buyer.

Enron: Anatomy of a Failure

In the Feb. 7, 2002 congressional hearing, Rep. Cliff Stearns (R-Fl) asked Jeff Skilling if the failure of Enron was a failure of Skilling's much publicized asset-light strategy. Skilling did not give a direct answer, but my analysis supports the thesis that asset-light did succeed in the two businesses it was originally applied to—wholesale gas and electricity—but failed when the logic of asset-light was improperly applied in later diversifications. Let us first try to understand the antecedents of the asset-light strategy: Enron's risk-management competency.

Risk Management: The Kernel of Enron's Early Successes

Enron's first stepping stone to success was EGS. EGS was highly profitable for two reasons:

1. By virtue of its contracts with depressed producers, Enron's cost of gas was lower than most integrated producers.

2. By virtue of its contracts with depressed producers, Enron could market huge volumes of gas without investing in production assets.

However, Enron could write these contracts because if it could secure the volatile payment streams from depressed producers by virtue of very sophisticated hedging strategies—risk management (refer to Figure A.1). While these strategies are complex, EGS was focusing on only *one commodity*—natural gas, and they had taken 18 months to refine this expertise.

The successful application of risk management laid the foundation for new, and *real*, profit opportunities that has since been supported by theoretical and empirical research.[19] For example, after renaming EGS as Enron Capital & Trade Resource (ECTR), ECTR successfully engaged in commodity and stock market hedging,[20] helped to smooth cash flows for both marketers and producers of gas, as well as optimize the complete energy requirements for industrial companies through its Enron Energy Services (EES) group. All of these ventures proved to be profitable.[21] None of these ventures required significant capital for physical assets. Likewise, Enron's success in the wholesale electricity market was *real* and based on the following sustainable advantages over all the other players in this business:

1. Electricity could not be stored, but Enron's gas business gave it the next best alternative. Enron could quickly produce any supply shortfall.

2. Enron had much better price and supply information than any other energy company. This reinforced its risk management competency. Thus, Enron had the freedom to aggressively write energy supply contracts that other energy companies could not even visualize. This included the gas for electricity trade.

3. Enron was early in the market and could, therefore, shape the manner in which the wholesale trading market developed.

Following the successful entry in the wholesale gas and electricity markets, Enron formalized its risk management and trading competencies as the famous asset-light strategy.

Asset-Light

Enron's business model in the wholesale gas and electricity markets drew upon well-established portfolio and hedging theory. Asset-light needed one more, yet to be discovered, theoretical concept: real options. Enron realized that after it created efficiency in the *distribution* of gas and electricity, it could divest the assets acquired to guarantee supply so long as it controlled the "switches" in the gas and electricity distribution business. With access to switches, Enron could use its ability as a market-maker to deliver these commodities at very short notice. Further, because the producers of electricity (and gas pipelines) realized there was a liquid market for electricity, it could run its generating plants more efficiently, which led to increased valuation for these generating plants. Enron capitalized on this trend by unloading most of their generating plants, including the short-term peaking generators of electricity and many miles of gas pipelines. Further, the increased valuation of these assets allowed Enron to book these asset sales as profits, which quickly amounted to over two-thirds of the wholesale business. However, Enron, presumably with the acquiescence of Arthur Andersen, booked these asset sales as *recurring* profits, which perplexed many analysts. With the treatment of asset sales as recurring profits, Enron pegged its future growth:

- Entering any and every commodity market where it perceived inefficiencies existed.

- Acquiring assets to gather information for hedging the price, supply risks, and physical delivery.

- Creating efficiencies by creating a market for trading these commodities.

- Selling the acquired assets at a profit when liquidity had been established in the market.[22]

The freed-up capital would then be used to pursue the next market in need of efficiency. In other words, in the latter part of the 1990s, Enron saw itself in the industry transformation business and not in the energy trading business. According to Skilling, "the purpose of a firm is to create options." Enron considered its entry in all-commodity markets as (real) options that could be exercised when Enron had managed to create liquidity and efficiency. Obviously, Enron realized that some of these options would expire worthless, but they expected most to be successful. It turned out that most of these options failed, and then the cover-up of these failures led to Enron's bankruptcy. I first will develop some general lessons from these strategic errors and then, drawing on organization theory, provide some insights on the process that led to these strategic errors. Finally, I will analyze the role of the limited partnerships and the capital market in this saga.

Enron's Successes and Failures: An Overview

I summarize the various diversification moves undertaken by Enron in Table A.1. The key thing to note from Table A.1 is that in all its successful diversifications, Enron entered the market by first offering risk management products. This had two positive effects. By initially offering risk-management products in the new markets, Enron became much better informed about the price and supply dynamics than other possible entrants. Note that this sequence to enter markets was fairly low risk—all Enron had to do was suspend its trading if the entry proved to be a failure. The success of asset-light was contingent on the ability of Enron to quickly focus the bulk of its activities in market-making and trading rather than production. This allowed Enron to leverage its capital tremendously. This was the strategy that Enron adopted in entering the gas trading business, wholesale electricity, the creation of EES, and European markets, as well as some of the industrial commodity markets and the success of EnronOnline. On the other hand, Table A.1 clearly suggests that Enron failed where it could not or did not use its risk management core competency as the basis for market entry. These failures lead to four general lessons for any organization that depends on a complex business model for its competitive advantage.

TABLE A.1   Enron's Diversification: The Antecedents of Success and Failure

	Enron's Successful Diversification				Enron's Failed Diversification			
	EGS	Wholesale Electricity & EES	European Energy	Metals, and Commodity Markets	Third World Energy	Water	Retail Electricity	Broadband
Customer Outcomes	Price and Guaranteed Supply	Price and Guaranteed Supply	Price and Guaranteed Supply	Price and Guaranteed Supply	Capacity	Capacity	Simplify Household Accounts	Customized Capacity
Utility of Risk Management	High	High	High	High	Low	Low	Some	Low
Utility of Trading Capability	High	High	High	High	Low	Low	Low	Low
Other Capabilities	Minimal	Minimal	Minimal	Minimal	Project Management and Third World Bureaucracy	Project Management and Third World Bureaucracy	Help Consumers Organize Household Accounts	Circuit Switching, Network Management
Initial Market Entry Strategy	Trading and Risk Management	Trading and Risk Management	Trading and Risk Management	Trading and Risk Management	Asset Acquisition	Asset Acquisition	Asset Acquisition	Asset Acquisition

Lesson 1: Codify the Business Model

At its peak, strategy gurus were extolling the virtue of Enron's culture of decentralized innovation that motivated every employee to transform markets using Enron's asset-light strategy. However, to my knowledge, no one within Enron had ever codified this process to rein in the cowboy mentality where everyone was given a free hand to try to enter any market they felt could be commoditized.[23] The paper industry commoditization effort is a case in point.

David Cox, a high school dropout and former commercial fisherman, took a menial job at Enron's printing department just to work for the company. Cox's father, who ran supply boats out to offshore oil rigs, had been outfoxed in a deal by Ken Lay years earlier. His father, impressed, told Junior to find a way to work for the man. Eventually, young Cox got to know Lay and Skilling and persuaded them that Enron should fund the startup of an outside printing company to handle its publications, with Cox in charge. They agreed, and soon Cox was handling annual reports and other jobs for numerous Houston companies. When rising paper costs began to cut into profits in 1995, Cox did what any Enron-trained person would: he tried to sign a long-term, fixed-price contract with a supplier. "I found that such contracts didn't exist," says Cox, a burly Cajun from southern Louisiana. "I called up Jeff Skilling and told him, 'Here's a $175 billion commodity industry, and there are no price-risk management tools.'"

You can figure out the rest. Pulp and paper executives argued that it wasn't needed, that Enron had no experience, and that even investors liked fluctuating paper prices. Cox, until recently the head of Enron paper trading, says he did about $4 billion in trades last year and expects that figure to double this year. "It's become quite a market," says Frank Dottori, CEO of Tembec, a big Canadian newsprint maker. "It's going to change the industry."[24]

Perhaps. But no one took David Cox under his or her wings and explained how asset-light may not work in all industries. Consider the following success factors that the early users of asset-light in EGS and ECTR were well aware of but never codified:

1. Customers want price and supply stability and are willing to comparison shop.

2. The product needs to be homogeneous and not come in different shapes, sizes, or grades.

3. The product could be seamlessly distributed using a national network where Enron controlled the switches.

4. Price and supply information can be readily obtained. Inefficiencies in distribution can be corrected by increased liquidity of the market.

5. Enron could initially enter the market by offering risk management products, not acquiring assets. This reduced the exit barriers in case of failure. Assets would only be acquired to guarantee initial supply and divested as soon as liquidity was established.

I will now demonstrate that all the failures of Enron were caused by not adhering to this codification.

Straying from Asset-Light

Clearly, the gas and electricity markets matched the requirements of asset-light almost perfectly. On the other hand, most of the industrial markets were not appropriate for the asset-light strategy, especially with respect to the inherent lumpiness of their products. Further, paper and steel all had different grades, unlike electricity or gas. This lack of homogeneity implied that most of these markets required a degree of industry-specific knowledge. The lack of homogeneity also implied that these markets could not have supply-demand dynamics that were as well established as the gas and electricity markets. As I have demonstrated, Enron's hedging expertise depended on the precise analysis of the price and supply information. However, these industrial markets, while not ideal for an asset-light strategy, were the least problematic because Enron could still make money by trading the underlying commodities. It is quite possible that had Enron survived, it may have been able to generate some degree of efficiency in *some* of these markets. However, as I demonstrate in the following section, Enron's trading capability was of no use in the retail electricity market.

(Mis-)Matching Customers to Asset-Light

Enron's entry into the retail electricity market failed to recognize one simple fact: *Residential customers were not very interested in comparison-shopping*. Thus, Enron's ability to provide electricity cheaply by leveraging its risk management competency was of no value to the retail customer base. Sadly, Enron did not learn from the California experience. Enron felt that by outsourcing the marketing to AOL, Enron could finally convince retail consumers to comparison shop through TNPC. Unfortunately, just like the California experience, AOL failed to deliver the retail customers. I tried to repeatedly find out the rationale for TNPC from my sources in Enron without much success. The announcement on Oct 16, 2001, and the associated loss of half a billion dollars, provided clarity—Enron had finally realized its mistakes internally.

Abandoning Asset-Light

The retail electricity entry as well as the other failures summarized in Table A.1 marks an important departure from Enron's successful diversification. Instead of taking the low-risk approach of entering a market by using its trading capabilities, in all its major failures, Enron acquired the assets first and then tried to start trading in a market—sometimes by creating the trading market from scratch. This had two adverse consequences. Anytime Enron invested in production capabilities, it tied down Enron's capital in one industry. Further, straying away from trading and market-making activities implied that Enron had to acquire other core capabilities to deliver the value that customers wanted. If either Enron's partners failed to deliver in those core capabilities (AOL in retail customers) or Enron itself (such as project management in the Third World energy and water market), Enron failed badly. I will now illustrate this analysis by using the broadband market entry as an example.

Enron entered the broadband market in the most risky way possible—by laying down fiber. What Enron did not explain was how it was going to liquidate the fiber assets and over what time frame, which is the key to asset-light. Further, Enron was directly competing with the asset-heavy major backbone providers. Finally, there was no market for trading in broadband; the major backbone providers were not interested in trading. Thus, Enron could not possibly use its core risk management competencies to become a market-maker and ended up being a supplier of broadband—a classic vertically integrated strategy. That may be fine if the potential demand was roughly in equilibrium with the existing capacity. However, in an economy that is two-thirds consumers, it is unclear how the broadband capacity could possibly be utilized unless consumers use the Internet for the bulk of their transactions. Such widespread use of the Internet is impossible unless the last mile has broadband, absent that most of the fiber capacity will remain unused. So it was unclear how liquidity could ever be achieved in this market. The broadband decision was completely at odds with the asset-light strategy. Enron acquired the physical assets first without understanding the price mechanisms and with no exit strategy for creating liquidity and divesting the assets. Yet Enron, as usual, had its supporters. "We haven't seen any [investments in bandwidth infrastructure] that have proven to be a waste of money," said analyst Richard G. Klugman of Donaldson, Lufkin, and Jenrette, Inc.[25]

Lesson 2: Have Clarity in Strategic Vision

The broadband strategy had all the characteristics of a vertically integrated (asset-heavy) strategy that was the original vision of Ken Lay when he formed Enron, even though by the mid-1990s it was obvious that all of Enron's successes came from the asset-light strategy (refer Table A.1). While the Dabhol project was initiated before asset-light was formerly established, subsequent Latin American energy asset acquisitions, the water (Azurix) venture, and the retail electricity market were symptoms of confusion at the very top because Skilling's asset-light strategy had to co-exist with Ken Lay's vertical integration strategy. Some of the confusion was well known to the business press. According to press reports,[26] the PGE acquisition, well after asset-light had firmly taken root, was motivated by Ken Lay's original vision of a vertically integrated company. However, three years after the acquisition, even Ken Lay acknowledged that Enron's strategic focus had changed, "We are extending our network skills...and are pursuing a market-oriented, low asset approach, patterned after our very successful global energy business."[27] However, in other instances, Enron would not or could not clarify this. For example, Enron was repeatedly asked if it was backing out of the asset-light strategy and competing with backbone providers by building fiber-optic capacity in 2000. Enron would only say that it was not abandoning asset-light. Within Enron, there was an expectation that the fiber capacity investment was needed to guarantee delivery in the initial stages, but as soon as the market for trading broadband capacity was established, Enron would divest all its fiber assets. Of course, that violated all the principles of asset-light, just as the business press suspected.

You may wonder if asset-heavy and asset-light strategies can coexist within Enron. I will now argue that these two strategies were mutually incompatible given the growth trajectory that Enron followed.

Success Factors for a Vertical Integration Strategy

Let us consider the determinants of success of a vertically integrated strategy. According to Clayton Christensen,[28] "vertical integration is an advantage when a company is competing for the business of customers whose needs have not yet been satisfied by the functionality of available products. Integrated companies are able to design interactively each of the major subsystems of a product or service, efficiently extracting the most performance possible out of the available technology." Clearly, vertically integrated strategies are called for in delivering the energy requirements of developing economies. However, the major subsystems of such a value-added chain called for project management capabilities and expertise in building power plants that Enron was abandoning in the U.S. energy market. Moreover, the trading and market making capabilities that distinguished Enron in the asset-light strategy were completely useless in the Third World market.

Consider the water venture. The Azurix venture did not match any of the success factors of the asset-light strategy except that water is not lumpy and heterogeneous (unlike paper or steel). Enron was well aware that none of its risk management or trading competencies could be leveraged in the water business. It is very difficult to envision a market for trading water in most Third World countries where water is considered to be a free good or heavily subsidized by local governments. Thus, it is very difficult to get an adequate return on the capital investment needed to upgrade Third World systems. Moreover, Enron repeatedly made mistakes in dealing with governments and managing their water projects in Third World countries. Thus, strictly from a strategy point of view, Enron did not have the capabilities to compete with traditional utilities from the developed economies that maintained their expertise in the asset-heavy strategies.

On the other hand, consider what Christensen suggests are the main requirements for an outsourcing (asset-light) strategy. "To be successful at outsourcing a piece of that (value-added) chain to a supplier, a company must meet three conditions. First, it must be able to specify what attributes it needs. Second, the technology to measure those attributes must be reliably and conveniently accessible, so that both the company and the supplier can verify that what is being provided is what is needed. And third, if there is any variation in what the supplier delivers, the company needs to know what else in the system must be adjusted." Enron's competitive advantage in the asset-light strategy came from precisely knowing the supply and demand requirements in the U.S. economy. This information advantage became even stronger when Enron developed EnronOnline, which eventually cornered the bulk of the wholesale energy trading business. (I strongly suspect that Enron used this advantage to manipulate prices in the California crisis.) Finally, if and when there are variations from the optimal supply and demand requirements, Enron's risk management competency could adjust for such variations better than any other company. In other words, Enron was clearly suited to succeed with the asset-light strategy provided it followed the codification identified earlier.

It was not clear both from my private conversations and public pronouncements whether Enron was wholeheartedly pursuing an asset-light strategy (sometimes mistakenly as in broadband) or only pursuing it in certain markets. Further, pronouncement by the CEO that "we are a cool company" did not provide much clarity regarding the vision. This is critically important, because even the best companies can only develop capabilities around one unifying vision. No one questioned the validity of pursuing asset-heavy strategies in a company like Enron, whose competitive advantage rested in its asset-light strategy.[29] While confusions at the strategic level, which I have just described, may be caused by the presence of two de facto CEOs (Lay and Skilling). This type of confusion is quite common in mergers or acquisitions where multiple champions with different agendas can drive a company into the ground.

Lesson 3: Control Systems Are Critical for Complex Business Models

A published report suggests that Rebecca Mark was given the go ahead for Azurix just to get her out of Houston![30] This can only happen if political considerations supersede sound strategic analysis.

Likewise, David Cox was single-handedly allowed to enter the paper business. In his testimony to Congress, Jeff Skilling claimed that he is a controls (as opposed to control) freak. The freewheeling adventures of Rebecca Mark, David Cox, and the broadband market entry are three prime examples to the contrary. The obvious question to ask is why so many strategically inappropriate ventures were ever allowed to go as far as they did. Research in organizational theory suggests several intriguing possibilities.

The Role of Hubris

Let us now examine the role of hubris in the fall of Enron. A recent article[31] analyzed the uses and consequences of hubris that perfectly illustrate the situation at Enron. The article suggested the sources of hubris are as follows: narcissism, a series of successes, uncritical acceptance of accolades, and exemptions from the rules. The consequences of the aforementioned are that confidence turns to arrogance, firms tend to rely on a simple formula for success, and they fail to face changing realities.

Uncritical Acceptance of Accolades and Narcissism

From 1993 onwards, business gurus as well as financial analysts heaped high praise on Enron's strategy, culture, and decentralized organization. To quote: "as much as any company in the world, Enron has institutionalized a capacity for perpetual innovation...(it is) an organization where thousands of people see themselves as potential revolutionaries."[32] There is no doubt that these kinds of accolades contributed to the narcissistic statements such as "we are a cool company." Behavior Decision Theory (BDT)[33] suggests that, even under normal circumstances, firms make the mistake of thinking that they are protected from common risks and overestimate their ability to control random events. This situation is exacerbated by narcissistic tendencies and, for Enron, confidence turned to arrogance; it felt it could transform any market, and control systems would only add friction (recall Skilling's quote about Silicon Valley).

Series of Successes and Exemption from the Rules

In the early 1990s, it took Enron about 3 years to become fully comfortable in its gas hedging operations. In the latter part of the 1990s, Enron's employees scattered all over the world were coming up with ideas to enter new markets and getting approved within weeks, without any kind of senior management oversight. I submit that this is not revolution, but closer to anarchy. Contrast Enron's attitude to that of Cisco's. Every single Cisco employee carries 10 priorities they need to attend to when submitting a new project proposal. Let me be perfectly clear. I still think Enron's initial strategy of creating a gas bank was absolutely brilliant, and its initial series of successes were real. Further, I do believe Enron created efficiencies in the energy markets. However, I also believe its successes contributed to arrogance that led to a simplistic formula for success—transform industries— without considering the underlying complexities of the asset-light business model. Finally, even when it was clearly apparent that many of its ventures were failing, Enron refused to face reality and come clean and instead decided to cover it up (using the same SPEs that were key to its successes), hoping something would turn around and, possibly, the market was not smart enough to uncover these complex transactions. Had Enron instituted the proper controls early on or, at the very least, preserved the organizational memory about the difficulty, rigor, and deliberate development of the gas and electricity asset-light strategy, many of these mistakes may have been prevented. Despite Mr. Skilling's protestation, it is apparent the lack of controls fueled the hubris, and this unregulated expansion may have also stretched Enron's capability to handle the sheer magnitude of the complex trades it was carrying out in the late 1990s.

Lesson 4: Every Strategy Has a Natural Size

The fourth factor that may have contributed to Enron's problems was the totality of all the different commodities (reportedly 1,400) that Enron started to trade in. This may have become too much even for a company as sophisticated as Enron. In 1992, Enron was only trading in gas and could offset the commodity risk of gas trading by focusing on that single commodity. I once heard Bill Gates say that every company has a natural size. I interpret his comments to mean that every strategy has a natural size. Long Term Capital found that out the hard way. It is difficult to say whether Enron's core trading business (even with 1400 commodities) was in any jeopardy, but it required full attention from senior management, and this attention was diverted by all its other strategic mistakes. I think by the late '90s, Enron realized its risk exposure might be getting out of hand. Just compare these two excerpts from Enron's annual statements.

> **"EGS will continue to offer reliable gas delivery at predictable prices, all of which will be accomplished *with limited commodity risk (emphasis* mine) to Enron." Enron Annual Report, 1992**

> **"The use of financial instruments by Enron's businesses may expose Enron to market and credit risks resulting from adverse changes in commodity and equity prices, interest rates, and foreign exchange rates." Enron Annual Report, 1999**

The central takeaway from these lessons is captured in Table A.2. Basically, if a firm can leverage its competency into creating a new capability for delivering value in the target market, then the diversification is a relatively low-risk entry. However, if the diversification requires extensive capability building, it is a risky proposition. This does not mean that such a diversification should not be undertaken. However, it does mean one needs to pay very careful attention to the risks. In the next section, I provide an analysis of the limited partnerships, the role of the capital markets, and some summary thoughts.

TABLE A.2   A Framework for Diversification Success

		Need for new capabilities	
		High	Low
Ability to leverage existing competencies	High	Emergent Markets — High Risk High Return	Least risky
	Low	High risk	Probably Unattractive market

The Role of the Limited Partnerships.

The limited partnerships and the SPEs it created were both instrumental in Enron's success and its bankruptcy. There is now a rush to judgment in characterizing all of Enron's SPEs as unethical[34] and contributing to Enron's bankruptcy. This is simply not the case. Enron's SPEs can be characterized into three different types.

Innovations in raising capital. The first batch of SPEs, such as the Cactus Fund, were primarily instruments to raise capital to procure gas and electricity supplies. Further, the Cactus Fund was developed deliberately, rigorously, and backed up by *tangible* gas revenues. Irrespective of Enron's future strategic mistakes, these SPEs remain a brilliant competitive innovation and also generated significant returns for investors that invested in these SPEs.[35]

Hide the losses. In contrast, the SPEs that Enron floated in the latter part of the 1990s had one primary goal: hide the losses from the strategic errors made by Enron[36] by moving the assets to limited partnerships.[37] Unfortunately for Enron, some of the investors in these latter SPEs were not convinced of Enron's strategies and negotiated a structure where Enron took all the risk[38] (see Endnote 8 for a description of how SPEs are structured). Note that this by itself is not a nightmare scenario. If the underlying investments (such as the Azurix venture) were successful, then Enron had little liability. Even if the underlying investments failed but Enron's stock price held up above certain trigger levels, Enron's risk exposure would not become public. Unfortunately, these SPEs invested in the diversification moves that I have demonstrated to be a *strategic* mistake for Enron. Further, due to the bursting of the telecom bubble, Enron's stock price also declined below the trigger point (see Endnote 38) leading to basically a "run on the bank."

Venture capital. The final type of SPEs, through partnerships such as ECB Merchant Investments and Broadband Ventures, invested in failing dot coms just before the market collapsed. Some of these actually invested in companies, such as ChemConnect that competed with EnronOnline! Further, Enron valued the use of SPEs not from tangible gas revenues (Cactus Fund) but with smoke and mirrors. Enron created a SPE called Braveheart that held the assets in a joint venture with Viacom's Blockbuster unit to deliver movies on-demand to residential customers. The joint venture never managed to sign up more than 1,000 customers, but showed $110 million in profits using mark-to-market techniques (future potential). Collectively, these SPEs lost nearly $2 billion![39]

Limited partnerships and SPEs will continue to play an important role in the global economy. The lesson we should takeaway is that these instruments are only as good as the strategy and the organizational processes supporting them.

The Complicity of the Capital Market

In retrospect, the capital market was not the watchdog that efficient market theorists expect it to be. The semi-strong form of market efficiency suggests that all publicly available information should be reflected in the stock price. In retrospect, it clearly was not. The question is, who is to blame? I can categorize three broad categories of players that failed the investing public. These are the financial analysts, the investment bankers, and the credit rating agencies.

Of these three, the first two probably failed because of greed and conflict of interest. The financial analysts were beholden to the investment-banking arm as is increasingly becoming apparent in both academia[40] and the popular business press. The investment bankers were falling over each other to get Enron's business because it was perceived to have the Midas touch, and details such as due diligence of the merits of Enron's strategies clearly suffered. However, what surprised me the most was the failure by credit rating agencies, such as Standard & Poor's, that did not have an obvious conflict of interest. As reported in *BusinessWeek*[41]:

> **The off-balance-sheet structures...were revealed in Enron's financial filings and even rated by the big |credit-rating agencies. But almost no one seemed to have a clear picture of Enron's total debt, what triggers might hasten repayment, or how some of the deals could dilute shareholder equity. "No one ever sat down and added up how many liabilities would come due if this company got downgraded," says one lender involved with Enron. Many investors were unaware of provisions in some deals that could essentially dump the debts back on Enron (see Endnote 38, emphasis mine).**

Yet, in June 2001, Standard & Poor's put Enron on credit watch, but ultimately *reaffirmed* its credit ratings, provided Enron divested its underperforming assets. It seems that Enron did manage to stretch the limits of market efficiency.

Summary Thoughts

I feel that the capital market became overly enthusiastic of Enron perhaps because it was profitable, not just compared to the typical dot.com but many blue chips. By now, it is well known that many e-commerce firms, including Amazon.com, were forced to diversify out of their core businesses in seeking growth to justify the stock price. I speculate that Enron followed the exact same path, not to prove profitability, but to support the stock price by demonstrating continuing growth. In the process, the rigor and discipline that Enron had brought to bear in its core businesses were abandoned. I would not be too surprised if it turns out that Enron did manipulate the California Electricity market, as profit growth at all costs became its driving mantra in the late 1990s. EnronOnline was in a unique position to do such manipulation because it was at the center of supply-and-demand information of the U.S. energy markets. The tragic ending to all this is that Enron could possibly have come clean even as late as 2000 and still survived as a vibrant trading company. Instead, the brilliant financial innovation that gave rise to EGS and the asset-light strategy became a tool to cover up its strategic mistakes. The Enron saga is truly a business story of epic proportions that will be discussed for a long time to come. I hope I have managed to shed some light on the antecedents to the tragic events and how to avoid a repeat of this in the future.

Endnotes

1 This Appendix is based on Sayan Chatterjee "Enron's Incremental Descent into Bankruptcy: A Strategic and Organizational Analysis." *Long Range Planning*, Vol 36 No 2, 2003. This article was selected as one of the top 50 business articles in 2003 by Emerald Group Publishing Limited. Used with permission from *Long Range Planning*.

2 Ann de Rouffignac. "Enron Pursues 'Asset Light' Strategy." *Electric Light & Power*, Volume 9, Issue 2, February 1, 2001.

3 Even these are now being questioned regarding their accuracy because they have been marked to market and not realized profits.

4 This is coming under some challenge recently, even though no evidence of earnings tampering has been demonstrated. However, there have been stories in the press that Enron made an effort to make this business look "busy" to visiting analysts by flooding the trading floor with non-traders pretending to be trading energy.

5 Rebecca Smith and Kathryn Kranhold. "Enron Knew Foreign-Assets Portfolio Had Lost As Much As Half of Its Value." *The Wall Street Journal*, May 6, 2002.

6 Robert L. Bartley. "Enron: First Apply the Law." *The Wall Street Journal*. Feb 11, 2002: A23.

7 The model had the same risks as the Savings and Loan crisis of the 1980s, where there was a mismatch between duration of short-term deposits and long-term loans.

8 The limited partnership is an independent organization initiated by the parent firm, such as Enron, that creates multiple SPEs. SPEs pool together assets that have a (usually volatile) revenue stream. An SPE (rather the investors in the SPE) buys the pooled assets at a discount to the face value (the combined revenue stream), much like a bank that discounts accounts receivables of a company. It is estimated that in the U.S. alone, there are upwards of $1.3 trillion dollars worth of SPEs that hold pooled debts from relatively secured assets, such as aircraft leases, and everything from consumer loans to unsecured loans, such as credit-card receivables. There is one difference, however, between the SPEs and simply a discounting of accounts receivables. If the promised cash-flow did not materialize, the originating company *may* be liable, unlike a straight discounting of accounts receivables where the bank takes all the risk. The liability of the originating company depends on how the SPE is structured (see Endnote 38 for an example). Most of Enron's early SPEs (through the mid 1990s) did not require stringent guarantees from Enron.

9 This information is, of course, critical to carry out the hedging operations as well as manage supply and demand imbalances.

10 Guy Doyle. "Over Regulated, Over Optimistic, Over Here: US Power Companies Will Lead the Charge of Independents Into Liberalised European Markets." *Financial Times World Energy Review* Nov. 5, 6, 1998: 5.

11 Gary Hamel. "Reinvent Your Company." *Fortune*, June 12, 2000.

12 Wendy Zellner, Stephanie Anderson Forest, Emily Thornton, Peter Coy, Heather Timmons, Louis Lavelle, and David Henry. "The Fall of Enron." *Business Week* December 17, 2001.

13 According to Ken Lay, "developing nations, according to the World Bank, need to invest $70 billion a year in new water facilities over the next decade. Add annual investment of $30 billion in developed countries, and you get a potential global investment market of $100 billion." A. Taylor. "Enron Steps Into Global Water Market." *Financial Times* (London), Saturday July 25, 1998: 19.

14 Press Room. "Enron's Failure in Water Ventures Highlights Dangers of Privatization to Consumers, Taxpayers." *Public Citizen* April 2, 2002.

15 The key to Enron's ability to undercut state-run utilities was a process called "synthetic deregulation," where Enron assumed a (large industrial) customer's obligation to pay the regulated rate for electricity. Then Enron guaranteed the customer some other price, usually pegged to a regional index, and used its trading desk to lay off the risk, much like a swap dealer exchanges fixed-rate obligations for floating-rate ones. Utilities didn't like it, but there was nothing they could do. This process applied to states that were deregulated as well as those that still were not. Thus, Enron won customers even in states such as Georgia and North Carolina, where utilities still had a monopoly on selling electricity to end-users.

16 Financial Times World Energy Review, *Financial Times* (London) June 9, 1998.

17 Charles M. Studness. "Converging Markets: The First Real Electric/Gas Merger." *Public Utilities Fortnightly.* Oct. 1, 1996, 134:18.

18 Richard S. Green and Michael J. Parish. "Enron's End Run: Marriage of Convenience Eyes Retail Market." *Public Utilities Fortnightly* Oct. 1, 1996, 134:18.

19 For example, see K.A, Froot, D.S. Scharfstein, & J.C. Stein. "Risk Management: Coordinating Corporate Investment and Financial Policies." *Journal of Finance* Issue 8, 1993: 1629-1658.

20 Gregory Zuckerman. "Enron Quietly Ran Risky Hedge Fund That Turned Over Millions in Trades." *Wall Street Journal* April 11, 2002.

21 It is thus not surprising Enron showed a profit for EES in the Oct 16, 2001 earnings announcement. However, EES came under some challenge recently, even though no evidence of earnings tampering has been demonstrated. There have been stories in the press that Enron made an effort to make this business look "busy" to visiting analysts by flooding the trading floor with non-traders pretending to be trading energy. This was probably to impress Wall Street.

22 While I developed this conclusion based on my interviews with senior Enron executives and quotes such as "make the non-recurring recurring," this conclusion can also be corroborated by published sources; for example, see Erick Schonfeld. "The Power Brokers" *Business 2.0* January 2001.

23 Erick Schonfeld. 2001. op. cit.

24 Brian O'Reilly. "The Power Merchant." *Fortune.* April 17, 2001: 18.

25 Wendy Zellner, Christopher Palmeri, Peter Coy, and Laura Cohn. "Enron's Power Play." *Business Week.* February 12, 2001.

26 The original reports can be found in Guy Doyle, 1998. op.cit. In a recent story that describes how Enron wants to go back to the initial vertical integrated strategy, Enron expects to keep Portland General Electric as part of this integrated strategy. Rebecca Smith and Mitchell Pacelle. "Enron Will Try to Reorganize Itself As a Small Firm With a New Name." *Wall Street Journal.* May 2, 2002.

27 Arnett, David. "Enron Unloads PGE." *Independent Energy* 29: Dec 1999: 10.

28 Clayton M Christensen. "The Past and Future of Competitive Advantage." *Sloan Management Review*; Cambridge. Winter 2001.

29 Smith and Pacelle. 2002. Op.cit.

30 Zellner et. al. 2001. Op.cit.

31 Mark J. Kroll, Leslie A. Toombs, and Peter Wright. "Napoleon's Tragic March Home from Moscow: Lessons in Hubris." *Academy of Management Executive* Volume 14(1) 2000.

32 Gary Hamel as quoted by Simon London. "Inside Track." *Financial Times.com.* Dec 4, 2001.

33 Max Bazerman and Northwestern's David Messick. "Ethical Leadership and the Psychology of Decision Making." *Sloan Management Review* January 1996.

34 For example, see John R. Emshwiller. "Enron's 'SPE' Transactions Raise Questions on Roles of Executives." Monday, September 30, 2002. This article "discovered" that Enron had been engaging in SPEs well back into the early 1990s and then tried to make the case that Enron's unethical behaviors could be traced back to the early SPEs. An earlier draft of this paper, available in the Darden website since January 2002, had maintained this claim all along.

35 For example, the 1993 SPE called Jedi returned an annual rate of 23 percent to one of its chief investors, CalPERS, which invested $230 million. CalPERS invested a further $175 million in Jedi II, but stopped during the California energy crisis in 2000.

36 Two examples of these SPEs are Osprey and Marlin, which were used to acquire the failing Third World energy and European water assets, respectively, and remove them from Enron's balance sheet. Osprey raised nearly $2.4 billion from U.S. and European investors.

37 No one has yet claimed that this is illegal under FASB.

38 Osprey was initiated under a limited partnership called Whitewing Associates. The investors in Whitewing may have been the catalyst for Enron's demise. They were not convinced of Enron's Third World energy strategy and insisted on additional Enron shares if the energy assets did not produce cash to service the debt. It was Whitewing that also insisted on the $48.55 trigger for Enron's share price when Enron became liable for *all* of Whitewing 's debts and had to disclose the debt obligations to Enron's shareholders. It was this disclosure that started the fatal run for Enron.

39 Matt Marshall. "Enron VC Units Had Some Bad Habits." *Mercury News.* Dec. 05, 2001.

40 For a summary of the recent works, see AScribe Newswire. "Stanford Graduate School of Business Research Analyzes Patterns of Bias in Work of Financial Analysts." *AScribe Inc.* August 19, 2002.

41 Zellner, et. al., op.cit. 2001.

INDEX